MW00573111

COVERT CITY

COVERT CITY

THE COLD WAR AND THE MAKING OF MIAMI

VINCE HOUGHTON

AND ERIC DRIGGS

PUBLICAFFAIRS

New York

PublicAffairs
Hachette Book Group
1290 Avenue of the Americas, New York, NY 10104
www.publicaffairsbooks.com
@Public_Affairs

Printed in the United States of America

First Edition: April 2024

Published by PublicAffairs, an imprint of Hachette Book Group, Inc. The PublicAffairs name and logo is a registered trademark of the Hachette Book Group.

The Hachette Speakers Bureau provides a wide range of authors for speaking events. To find out more, go to hachettespeakersbureau.com or email HachetteSpeakers@hbgusa.com.

PublicAffairs books may be purchased in bulk for business, educational, or promotional use. For more information, please contact your local bookseller or the Hachette Book Group Special Markets Department at special.markets@hbgusa.com.

The publisher is not responsible for websites (or their content) that are not owned by the publisher.

Print book interior design by Sheryl Kober

Library of Congress Cataloging-in-Publication Data

Names: Houghton, Vince, author. | Driggs, Eric, author.
Title: Covert City : the Cold War and the making of Miami / Vince Houghton and Eric Driggs.
Description: First edition. | New York, NY : PublicAffairs, 2024. | Includes bibliographical references and index.
Identifiers: LCCN 2023028506 | ISBN 9781541774575 (hardcover) | ISBN 9781541774582 (ebook)
Subjects: LCSH: Miami (Fla.)—History—20th century. | Cubans—Florida—Miami—History—20th century. | Espionage—Florida—Miami—History—20th century. | United States—Foreign relations—Cuba. | Cuba—Foreign relations—United States. | Cold War.
Classification: LCC F319.M6 H675 2024 | DDC 975.9/381—dc23/eng/20240110
LC record available at https://lccn.loc.gov/2023028506

ISBNs: 9781541774575 (hardcover), 9781541774582 (ebook)

LSC-C

Printing 1, 2024

For Jordan, Grayson, and Sloane.
And, as always, to Jon and Rae.
—V.H.

For my family, and the sacrifices they made so I could write this.
—E.D.

Contents

Contents

Prologue
Vince Houghton

I lived in Miami continuously from 1978 until I left for college in the fall of 1994.[1] After that, I lived in Miami off and on for the next decade—for a time after I got out of the army, and then again before I left for grad school. Even during the years I spent elsewhere, I always worked my way back to Miami multiple times a year. Certainly for the major holidays, but also random visits to see my parents and my friends. If my memory serves, in the two-plus decades after I left for college, I missed Thanksgiving in Miami only twice: during basic training in 1997 and when I was deployed to the Balkans in 1998. Every other year I dutifully braved the insanity of holiday travel stupidity and schlepped southward.

I kept traveling every year until 2016. I had traveled a lot that year. Far more than normal. This included a trip the week before Thanksgiving. I'd had enough of airports and living out of a suitcase. After all, what could possibly happen that would make it worth yet another day of packing? Another fruitless search for convenient airport parking? Another security line? Another flight?

Fidel Castro died the day after Thanksgiving 2016.*

I had two immediate feelings when I first heard the news: (1) a sense of severe disappointment—I was going to miss the greatest party in the history of Miami. The feeling of FOMO was overwhelming; and (2) an acute sense of fear—would all my Cuban friends and their families be leaving now to reclaim their lost property? The Beard was dead. I had been told since I was little that once Fidel was gone, Cuba could be free. Cuba *would* be free.

---

* Dozens of rumors of Castro's death had made their way to Miami over the years. Most of us had learned to take them with a grain of salt. But this time, it was for real.

To this day I'm still annoyed I missed the celebration of Castro's death. I might never get over this. But the fear of a mass exodus of the Cuban community from Miami was quickly forgotten. Although Fidel Castro was dead, the Cuban government and its repressive policies remained. During his long life, Fidel had successfully entrenched within the Cuban regime his ideological mix of Marxism-Leninism, authoritarianism, and nationalism, with a dash of egomaniacal narcissism.[2] His death changed nothing.

Years earlier, Fidel had ceded power to his brother, Raúl, who promised some reform, but delivered very little. Now, a member of a younger generation leads Cuba—someone who wasn't even alive when Fidel first came to power. But, so far, the Miguel Díaz-Canel regime has been business as usual. Cuba is still Cuba.

And the Castro ideology continues to metastasize throughout Latin America and the Caribbean. In some nations, it presents a minor nuisance, a political insurgency that shouldn't be ignored, but has no real power. In other countries, such as Venezuela, the power of the Fidel Castro acolytes is absolute.

Unlike my coauthor, I am not of Cuban heritage. My family was not displaced by the Castro revolution. The first Houghtons in the US came over in the early seventeenth century. I am not directly *part* of this story. Instead, I'm trying to approach this topic from the lens of an intelligence historian. I'm trying to tackle this issue from the perspective of American national security, foreign policy, espionage, and military power.

I'd like to say this makes me more objective, and less likely to allow personal feelings to interfere with my analysis. But who am I kidding? I grew up in Miami. The Cuban refugee experience is interwoven into who I am today. I cannot pretend I'm not biased. I promise you, I am.

But that doesn't mean this history should be ignored or dismissed (as it has been, up to this point). This story is an integral part of the narrative of the Cold War. And it continues to play an essential (and at times, absolutely bonkers) role in the understanding of current American foreign policy. It's not just the story of a city. It's a story of America.

Introduction

Would you be willing to indulge us for a moment? We'd like to engage in a brief thought experiment.

If we polled one hundred moderately educated people—perhaps on a college campus, or at an academic conference—and asked them to name the cities they most associate with the Cold War, what would the most common answers be?

It's likely we would get a lot of Washingtons, Moscows, Berlins, and Beijings.

If there were some intelligence historians in the crowd, we could hear some Viennas, Londons, possibly a Paris here or there.

Maybe some military buffs would be among the polled, and we would have a Saigon, a Pyongyang, or a Kabul sprinkled in.

But would anyone say Miami? Before you picked up this book, would you have?

Not very likely. Miami's role in the Cold War has been woefully understudied by the academic community, and consequently underrepresented in much of the existing literature written on Cold War history.

Don't believe me? Just grab any mass-market Cold War history off the bookshelf. Now open it to the index and look for Miami. We'll wait.

Not much to see, is there? With very few exceptions, Miami is not part of the broader narrative. And even in those few books that take the time to include Miami, the story of the city's role in the Cold War is presented as tangential, not primary. There's a lot of "a force of Cubans from Miami landed at the Bay of Pigs," and then . . . nothing.

For most, Miami conjures up images of sun-soaked beaches and cocktails, a tropical playground complete with fancy cars, massive boats, and fast living. It's been dubbed the "Magic City," a nod to its enchanting beauty and tropical charm. But everybody knows that while enchanting and charming, magic is also an art of sleight of hand and trickery, creating a world where nothing is as it seems. And throughout its history, Miami has had plenty up its sleeves.

Miami is a city that over the decades has grown from the tension between the law and lawlessness. It was built by vices: intoxicating liquors, narcotics, and yes, even a glitzy TV show with cops in Ferraris. While *Miami Vice*—through the adventures of Crockett and Tubbs—launched the city into the nation's imagination as a paradise built on a seedy, crime-ridden foundation, Al Capone and swarms of enterprising rumrunners helped write that script in real life far before the 1980s, and before Tony Montana decided to get creative with power tools in a Miami Beach bathtub.

Miami has also been shaped by significant events throughout the Western Hemisphere—political, economic, and natural. Calle Ocho, Little Havana (which is now largely populated by Central Americans), Little Haiti . . . the city is a patchwork of the region, and is a reflection of the geography, culture, and struggles that challenged the countries many left behind. Wars and revolutions helped swell the population of Miami. Many came to the city to flee these events. Others came with the intent of influencing them.

Miami's formative years were shaped by its role as a clandestine battleground for intelligence, and the city's growth closely paralleled the growing need for information as threats became more imminent. As the only major American city with a direct line of sight to both Latin America and Europe, its powerful undercurrents of burgeoning criminal enterprise, passionate political intrigue, extensive international influence, and exorbitant wealth made Miami a capital of secrets. Those secrets had people sworn to protect them. And others equally dedicated to revealing them. The city became not only a backdrop to the struggle between these players, but also a major character itself in a complex drama with impacts far beyond the city limits.

The city was built by those who were there to keep tabs on our adversaries. The city was built by those gathering information to help the United States maintain its national defense. The Miami of today was built by the need for strategic and tactical intelligence, to warn American leaders of an impending attack, or to help them win when war became the only remaining option. And it was built by those focused on keeping illicit organizations at bay.

Miami is a city built by spies.

At its heart, this is a book about a place—a city both its authors call home. But how we both got here is emblematic of the theme of the book. One of our families came due to a world at war. The other, because a revolution upended his family's lives and threatened their very existence. But this isn't just our story. It's the story of so many of our fellow Miamians. This city's population growth and economic expansion are deeply tied to its unique geography and culture, but also to decades of fighting America's battles and stealing others' secrets to protect the American Dream.

And we aren't talking about the transplants from New England, New York, and New Jersey. They went to Boca Raton, West Palm Beach, Mar-a-Lago, Jupiter.

The spies moved to Miami.

Part I

1

In the Apostle's Footsteps

A crowded room of workers sat mesmerized. Despite a full day of labor, they delayed heading home that evening. They all were there for the same reason: to hear the words of the eloquent, well-dressed man who was speaking. He, like them, had left their beloved island home of Cuba, and had spent years in the United States yearning to go back. He knew exactly what they were going through and spoke of their shared understanding. He had lived the immigrant experience of being surrounded by people and yet feeling utterly alone. Of feeling uprooted, of living a life he called "flavorless"—he knew the unrelenting yearning for home.

But this was a meeting filled with hope, a fundraiser for an organization that was working toward freeing Cuba. He spoke of their homeland that was falling to pieces, and how they needed to bring what was being created in exile back to the island. They all left inspired, full of hope that their contributions to the greater cause would help hasten freedom in Cuba, maybe next year, but definitely by the turn of the century. The year was 1891. That man was a poet named José Martí. And there's no way to truly understand the Cuban exiles in Miami who suffered the same experience decades later without understanding a bit about his story first.

José Martí is an absolutely central figure in Cuba; he is referred to as the "Apostle" of Cuban independence. Cuba had been a Spanish colony of strategic importance since the age of galleons, but in the 1800s the Spanish Empire had been splintered into various new republics, and independence movements swept through the colonies. Cuba had fought two separate wars of liberation against Spain, and Martí's efforts were in support of a third, and hopefully decisive, war of independence. He gave voice to Cuba as an independent country and to the concept of Cuban identity in a way that had never been heard before. This helped to galvanize Cubans, and still does today. He was a prolific writer, poet, political philosopher, essayist, and orator, producing soaring verses and eloquently speaking on behalf of the Cuban cause. He also created a blueprint for building support for Cuba within the United States, particularly among the growing Cuban exile communities who fled violence on the island. Years later, when a new group of exiles fleeing Castro's revolution were displaced to the United States, their efforts were clearly inspired by, and often modeled after, those of Martí.

Martí recognized that the exile community was sizeable and, if channeled, could be a significant resource in support of change on the island. He spent years in the United States organizing, fundraising, educating, and planning for a free and independent Cuba. Martí organized the Partido Revolucionario Cubano, or Cuban Revolutionary Party (PRC), establishing clubs in cities with concentrations of Cubans and Cuban sympathizers throughout the US and the Caribbean. He was a tireless organizer and his efforts bore considerable fruit. By November 1894, the PRC had 126 clubs in eighteen cities, including sixty-two in Key West, fifteen in Tampa, eleven in New York, seven in Mexico, six in both Philadelphia and Jamaica, three in New Orleans, and clubs in Atlanta, Chicago, Boston, Santo Domingo, and Panama.[1] One of the key purposes of these clubs was to raise funds for what he and many others saw as an inevitable and justified war for Cuban independence.

Martí penned a document that encapsulated the guiding principles of the effort to free Cuba. Called the Montecristi Manifesto (it was signed in Montecristi, Dominican Republic), it explained the current situation in the sweeping prose Martí is known for:

> The war . . . is not merely a pious longing to give full life to the
> nation that, beneath the immoral occupation of an inept master, is

crumbling and losing its great strength both within the suffocating motherland and scattered abroad in exile. The war of independence in Cuba . . . is a far-reaching human event and a timely service . . . to the stability and just interaction of the American nations and to the still unsteady equilibrium of the world.[2]

In the early days of the Castro regime, and as more and more Cubans fled to Miami, these words had a familiar echo. The beloved homeland under the thumb of an inept master, families and loved ones scattered in exile. And Martí's mention of the "still unsteady equilibrium of the world" rang as true in the age of the Cold War as it did in 1895.*

Martí himself also planned and participated in what was already a time-honored tradition in Cuban liberation efforts: clandestine maritime incursion into Cuba from the United States. It had been used multiple times in previous wars of independence from Spain. In January 1895, he master-minded a plan to use three vessels to smuggle weapons and ferry hundreds of fighters to support the Cuban cause. The "Fernandina Plan," named for the embarkation point of Fernandina Beach in northeast Florida, was a complete failure. One of the main challenges was that these expeditions ran counter to one of the oldest laws of the United States: the Neutrality Act, which was passed under George Washington and remains largely unchanged. The Neutrality Act prohibits private individuals from launching any hostilities against a country with which the US is at peace. This impeded Martí's incursion attempt and would prove troublesome to others looking to support another Cuban liberation movement later in this story.

Undeterred, Martí and senior revolutionary leaders eventually found other means of transportation and landed in Cuba in February. Three months after landing back in Cuba, on May 19, 1895, Martí would lose his life on the battlefield in one of the first skirmishes of the war. When Cuba raised its flag as an independent country in 1902, Martí's sacrifice would be an inspiration to a new island nation: he took his place as the country's founding father.

So when later Cuban exiles begin arriving in Miami in the early 1960s, looking to mount an effort based in the United States to free their country

---

* It would be one of the last things he wrote. Martí reached Cuba shortly after the manifesto and lost his life on the battlefield two months later in one of the first skirmishes of the war.

from a government antithetical to their beliefs, they didn't have to look very hard for inspiration. What began to take place among Cuban exiles in Miami—organizing in the US for the cause of Cuban liberty—wasn't new. It was woven into the fabric of Cuban history. It's very easy to see how they could have viewed their effort as an echo of their beloved country's origin story, one that was taught to schoolchildren across Cuba. It would be a bit like an American being asked to cross the Delaware or participate in a fight on Bunker Hill—the echoes are unmistakable. This was also a history that was still in relative infancy: the country gained its formal independence at the turn of the twentieth century, which was still in living memory. With all of this in mind, one can understand how many forced to flee to Miami could have envisioned themselves as patriots called upon by destiny to retrace Martí's steps and organize stateside to regain Cuba's freedom.

Cockpit of Jealousies

One potentially corrosive element of Martí's instructive experience in the United States was the glory he received as the primary organizer of the effort that eventually secured freedom for Cuba. It would be speculative to assume motivations of those leaders inspired by Martí's example, and this in no way diminishes the desire for freedom that inspired many of the exile organizers in Miami in the early 1960s. However, it must have been intoxicating to follow in Martí's footsteps: to see yourself as having the chance to reestablish democratic rule and be mentioned in the same breath as your country's founding father. Considering virtually everyone thought that exile was going to be a very temporary arrangement, many likely saw efforts on behalf of a free Cuba as a stepping stone to political or other advancements once they returned. One of the few points of agreement among the Cuban exile community was that they wanted Castro gone. Beyond that, anything from the means of unseating him to who should lead such an effort to a timeline was a source of debate and disagreement. As a result, and despite the fact that the goal was the same—returning home to Cuba—the exile community was hindered early and often by a lack of unity and an abundance of infighting.

There was plenty of both, to be sure. And it was everywhere.

As early as December 1960, the State Department was receiving reports that certain exile organizations in Miami were "nothing more than a cockpit of jealousies, personal ambitions, and frustrating inertia." The Assistant Secretary of State for Inter-American Affairs, when discussing some of the frictions that existed in the Cuban exile community, lauded the vast majority of exiles working toward the pursuit of freedom for their "betrayed and subjugated country." He did concede, however, that he "would be less than candid . . . if [he] obscured the fact that subjective considerations of personal advantage have sometimes influenced exile political activity," lamenting that "the personal attacks launched by one leader or group against another have bordered on irresponsibility."[3] The dispatches of the CIA and other agencies in Miami were full of reports of mistrust and infighting within organizations. Groups splintered off in protest of affiliations with certain individuals of questionable political leanings. Others suffered from fissures at the top, with leaders apparently joining forces against other leaders within the same organization, or multiple factions within an organization claiming allegiance to one particular leader or another.

Eventually, there would be literally hundreds of organizations vying for relevance in the effort to liberate Cuba. Only a few years after the Revolution took power in Cuba, the number of Cuban exile organizations, most of them based in Miami, required the CIA's authoring of the *Cuban Counterrevolutionary Handbook*, a guide for overwhelmed CIA personnel trying to navigate the dizzying number of counterrevolutionary groups. The handbook listed 415 separate organizations. There was the Anti-Communist Front (Frente Anti-Comunista, FAC), not to be confused with the Christian Anticommunist Front (Frente Anticomunista Cristiano, also FAC). The Democratic Liberation Movement (Movimiento Democrático de Liberación) and the National Democratic Liberation Movement (Movimiento Democrático de Liberación Nacional) were separate and apart from the Democratic Revolutionary Movement (Movimiento Democrático Revolucionario), and the Democratic Revolutionary Liberation Movement (Movimiento Demócrata Revolucionario de Liberación). Any mention of the FARI could have referred to the Independent Revolutionary Anticommunist Front (Frente Anticomunista Revolucionario Independiente), the Integrated Revolutionary Anticommunist Front (Frente Anticomunista Revolucionario Integrado), or the

Internal Revolutionary Anticommunist Front (Frente Anticomunista Revolucionario Interno). And who could forget the National Anticommunist Liberation Front, known in Spanish as the Frente de Liberación Anticomunista Nacional, or FLAN?* The constellation of organizations included 119 separate "Movements," 72 "Fronts," and 22 organizations identifying themselves as "Armies."[4]

A significant consequence of having such a wide panoply of organizations was that they were in essence all in competition with each other, both for funds and members. The competition between organizations made staying relevant an important consideration in garnering support. One of the most effective ways to do that was doing something bold in the name of a free Cuba. Any action that was perceived as a slap in Fidel's face was met with approval by large swaths of the exile community. That support was often leveraged into appeals for financial assistance to continue those kinds of efforts. In years to come, that cycle of clandestinely striking at Cuba to generate publicity, interest, and funds would be a dominant exile-organization dynamic.

Organizing Organizations

One of the most notable and consequential efforts to coordinate among these disparate organizations was created in May 1960, when an alliance of five previously established exile groups combined to form the council of the Frente Revolucionario Democrático, or Democratic Revolutionary Front (FRD). A number of the groups in this council had significant presence in Cuba. The Organización Auténtica was an offshoot of a Cuban political party founded in the 1930s and included a former president of Cuba, Carlos Prío Socarrás.† He was the last elected president of Cuba, and was deposed by the 1952 coup that brought Fulgencio Batista to power. Batista himself was unseated by Castro's revolution later in the 1950s. The Auténticos were led by Manuel Antonio "Tony" de Varona, who was once prime minister of Cuba under Prío, and served as the head of the FRD council.[5] The Organización Triple A was represented by Aureliano Sánchez Arango. José Ignacio Rasco was a lawyer

---

* Yum.
† The "authentic" part of their name comes from the political party they grew out of. It was called the Partido Revolucionario Cubano (Auténtico), meaning they traced their inspiration directly to Martí's PRC.

and former classmate of Castro's and the leader of the Christian Democrat Movement, or Movimiento Demócrata Cristiano, in Cuba, originally created as a political party but forced to move underground after they published a manifesto pointing out Castro's constitutional violations.[6] The Agrupación Montecristi, named for Martí's manifesto, was headed by Justo Carillo, who in Cuba had been president of the Agricultural and Industrial Development Bank under Castro. Finally, the Movimiento de Recuperación Revoluciona-ria (Movement for Revolutionary Recovery, MRR) was established in Cuba in 1959 by Manuel Artime. Artime had fought in Castro's revolution, and was appointed to the National Agrarian Reform Institute after the revolution's victory. However, in October 1959, upon hearing rumblings of Castro's poten-tial plans to establish communism in Cuba, he resigned, denounced Castro, and then fled the island in December of that year after becoming disillusioned with the autocratic turn the regime was taking.[7]

The FRD alliance was not a ragtag group of adventurers improvising as they went along. This was an organized operation that clearly saw their role in historical terms. The FRD viewed this as another War of Independence, another "immoral occupation by an inept leader," this time from a totali-tarian regime and its external allies that had imposed their will upon their country.[8] By December 1960, the FRD had drafted a number of documents in preparation for what they saw as inevitable hostilities to liberate Cuba. They included a Declaration of a State of War on behalf of the Cuban people to expel Castro and the Sino-Soviet influence from the island and reestablish the 1940 constitution. There was a plan for an eighteen-month provisional government to help with the transition back to constitutional democracy.

The FRD was an umbrella organization that tried to unite some of these groups, coordinate their efforts, and importantly, funnel US government funds toward a single goal: the reestablishment of democratic government in Cuba, primarily through military force. There were basically two ways to do this: sup-porting resistance movements that already existed on the island or organizing a military capability and infiltrating Cuba. The FRD was involved in both.

Some of the organizations within the FRD were anti-revolutionary groups that were originally founded in Cuba, and still had presence on the island. These were very useful channels and were seen by the CIA as the best investment of their time and resources due to existing networks that could be used against the Castro regime. The earliest examples of clandestine infiltrations from Miami to Cuba—which became a surprisingly regular part of South Florida boating traffic and will be discussed in far more detail—were in support of these networks. Some were running guns and ammunition to operatives on the island as early as 1960. For example, in August 1960, the Christian Democrat Movement claimed to have between eight and ten thousand men in Cuba and would use the material support to carry out acts of sabotage throughout Cuba in early 1961.[9]

The creation of the FRD in Miami, and the resources it had access to, actually inspired the consolidation of a number of organizations in Cuba itself into a similar entity. In December 1960, twenty-seven underground resistance organizations in Cuba unified into the Revolutionary Unity (UR) organization to not only help better coordinate efforts on island but also streamline their ability to get weapons and needed supplies from the FRD. It was clear that the need was palpable: one of the UR's first sources of income was a holdup of the Tropical Brewery, which at the time produced about 60 percent of Cuba's beer—so something similar to robbing Budweiser in its prime—and netted $20,000. Within two months, the UR was receiving clandestine shipments of weapons and matériel from Miami for their anti-Castro efforts.[10]

The FRD was also central to the other planned method of democracy through arms. If the first was akin to helping the French Resistance in World War II, the second was preparing for D-Day: readying an invasion force to establish a beachhead and eventually liberate the country.

The FRD created a naval commission to coordinate the maritime piece of any operations: with Cuba being an island, this was obviously an important consideration. They compiled a register of private vessels that could be used for operations, as well as a naval reserve to operate them: a Cuban version of the "Corsair Navy" utilized in the United States during World War II to recruit private boat owners for the war effort. By March 1961, they had identified a flotilla of thirteen vessels and over a hundred volunteers. They also recognized that they likely would need additional and more mission-appropriate vessels in order to effectively mount a campaign against Castro's Cuba, and raised thousands of dollars to support the creation of a larger fleet.[11]

In September 1960, the naval office of this Cuban Navy in exile began operations in Miami. Shortly thereafter, they launched one of their first clandestine voyages, which was apparently enough of a failure—both in terms of the selection of the vessel for the mission and other logistical reasons—for them to form task forces and working groups to better plan these incursions. Their working relations with the CIA were more formally established by November, and they held increasingly structured discussions about operations, as well as attempting to unify a disparate number of similar efforts among exiles.[12]

They also needed men and matériel. The FRD had an organized and efficient recruiting mechanism to recruit military-aged men in Miami for the cause: registration cards, an internal intelligence check to try to weed out infiltrators sympathetic to Castro, and an oath of allegiance. Here is what the young men who registered for the FRD signed:

> I, _____, convinced that the tyranny in Cuba can only be overthrown by revolutionary means, apply for entry into the Democratic Revolutionary Front to fight towards that end, for that purpose, I invoke the most sacred memories of my life and with my body and mind set on the highest interests of my country.
> I solemnly swear on my honor as a revolutionary and as a man to support with all my might the Cuban revolution, even at the risk of my life, fighting within the Democratic Revolutionary Front in defense of our democratic system and the restoration of the Constitution and the Law, submitting myself to the established discipline and Military Code.
> So help me God.
> LET US FIGHT TOGETHER FOR
> THE FREEDOM OF CUBA![13]

These recruits were individuals who felt that this was a duty, a calling to rescue their country from autocratic rule and to restore democracy in Cuba. This was deeply personal, a point of honor, and an exhilarating opportunity. In a country whose first stirrings of independence were less than a hundred years earlier, it surely felt like their efforts were momentous. It was lost on no one that the young revolution they were organizing to overthrow began in very much the same way: a small group of individuals infiltrating the island by sea. The story of the *Granma*, the rickety old boat used by Castro to land in Cuba, had already become a part of the regime's own legend. The revolutionary government even saw fit to eventually rename a province in the vessel's honor. The opportunity to defeat this movement by the same means and method was almost poetic in its symmetry. They felt that this was an opportunity to participate in another liberation of their young country, and they expected to be primary authors in the writing of that history. These recruits would become part of the military arm of the FRD, a group that would play a major part in a critical chapter in the Cold War.

The Brigade

One of the first recruits was Manuel Artime of the MRR, who was added to the board of the FRD. Along with the San Román brothers, both former Cuban Army officers, he and twenty-five others formed the original nucleus of this effort, which was created and approved under Eisenhower. They received extensive guerrilla training and were sent to facilities specially built for this purpose in Guatemala. Men continued to come in from Miami to receive training from US Green Berets and await orders. The unit started with around 400 and ended up with nearly 1,500 men, and they were a diverse group from all social groups and political leanings.[14] Only 135 of them had military experience. Students, who numbered 240, were the most represented occupation. The average age was twenty-nine, but the youngest member of the Brigade was sixteen, and the oldest was sixty-one.[15]

The Brigade would become a crucible for the Cuban exile community in Miami, and numerous leaders and major players in later years started their anti-Castro experience with this unit. Félix Rodríguez, who would have a long and storied CIA career, was a member of the Brigade. Jorge Mas Canosa, a future exile leader, was among the ranks. José Basulto, who would be at the center of a major international incident over the Florida Straits, served. So did Erneido Oliva, who would join the US Army and retire as a major general and would be the only individual to serve as a second lieutenant in four armed forces involved in this unfolding drama: Cuba's Constitutional (pre-Revolutionary) Army, the Revolutionary Army, the Brigade itself, and the US Army.[16]

Every member of the Brigade was given a serial number. To disguise the number of men available for an assault on Cuba, the numbers were assigned starting with 2500, not 0. During training, a man by the name of Carlos Rafael Santana slipped and fell off a mountain cliff to his death. He was the first of the unit to lose his life. In his honor, the unit took up his serial number as the name they would carry into battle: they would be known as the 2506 Assault Brigade.[17] The unit would be part of a significant effort to shape the history of Cuba and would fight to establish a beachhead for its eventual liberation—these men would storm the beaches at the Bahía de Cochinos, known to history as the Bay of Pigs.*

The US government was interested in shaping that history as well and made that interest very clear. While recruits for the 2506 were being brought from Miami to clandestine training camps, Washington wanted the FRD to broaden its political base. Later in 1961, that desire, which was reportedly "terribly important to the White House," led to the FRD's retooling and renaming as the Consejo Revolucionario Cubano (Cuban Revolutionary Council, CRC). The US-selected chair of the council was José Miró Cardona, a jurist who served as Castro's first prime minister before breaking with him and leaving the country. The CRC was not an entity with assets or operational capabilities of its own but, like the FRD before it, served as an umbrella organization to consolidate exile efforts and provide a single touch point for American agencies.

Much like José Martí had done years before, the CRC organized committees in numerous cities. Headquartered in Miami, with offices in New York, Washington, and New Orleans, the CRC had delegations in every Latin American country as well as in France and Spain.

The most important characteristic of the FRD's retooled self as the CRC, however, was its relationship to the US government. In terms of practical impact, the fact of government financial support—largely cash flowing through the CRC—was critical to bringing Miami exile organizations into the fold. The council reportedly received $90,000 a month in support from Washington, resources that made the CRC a central player.[18] The council also had direct access to senior White House aides and the president, and served as a primary conduit between Washington and the Cuban exile counterrevolutionary efforts in Miami.

---

* The "Bay of Pigs" has always seemed like a strange name. In Cuban slang, the triggerfish, a colorful tropical fish common to those waters, is called a *cochino*, which is also a term for pig. In light of that fact, we should have been calling it the "Battle of Triggerfish Bay" all along.

Miró Cardona met with President Kennedy on a few occasions.[19] One of those meetings included a reaffirmation of the president's support for the CRC. Kennedy ended the meeting with words of encouragement: "Do not waver. You have my support. Pass on to the Council my most cordial best wishes." But it was the one phrase before that show of the president's support that resonated with Miró Cardona more than any other, and one that proved ominously prophetic for him and for the entire Cuban exile community: "Your destiny," Kennedy told him, "is to suffer."[20]

Sadly, the president was correct on all accounts, and he had no way of knowing just how predictive his words would be. Miró Cardona did have unique access to the American government, and was a gatekeeper of sorts for resources to Cuban exile organizations, but that came at a heavy price. Over time, his vision for protecting Cuba began to diverge significantly from that of the US government. Because of his proximity to Washington's power, frustrations with the Americans were often aimed at him: not being aggressive enough to overthrow Castro, not enough resources, favoritism toward one organization over another. Years later, Miró Cardona became exhausted by infighting and criticism, and intimately familiar with an unfortunate reality of the exile community's efforts: fragmentation and lack of cohesiveness.

For now, however, the table was set for what everyone hoped would be a definitive blow to the Castro regime. The 1,443 men of the 2506 Brigade were ready to fulfill their destiny and follow in Martí's footsteps.[21] Miami, now a critical recruiting and logistical hub for anti-communist efforts, would soon become a smaller, tropical Portsmouth used as a staging area for a Caribbean Normandy.

2

"You Can't Mañana This Thing"

It was an introvert's paradise.

Two weeks after Fidel Castro forced Fulgencio Batista from power in 1959, Justin Gleichauf found himself as the one and only employee of the new CIA operation in Miami. Part of the Domestic Contacts Division of the Directorate of Intelligence, the CIA field office (meaning Gleichauf) was tasked with monitoring and reporting on developments in Cuba.[1]

Gleichauf missed the fighting in the Second World War because he was too underweight for combat action (he was the water boy in college at Notre Dame because he was so skinny). Instead, he served as a technical advisor in the Office of Price Administration and on the Board of Economic Warfare. In 1950, he joined the CIA, and was assigned to an office that debriefed American professors and businessmen who had just returned from trips to Europe. During the Hungarian revolution in 1956, Gleichauf directed the interrogations of Hungarian rebels who came to the US after fighting Soviet troops.[2]

When he first got to Miami, the first wave of exiles had already arrived, and he set out to learn what government agency was doing what with the new Miami residents. According to Gleichauf, thirteen different federal agencies were working the problem, including the INS; Border Patrol; Customs; the Coast Guard; the State Department; the Department of Health, Education, and Welfare (HEW); FBI; and Army, Navy, and Air Force intelligence (along with a myriad of local law enforcement agencies).

And now the CIA.

At this time, the US government still hadn't decided what it was going to do about the new regime in Cuba. The US intelligence community had very little information about what was happening there, so Gleichauf collected as much open-source intelligence as he could, like newspapers, magazines, and any other printed material that might have relevant information. This open-source sweep also included *Granma*, the official newspaper of the Cuban Communist Party, and *Verde Olivo*, which gave some insight into the Cuban military.

To attract new contacts, he listed his CIA phone number in the telephone book and handed out business cards with his home number. The results were mixed. For every solid lead, Gleichauf explained, there was "a motley collection of weirdos," and opportunists who were looking for a way to earn some money from the US government. There were also "lots of would-be Mata Haris, eager to do anything for the cause," and American mercenaries, who thought Cuba would be a quick and easy way to get glory and riches. Gleichauf consistently tried to warn them off, with limited success.

There were also Castro sympathizers in Miami:

> A brick was thrown through the windshield of my car parked outside the house, and my wife received a number of threatening calls along the lines of ". . . [x-date] will be a day that you and your family will never forget . . ." I received a barrage of late-night phone calls, with the caller remaining silent while I answered. I memorized Spanish insults, which I directed at Fidel via the open line. The calls eventually dwindled.

With so many exiles entering Miami at that time, the CIA finally realized Gleichauf could not do this all by himself, so it beefed up his office's staffing. To four. The new additions were one air force and two army intelligence officers. Thankfully, they all spoke Spanish.

In the meantime, the government had finally figured out how it was going to react to Fidel Castro: he had to go. The CIA was working on multiple different operational plans against the new Cuban government. One of these involved air-dropping supplies to resistance forces still in Cuba. In late September 1960, the CIA made its first airdrop of supplies to rebels in Oriente Province (enough for one hundred soldiers). The operation, however, did not go as intended. Instead of supplying rebel forces fighting Castro, the airdrop landed seven miles from where it was expected—right into the hands of the Cuban revolutionary militia the arms were meant to be used against.[3]

And this wouldn't be the last time something like this went awry. Richard Bissell, the CIA Deputy Director of Plans, lamented, "We never got to first base in Cuba in building an underground organization. . . . We only had one [supply drop] where we were reasonably sure that the people the supplies were intended for actually got them."[4]

Then there was the story you might already have heard of—the CIA's use of the mob against Castro.

The Mafia was motivated. Before Fidel Castro came to power, Havana had been "the empress city of organized crime," and a "free port for the mob."[5] Havana was *the* main tourist destination in the 1950s, and people came there from all over for the gorgeous weather, the beaches, the gambling, and the bordellos. Even tourists from Miami headed south for activities forbidden at home.

Batista was a supporter of this world, at least for the right price (he received serious kickbacks for his protection). Now he was gone, replaced by a regime that was taking it all away.

The Mafia could not find a way to control Fidel Castro, which meant he had to go. It was nothing personal, just business.

In August 1960, Bissell approached the CIA's Office of Security to see if they had any assets that "may assist in a sensitive mission requiring gangster-type action. The mission target was Fidel Castro."[6] The CIA had used a man named Robert Maheu in the past for some of their shadier operations. A former special agent in the FBI, Maheu left the Bureau and opened a private investigation office in Washington, DC, in 1956. He was what was known as a "cut-out," a middleman, or someone that allowed the Agency to maintain distance from these kinds of things. According to CIA documents, "over the years he [had] been intimately involved in providing support for some of the Agency's more sensitive operations."[7] He had contacts in the underworld and would be the person who insulated the CIA from any direct contact with the mob.

Maheu reached out to Johnny Roselli, whom he had met on more than one occasion in Las Vegas. Roselli would eventually link Maheu (and the CIA) with Momo Salvatore "Sam" Giancana and Santo Trafficante Jr., two men, incidentally, on the list of the attorney general's ten most-wanted. Trafficante was the head of the Mafia's Cuban operations, and Giancana was the chief of the Chicago branch of the Mafia and considered the successor to Al Capone.[8] Together, Roselli and Giancana had controlled a massive Mafia empire, reportedly larger than the organization run by the five families of the New York Cosa Nostra—combined.[9]

Maheu had been authorized to offer the mobsters $150,000 for the job, but they declined. They would do it for free. Why? Well, for one, they stood to make far more money if Castro was removed from power, and they could restart their gambling interests in Cuba. Also, they likely assumed helping the US government in such a way could pay off later if they found themselves in, say, legal trouble.

In September 1960, Maheu met up with Johnny and Sam at the Boom Boom Room at the Fontainebleau Hotel in Miami.* The men discussed a variety of options for taking out Castro. The CIA was originally thinking along the lines of a "typical, gangland-style killing in which Castro would be gunned down," but Giancana said absolutely no to the use of firearms. He argued that no one could be recruited to do this kind of job, "because the chance of survival and escape would be negligible."†[10]

Instead, the mobsters suggested the use of a poison pill. Giancana said he knew a guy, whom he identified only as "Joe" (it was Trafficante), who would serve as a courier to Cuba and could make arrangements there to get the pill into Castro's drink. The individual who could get close to Castro in Cuba was Juan Orta, who was described as a "disaffected Cuban official with access to Castro and presumably of a sort that would enable him to surreptitiously poison Castro." According to Roselli and Giancana, Orta had once received kickbacks from gambling profits, and now that that was gone, "he needed the money." Orta was, at that time, the office chief and director general of the office of the prime minister, Fidel Castro.

---

* Can't you just picture the Boom Boom Room in your head? Is there a more aptly named establishment that just screams out "mob hangout"? Maybe the Bada Bing!, but it's close.

† I doubt Giancana used the word "negligible," but OK.

After Maheu reported back to the Agency, the chief of the CIA's Technical Services Division (TSD) was asked to develop a pill that "had the elements of rapid solubility, high lethal content, and little or no traceability."[11] The poison itself had to be "stable, soluble, safe to handle, undetectable, not immediately acting, and with a firmly predictable end result." Botulin toxin met all those requirements and could be made into a pill. Six of these were produced and tested.[12]

And they didn't work.

When they were dropped in water, they didn't even disintegrate, let alone dissolve completely, with "little to no traceability." The TSD tried again, and successfully made a new batch that "met the requirement for solubility." But would they kill someone?

No.

Guinea pigs were acquired for the test, but when the TSD tested the pills on the poor animals, they were found to be "ineffective."[13]

Well, that didn't work. Perhaps we should scrap this idea and move on to plan B?

No.

Roselli was given the useless pills and passed them along to Trafficante, who said they had then been delivered to Orta in Cuba. A 1966 CIA document states that, after several weeks of aborted attempts, Orta "apparently got cold feet and asked out of the assignment."[14] But by 1967, the CIA knew the real story: Orta had lost his position in the prime minister's office in January 1961, while planning for the operation was still in full swing in Washington and Miami. Did Roselli, Giancana, and Trafficante know this? According to the CIA, yes. So why did they say they could deliver when clearly they knew they couldn't? Only the three of them truly know, but one could surmise that they hoped to curry favor with the government by showing they'd tried.[15]

Operation Zapata

The CIA scheme to kill Castro with the mob was not, of course, the only such idea making its way through the corridors of power in Washington. The Pentagon had been instructed by the Eisenhower administration to develop a plan for paramilitary and covert actions against the Cuban regime. The military and the CIA would train Cuban exiles in the Miami area and then eventually in Central America. In the summer of 1960, word began to spread like wildfire through the Miami exile community—the US government was looking for volunteers to take the fight to Castro. According to Félix Rodríguez, who was among these volunteers, only one Cuban in a thousand "knew what the CIA was back in the summer of 1960"—it didn't matter. They were going to get the chance to fight.

In May, the CIA opened a headquarters in Coral Gables for its operations against Castro. The cover name of the facility was "Clarence A. Depew and Sons," supposedly a New York career development and placement firm.[16] At the same time, small training camps were popping up around Miami, the Everglades, and the Florida Keys.

Interestingly, this was not the first time Cuban exiles had used Miami and its surrounding areas for training purposes. It was also not the first time they were training to unseat an oppressive regime in Cuba. In 1958—before Castro even came to power—Everglades National Park staff discovered heavily armed Cubans walking through the park, looking for a location to place a shooting range. These Cuban exiles were not trying to unseat Castro, of course; they were trying to help him. They identified themselves as "anti-Batistianos" to the (very confused) park rangers.[17]

Also in 1958, an airborne Everglades park ranger spotted a ship loading cargo on Key Largo—but in a very unusual place that raised immediate suspicion. The park rangers contacted the Border Patrol, who investigated the ship. Turns out it was loaded to the brim with ammunition headed to Cuba to support Fidel and his fight against Batista.[18]

But starting in 1960, CIA-sponsored training camps, supply depots, weapons and ammunition caches, and the like were spreading across the South Florida landscape, intermingling with the city's residents in sometimes unpredictable ways. On the night of August 25, 1960, five teenage boys decided to play a prank on the residents of 26145 SW 195th Avenue by throwing firecrackers into the driveway of the house. It was a foolish plan in the best of times, but it turned out to be even more foolish than they could have realized: this house was actually a CIA-sponsored anti-Castro training camp. Thinking they were under attack, the Cuban exile trainees came out shooting, firing blindly into the darkness. One of the teenagers was grazed in the back of his head by one of the bullets. He was fine, but the secret CIA training facility was no longer very secret. Metro-Dade police closed down the facility a few hours later and detained "15 toughened Cubans" who had been using the property for jungle-warfare training.[19]

As training continued throughout South Florida, attention elsewhere in the United States turned to national politics. The 1960 presidential campaign pitted Senator John F. Kennedy from Massachusetts against the sitting vice president, Richard Nixon. In November, Kennedy won the election and, as part of the transition, was handed the plan for the exile-led invasion of Cuba by the outgoing Eisenhower administration. Why did Kennedy so readily accept this course of action? Why didn't he, as some historians and commentators have argued, have the courage to decide upon his own solution for the Castro situation? We are not about to try to get into Kennedy's head—his motivations are his own. However, it seems disingenuous for the Monday-morning quarterbacks to criticize Kennedy in this situation. Dwight Eisenhower was a five-star general. He ran the entire European Theater of Operations in World War II. He was the NATO Supreme Allied Commander.

JFK was a lieutenant in the Navy during World War II. His claim to fame was helping to save his marooned crew after his PT boat was run over by a Japanese destroyer. If you were Kennedy, would you have questioned the military wisdom of Dwight Eisenhower?

Yet others in his administration did. Just a few weeks after Kennedy's inauguration, one of his top aides and advisors, Arthur Schlesinger Jr., sent him a top-secret memorandum that spelled out his objections to the invasion plan. While acknowledging the "great pressure within the government in favor" of a military solution to the Cuba problem, Schlesinger contended that the arguments against this decision were important to note. He said:

> However well disguised any action might be, it will be ascribed to the United States. The result would be a wave of massive protest, agitation and sabotage throughout Latin America, Europe, Asia and Africa (not to speak of Canada and of certain quarters in the United States). Worst of all, this would be your first dramatic foreign policy initiative. At one stroke, it would dissipate all the extraordinary good will which has been rising toward the new Administration

throughout the world. It would fix a malevolent image of the new Administration in the minds of millions.

Schlesinger then proposed some alternatives. Could the US "induce Castro to take offensive action first?" Noting Castro had already launched small expeditions against Panama and the Dominican Republic, Schlesinger said he could "conceive a black operation in, say, Haiti which might in time lure Castro into sending a few boatloads of men on to a Haitian beach in what could be portrayed as an effort to overthrow the Haitian regime." If Fidel was tricked into making the first move, "then the moral issue would be clouded, and the anti-US campaign would be hobbled from the start."

Or, perhaps Kennedy could give a speech addressed to the whole Western Hemisphere in which he set forth "in eloquent terms" his ideas on inter-American progress toward freedom and justice. This would make the Cuban operation seem as though it was part of a broader Latin American policy that was in lockstep with the "aspirations of the plain people of the hemisphere." If Kennedy could pull this off, "action against Castro could be seen as in the interests of the hemisphere and not just of American corporations."

Finally, Schlesinger asked about the possibility of ousting Castro *and* right-wing Dominican Republic dictator Rafael Trujillo at the same time. If the overthrow of both could be coordinated, or if Trujillo could be deposed *before* Castro, then "it would show that we have a principled concern for human freedom and do not object only to left-wing dictators."[20]

Powerful arguments from one of Kennedy's most trusted advisors.

But the president was getting conflicting advice from some of his top people as well. McGeorge Bundy, JFK's National Security Advisor, sent a letter to the president three days before Schlesinger's. In the letter, he conveyed far more confidence in the potential of success for the Cuba operation. Acknowledging the hesitation from the State Department and others in the diplomatic community, Bundy reminded Kennedy that "Defense and CIA now feel quite enthusiastic about the invasion from Guatemala [where the exiles had been sent to train and stage for the eventual mission]—at the very worst they think the invaders would get into the mountains, and at the best they think they might get a full-fledged civil war in which we could then back the anti-Castro forces openly."[21]

The CIA had their reasons for moving forward with the plan, but one reason stands out—at least for this book. According to Schlesinger, on March 11, 1961, CIA Director Allen Dulles warned President Kennedy to not "forget that we have a disposal problem." Meaning what, you might ask? Meaning that there were hundreds of trained Cuban exiles in Miami and Guatemala waiting to invade Cuba. If Kennedy called off the operation, all of those men would be left to their own devices, with potentially disastrous consequences. CIA Deputy Director of Plans Richard Bissell worried the entire operation would collapse if Kennedy didn't make his decision, and make it soon: "You can't mañana this thing."[22] Four weeks after Dulles's and Bissell's warnings, Kennedy is said to have told Schlesinger, "If we have to get rid of these 800 men, it is much better to dump them in Cuba than in the United States, especially if that is where they want to go."[23] A true profile in courage.

Of course, the Bay of Pigs invasion was a disaster. Of the 1,400 Cuban exiles who were part of the operation, more than 100 were killed and almost 1,200 were captured. The 2506 Brigade POWs spent twenty months in Cuban prisons, before they were finally exchanged for $53 million worth of baby food and pharmaceuticals. There are now hundreds of books, articles, analyses, dissections, studies, and investigations about that mission and why it ultimately failed.*

But fail it did. The Kennedy administration (rightfully) took much of the blame. Heads rolled at the CIA as Kennedy replaced Allen Dulles and most of his leadership team. In Cuba, Castro used the Bay of Pigs as an excuse to crack down on anyone who could maybe one day, some day rise up to challenge his authority. In the month following the invasion, Castro's regime arrested twenty thousand people for "counterrevolutionary activity."[24] In a conversation with Kennedy administration official Dick Goodwin later that year, Che Guevara thanked the Americans for the Bay of Pigs, saying that "it had been a great political victory for them—enabled them to consolidate—and transformed them from an aggrieved little country to an equal."[25]

Félix Rodríguez, a 2506 member who went on to do a whole lot more within and outside the CIA (more of him to come), lamented what the mission's failure meant for the resistance inside Cuba:

---

* If we tried to list them, this footnote would be twenty pages long.

The fact is, in botching the invasion, the Americans did the very thing they were out to prevent: they caused Fidel to cement his power structure and crush any rebellion. Before the Bay of Pigs we had no trouble recruiting anti-Castro volunteers in Cuba. Before the Bay of Pigs, the Cuban people joked about Castro openly and talked in public about what would happen when he was thrown out. Afterward there was no talk in public—or anywhere else. Castro used the invasion as a pretext for arresting and executing virtually all of his current and potential political enemies, thus ending a generation's worth of protest. He sent agents provocateurs into the streets and countryside to kill those who spoke against him. I believe that before April 17 there had been a good chance of overthrowing Castro and returning Cuba to democracy. Afterward, that goal became 100 percent harder to achieve.[26]

A week after the failed operation, during a time when the Kennedy administration, the Pentagon, the CIA, and the Miami Cuban exile community were in the midst of a postmortem on what went wrong, Deputy National Security Advisor Walt Rostow sent a memorandum to the Secretaries of State and Defense, and the director of the CIA. In this prescient document, Rostow lays out the main threats to the United States from the Castro regime now that they had failed to remove him:

- It might join with the USSR in setting up an offensive air or missile base.
- It might build up sufficient conventional military strength to trigger an arms race in the hemisphere and threaten the independence of other Latin American nations.
- It might develop its covert subversive network in ways which would threaten other Latin American nations from within.
- Its ideological contours are a moral and political offense to us; and we are committed, by one means or another, to remove that offense, including our commitment to the Cuban refugees among us.

- Its ideological contours and success may tend to inflame disruptive forces in the rest of Latin America, accentuating existing economic, social, and political tensions which we, in any case, confront.[27]

He was five for five.

Despite the failure of the Bay of Pigs, the Americans weren't getting out of the oust-Castro business anytime soon. Plans began for the next phase of operations even before the last 2506 member was captured in Cuba. In short, the new plan was to create an "island-wide resistance organization responsive to [CIA] direction," and to support and guide "those anti-Castro groups who are revealed to have a potential for clandestine operations" (see Chapters 1, 3, 4, 5, 6, and some of 7 for more on this).

Arthur Schlesinger Jr., seemingly always the critic (but clearly someone Kennedy should have listened to more often), thought the plan made little sense: "What is intended is a CIA underground formed on criteria of operational convenience rather than a Cuban underground formed on criteria of building political strength sufficient to overthrow Castro."

Schlesinger's main point—"It is a fallacy to suppose that clandestine activity can be carried out in a political vacuum." The CIA claimed they weren't ignoring political conditions in Cuba, despite Schlesinger's skepticism. They were, in fact, supporting political organizations and not just paramilitary or covert activities. But, according to Schlesinger, the CIA was playing favorites with the political organizations "most willing to accept CIA identification and control," and they discriminated against any groups "most eager to control their own operations." That is to say, the plan discriminates "in favor of mercenaries, reactionaries, etc., and discriminates against men of independence and principle."

In essence, the CIA was backing the "people *least* capable of generating broad support within Cuba."[28]

Yet by November 1961, President Kennedy was secretly directing his administration to use all available American assets to help Cuba to overthrow the Castro regime. Many of his top advisors were bullish on the prospects. Dick Goodwin wrote in an Eyes Only memo to the president that "the beauty of such an operation over the next few months is that we cannot lose. If the best happens we will unseat Castro. If not, then at least we will emerge with a stronger underground, better propaganda and a far clearer idea of the dimensions of the problems which affect us."[29]

We can't lose! What could possibly go wrong?

All that was left was to give the new operation a code name. All Agency code names, or "cryptonyms," began with what was known as a "digraph," a two-letter sequence that served as a geographic designator for the code name. For example, AM was the digraph for Cuba—Fidel Castro was referred to in CIA documents as AMTHUG, while Che, a physician, was AMQUACK; JM was for locations and people related to programs fighting Castro—the Miami CIA station would be named JMWAVE.

To keep the operation as compartmentalized and secret as possible, the CIA looked for a cryptonym that didn't begin with AM or JM. Instead, they used a digraph from an area thousands of miles away from Cuba—MO.*

The name of the operation would be MONGOOSE.

---

* MO was the cryptonym for Thailand . . . we think.

3

Does the *C* in CIA Stand for *Coño**?

Operation MONGOOSE was officially launched on November 30, 1961, under the direction of US Air Force Brigadier General Edward Lansdale, who would serve as its chief of operations. Lansdale was an experienced insurgency and counterinsurgency officer, having served with the Office of Strategic Services in World War II. After the war, he worked in the Philippines helping the Philippine Army build up its intelligence capabilities and, in the early 1950s, assisted them in defeating the communist Hukbalahap insurgency. The Huks, as they were more popularly known—at least by the English-speaking press—had originally organized to fight against the Japanese occupation of the Philippines. But when the war ended, they had turned their attention to the US-allied government. After this successful mission, Lansdale was sent to Vietnam to try to do something similar there—train the national government in counterinsurgency operations.[1]

First the Japanese. Then the Huks. Then the Viet Minh. Castro's Cuba was next.

To make this work, the US government would need to pour massive resources into its base of operations in Miami. The CIA, of course, was there

---

* *Coño* in the chapter title translates more or less to . . . "shucks" . . . in Cubanese.

already, but not with the necessary personnel or financial backing for a program of this magnitude. There was also the legal question: the National Security Act of 1947, which established the CIA, mandated that the Agency would operate exclusively abroad. Was the Miami CIA presence consistent with this law?

Lawrence Houston, the CIA's General Counsel, was asked for his legal opinion. "You guys are responsible and reporting to the president," Houston argued, "so set it up anyway you want to."[2]

The Miami CIA station, code-named JMWAVE, had opened in September 1961, and now it was going to get an enormous expansion of its resources, personnel, finances, and capabilities. JMWAVE was modeled after the CIA's overseas stations, but there were two key differences. First, it was unprecedented for a full-service CIA station to operate in a US city. The CIA had smaller facilities scattered around the country, but nothing remotely this size, or with such a broad scope. Also, the CIA stations that operated overseas had a built-in cover—the United States embassies. CIA employees worked from the embassy and most of them had jobs as embassy staff. By day, the CIA case officer might be the "Second Deputy Agricultural Attaché," but at night he or she would be conducting a clandestine meet with a foreign asset—a spy—to collect intelligence on an adversary. But the Miami CIA station did not have this luxury. Their cover had to be commercial.

The main CIA headquarters for JMWAVE was Zenith Technical Enterprises. However, for JMWAVE's operations in Miami this was just the tip of the iceberg. Hundreds of millions of dollars of government money rushed into Miami to maintain this mission. The CIA controlled more than fifty front companies in Miami—not all at the same time, to be sure. They could only use front companies and properties for short periods of time before they needed to move on. The risk of exposure was far too high to get comfortable.

The names of these front companies were intentionally vanilla and nondescript—the kind of names you hear and then forget thirty seconds later. There was Actos Technology Inc. and the Pacific Corporation. The Double-Chek Corporation, the Gibraltar Steamship Corporation, and the Vanguard Service Corporation also protected CIA entities. Paragon Air Service provided logistics support for JMWAVE operations, along with Southern Air Transport, a CIA-run airline that flew out of the Miami International and Opa-locka airports. Of course, we can't forget Red Sunset Enterprises, which was set up to recruit underwater-demolition experts, or Transworld Marine, which purchased boats for the CIA to surreptitiously infiltrate exiles and weapons into Cuba.

Wait, I've already forgotten them.

Ceres Enterprises Inc., located on West Flagler Street in Miami, was supposedly established in order to maintain and operate boats for marine research. In reality, it provided cover for CIA maritime vessels (code-named the *Barb* and the *Jade*). Ace Marine Survey Inc.'s cover was also that of a research company, primarily focused on the study of marine life and the testing of marine equipment. In the spy world, it provided cover for the CIA's SONORA.[3]

In 1964, two journalists for *Look* magazine wrote an article that blew the cover on Zenith Technical Enterprises. No worries, though. The CIA just changed the name to the Melmar Corporation and kept on trucking.

We don't know the exact numbers for sure, but by the time MONGOOSE got really going the annual budget of the Miami operation was an estimated $50 million (in 1960s dollars). If you are wondering what that would be today, using the Bureau of Labor Statistics CPI inflation calculator it comes out to over $500 million annually.[4] This inflow of money funded purchases all over the Miami area: land for training camps, marinas, hunting camps, airlines, hotels, safe houses, leasing firms, transportation, publishing offices, boat shops, merchant shipping, travel agencies, and more. They had three or four people on staff who just worked on real estate, managing the myriad of front companies created to hold properties. They had more than one hundred cars under lease and operated the third-largest navy in the entire Caribbean (after the US and Cuba).

There were hundreds of CIA employees, hundreds of Cuban exiles on the payroll, more than a thousand contractors, and up to fifteen thousand Cuban exiles connected to JMWAVE in some kind of way. In the 1960s, the CIA became one of—if not *the*—largest employer in Miami, and one of the largest employers in the State of Florida.[5]

It would be hard to overstate how much of an economic impact the CIA's presence had on Miami. The CIA existed as what could be considered a jobs program for thousands of Cuban exiles, who came to Miami with nothing but the clothes on their backs. But it's far more than that. All these CIA employees, contractors, and new exiles needed *stuff*, and a lot of it. They needed to buy houses, cars, furniture, appliances, food, clothing, and the like. They bought groceries, ate out at restaurants, drank at bars, and went to movies. Some of their kids went to private school and, of course, they paid sales and municipal taxes. Much of that $50 million budget was dropped right into the local economy.

JMWAVE/Zenith Technical Enterprises occupied more than two thousand acres of land located in southwest Miami-Dade County. At one point, it was the Richmond Naval Air Station, an LTA (Lighter Than Air—read: blimp) base during World War II. Officially commissioned in September 1942, the Richmond NAS contained the largest wooden structure in the world—Blimp Hangar No. 1—which soared 16.5 stories high and measured over one thousand feet in length. During the war, airships from Richmond flew day and night, hunting for German submarines off the coast of Florida, until the air base was flattened by a hurricane in September 1943. With over $30 million in damage, this storm had meant the end for any operational role for Richmond NAS.

After the war, the Navy transferred the property over to the University of Miami, who expected an influx of discharged soldiers looking to use their GI Bill benefits and seek higher education. The university used the complex as their "South Campus" and housed freshman classes there. They also used the secluded and wooded area for tropical food and medical research. In the early 1960s, no longer needing the space for students or science, UM leased the property to the CIA.[6]

For much of MONGOOSE (and several years after), the Miami CIA operation was led by Chief of Station Theodore "Ted" Shackley. A South Florida native (he grew up in West Palm Beach), Shackley's first experience in the intelligence field was with the US Army's Counterintelligence Corps in the late 1940s. From there he moved over to the CIA, which was looking for personnel with skills in Soviet Bloc languages. Since Shackley spoke Polish (his grandparents were immigrants) he was hired and assigned to the Polish unit of the CIA's Office of Special Operations, where he learned how to be a spook. His career soon led him to West Germany, where he worked under the wing of legendary/infamous (depending on who you ask) CIA officer William Harvey, who introduced him to the world of paramilitary action. As Harvey moved up the ranks, so did Shackley. When Harvey, now at CIA headquarters, was looking for a chief of station to lead the newly revamped Miami operation, Shackley was his natural choice.[7]

Shackley in Miami reported to Desmond FitzGerald at CIA headquarters in Langley, Virginia. FitzGerald was the head of what was called the Special Affairs Staff (SAS), a mundane name for the office that oversaw all the James Bond stuff—the espionage, paramilitary, sabotage, and other intelligence actions against Castro. Like JMWAVE, the office went through a dramatic transition. Under his leadership, the SAS became the CIA's largest geographical office with more than 150 staffers. This, remember, was for only a single country. The SAS was larger than entire regional departments, some of which included a dozen or more countries. It was bigger than even the *Soviet* division. And the budget was four times the total spent in all twenty of the other Latin American and Caribbean nations . . . combined.[8]

So What's the Plan?

On February 20, 1962, Lansdale presented to the Kennedy administration "an operation plan for the overthrow of the Communist regime in Cuba, by Cubans from within Cuba, with outside help from the US and elsewhere." The plan included sections on political, economic, and psychological warfare, as well as military, sabotage, and intelligence support for Cuban anti-Castro forces on the island. In the plan, Lansdale acknowledges that the Americans "still know too little about the real situation inside Cuba," but there is clear "evidence that the repressive measures of the Communists, together with disappointments in Castro's economic dependency on the Communist formula, have resulted in an anti-regime atmosphere among the Cuban people which makes a resistance program a distinct and present responsibility."

The foundation of Lansdale's strategy:

Americans once ran a successful revolution. It was run from within, and succeeded because there was timely and strong political, economic, and military help by nations outside who supported our cause. Using this same concept of revolution from within, we must now help the Cuban people to stamp out tyranny and gain their liberty.

The document also included a timeline for the multi-phased operation:

Phase I. **Action.** March 1962. Start moving in.

Phase II. **Build-up.** April–July 1962. Activating the necessary operations inside Cuba for revolution and concurrently applying the vital political, economic, and military-type support from outside Cuba.

Phase III. **Readiness.** August 1, 1962. Check for final policy decision.

Phase IV. **Resistance.** August–September 1962, move into guerrilla operations.

Phase V. **Revolt.** First two weeks of October 1962. Open revolt and overthrow of the Communist regime.

Phase VI. **Final.** During month of October 1962. Establishment of new government.[9]

See? Nothing to it!

Also in February, Lansdale circulated a memorandum with ideas for potential MONGOOSE operations. Lots of ideas. Some were decent. Others were silly. A few were downright abhorrent. None of them were particularly practical. President Kennedy's top military aide, General Maxwell Taylor, recognized Lansdale as "an idea man," but added that "to find an idea that was feasible was a different proposition." An aide for CIA Deputy Director for Plans Richard Helms was less charitable: "He used to drive everybody crazy with his ideas. He'd bombard [Bill] Harvey with a million goddamn papers all the time."[10]

Here are a few of the many proposed operations:

Operation FREE RIDE
In an attempt to create "unrest and dissension" among the Cuban people, American pilots would air-drop hundreds of valid, one-way airline tickets for

flights from Cuba to Mexico City, Caracas, and a number of other US-friendly countries (but not the US itself). Whether people used them or not didn't matter all that much. The idea was to get the Cuban security services worried about a mass exodus.

Operation DEFECTOR

This was an idea with the expressed purpose of decreasing Cuban military capability. Combining the vague premise of "intelligence means" (whatever that is) with the promise of equally vague "rewards," Operation DEFECTOR was intended to induce Cuban soldiers (or even entire units) to defect along with their equipment. Not only would this reduce Cuban military readiness, but it would create "havoc" within Cuban security and intelligence agencies, as they scrambled to prevent military desertions.

Operation BREAK-UP and Operation FULL-UP

These two plans were intended to reduce Cuban confidence in the equipment of their Soviet benefactors. Operation BREAK-UP would "clandestinely introduce corrosive materials" to Soviet-supplied aircraft, vehicles, and ships, to cause accidents, increase supply and maintenance problems, and "seriously" affect combat capability and readiness. Operation FULL-UP called for an introduction of a "known biological agent" into jet fuel storage, which would multiply until it "consumes all the space inside the tank." The Cubans would believe that the fuel was contaminated when it arrived, and since it was supplied to them by the Soviet Bloc, it would create tension within the alliance.

Operation COVER-UP

As astronaut John Glenn prepared to become the first American to orbit the Earth, the United States military (mainly the Navy) was gearing up to support the operation. This meant dozens of ships—to monitor the launch, to take in scientific data from the mission, to preposition themselves in case of emergency, and even if there wasn't an emergency, to recover Glenn and his space capsule upon reentry. Operation COVER-UP would use this naval buildup and try to convince (the memorandum didn't say how) the Cubans that it was actually a smoke screen for something else. We aren't trying to be cagey when we write "for something else," because the document itself says that "it should not be revealed as to what the cover is." I suppose the obvious conclusion would be cover for an invasion force, but they apparently wanted to keep the Cubans guessing . . . or Lansdale hadn't thought far beyond that.

Operation DIRTY TRICK

This took Operation COVER-UP a step further. Remember, at this point the US had barely put two men into space. Alan Shepard's mission was barely high enough to be considered a space flight, and Gus Grissom's was similar—and then we lost Grissom's capsule to the bottom of the ocean, and almost lost Grissom too. So we didn't have a superb track record on sending people into space and recovering them safely back on Earth. There was a fairly decent chance John Glenn's mission would be a disaster (and it almost was—his flight was shortened due to a mechanical malfunction). If things didn't go well, we were ready to blame it on the Cubans. The objective of DIRTY TRICK was to manufacture "irrevocable" evidence that—should Glenn's flight fail—would show that Cuban "electronic interference" was the cause. Contingency planning at its worst.

Operation GOOD TIMES

The objective for this plan was to "disillusion the Cuban population" with fake pictures of Fidel Castro—such as a fat Castro standing in a room in his house, with "two beauties" (one on each arm). The house would be "lavishly furnished," and the dining-room table would have an enormous spread, full of "delectable" Cuban food. The air-dropped photos would be supplemented with an "appropriately Cuban" caption—something like "My ration is different"—all in the spirit of putting "even a Commie Dictator in the proper perspective" with the underfed and underprivileged Cuban masses.

Operation NO LOVE LOST

This plan called for exile pilots to confuse and harass Cuban pilots by use of radio conversations. Since the exile pilots might personally know many of the pilots still flying for Castro, they could engage them in a spirited argument. According to the plan, this "would be real trouble for Castro pilots in actual weather conditions." And finally, some guidance on the script for the exile pilots: "Argument could go, 'I'll get you you Red son-of-a-gun,' and call by name if appropriate."[11]

Lansdale's zeal and confidence won over the Kennedys (Jack and Bobby). Part of this might be due to the supposed timing of the operation: a free Cuba in the fall of 1962, just in time for the midterm elections. Lansdale was particularly politically astute—according to one highly placed Kennedy aide, Lansdale "knew who he was working for." But others in the administration and intelligence community were more immune to Lansdale's charms. The CIA, knowing its own limitations, tried to warn the Kennedys that covert action wasn't some magic bullet that could solve all their problems.[12]

The Pentagon was even less convinced the covert-action-heavy Operation MONGOOSE could bring about regime change in Cuba. They were adamant that time was not on their side, and more direct (read: US military) action would be required to oust Castro. In March, they proposed their own plan in a memorandum titled "Justification for US Military Intervention in Cuba." The proposal was known as Operation NORTHWOODS.

In a perfect world, Cuba could be goaded or provoked into attacking the United States. In this ideal scenario, Castro would make it unnecessary for the US to concoct an elaborate plan to convince the world that we were the victim. Castro would do the dirty work for us.

Fidel Castro was a lot of things, but he wasn't stupid. He wasn't about to give the US a perfectly valid excuse to invade his country.

This meant that the Joint Chiefs of Staff had to create the scenario themselves. They needed to make it appear as though the Cubans had attacked legitimate and vital American interests. At least they needed the rest of the world to agree to suspend their disbelief so that the US could claim victimhood, and retain a modicum of plausible deniability that it wasn't really the United States military that was behind all of it.

After a litany of caveats—the courses of action listed in the document were "only for planning purposes"; the document should be considered a "point of departure"; it would be desirable to use "legitimate provocation" as the basis for American intervention in Cuba—NORTHWOODS jumped right in to a list of ways to pretend the US had been wronged by Castro and the Cubans. It's a long list, but here are some of the particularly interesting ones:

NORTHWOODS provided an eleven-point checklist of operational ideas regarding a fake assault on the United States naval installation at Guantánamo Bay. First, using clandestine radio, the plan called for starting rumors of a pending attack by Cuban military forces on the American base, followed closely (step 2) by an actual assault on the base by Cuban exiles (the document called them "friendly" Cubans) dressed in Cuban military uniforms. Some of these "friendly" Cubans would be captured attempting to sabotage key Gitmo facilities (step 3), while other "friendlies" would start riots near the base main gate—the Cuban people rising up to demonstrate against the American occupiers (4). This was the point at which the mission went kinetic (or in layman's terms, when we would start to blow stuff up). Step 5 called for setting fires inside the base that would blow up ammunition stores, and burn aircraft parked on the airfield (step 6). Concurrently, the "friendly" Cubans would launch mortar shells into Gitmo, causing "some damage to installations" (7), and saboteurs would set fire to a ship in the harbor (10), or even sink one near the harbor entrance (11, which could be done in lieu of 10—this could happen along with the requisite funerals for "mock-victims"). These sabotage operations would occur simultaneously with a fake ground assault. After "capturing" the assault teams in the vicinity of Gitmo (8), and "capturing" the militia group that "storm[ed] the base" (9), the United States would have the necessary pretense to respond with "large scale" military operations to oust the Castro regime.

A more detailed proposal for the sink-a-ship idea was also on the docket in case Kennedy wanted to go in that direction. NORTHWOODS opined that a new "Remember the Maine" incident in Guantánamo Bay could be an impetus for a full-scale invasion. If you still retain your Spanish-American War history, you'll recall that the catalyst for that 1898 war was the mysterious explosion of the USS *Maine* battleship in Havana Harbor. While we know now (and probably they knew then, too) that the ship most likely blew up because of an accident, the United States government used the incident to instigate a war against Spain. If it worked once, why not again? A nice little touch at the end of the plan's explanation really makes it sing: "The US could follow up with an air/sea rescue operation covered by US fighters to 'evacuate' remaining members of the non-existent crew. Casualty lists in US newspapers would cause a helpful wave of national indignation."

Step 4 on the NORTHWOODS plan is especially callous. It begins: "We could develop a Communist Cuban terror campaign in the Miami area, in other Florida cities and even in Washington." The terror campaign (and it's extraordinary that they even use the words "terror campaign" here without a hint of self-awareness) would be primarily targeted at Cuban exiles in Miami or refugees seeking asylum in the US. "We could sink a boatload of Cubans enroute to Florida (real or simulated)." Real or simulated! It continues: "We could foster attempts on lives of Cuban refugees" in the US "even to the extent of wounding in instances to be widely publicized." So how do we carry out this terrorism? By "exploding a few plastic bombs" in specific locations around the Miami area.[13]

Fortunately for the civilians in Miami and Washington (and their offspring—including the two authors of this book), President Kennedy rejected the Joint Chiefs' plan. There would be no Operation NORTHWOODS.

So Lansdale's MONGOOSE was still the only game in town. As the spring and summer months turned to fall, Lansdale and his team continued their planning.

And then they planned some more.

And then they sent around memoranda on their planning.[14]

And then they planned some more.

Eventually it was October 1962 and time (according to the schedule) for phases V and VI of MONGOOSE: Open revolt! Revolution! A new government!

Or perhaps, more memos?

Maybe this is unfair. Maybe given the opportunity to continue unfettered, Operation MONGOOSE could have accomplished its mission and given the world a Cuba without Fidel Castro. But an international crisis would intercede, and thirteen days in October would make the MONGOOSE plan take a back seat to the abject terror of nuclear brinkmanship.

When the dust settled, the US-Cuban dynamic would be dramatically changed.

It's Poppin' in Opa-locka, Floppin' Them Candy Paints

Cubans fleeing the Castro regime were already undergoing a life-changing, disorienting, and confusing experience. Many of them must have felt that all the displacement and uprooting was some sort of terrible dream. For many who were processed into the country in a small Miami neighborhood called Opa-locka, their earliest impressions of the United States were complete with

Moorish minarets, sultanate palaces, and streets names torn from the pages of *Arabian Nights*.

Opa-locka was the vision of aviation pioneer Glenn Curtiss, who made millions manufacturing aircraft, and wanted to invest some of that wealth in the 1920s real-estate boom that helped jump-start the expansion of Miami. He envisioned an entire community inspired by the *One Thousand and One Nights* collection of Middle Eastern folktales and the recent smash-hit film of 1925, *The Thief of Baghdad*, starring that rakish heartthrob Douglas Fairbanks. The city has the largest concentration of Moorish Revival architecture in the Western Hemisphere, and boasts streets named Ali Baba Avenue, Aladdin Street, and of course, Sesame Street. With thousands of Cubans fleeing the island in the early months of the Castro regime, a huge treasure trove of intelligence was being collected just a few blocks from Sesame Street—but this intel was brought to you by the letters *C*, *I*, and *A*.

In much the same way that MONGOOSE jump-started the Miami CIA station JMWAVE, the program also gave a major boost to Justin Gleichauf's little-interrogation-center-that-could operation in Coral Gables. Their four-person team swelled to about fifty, and was moved to the old barracks on an unused World War II Marine Corps air base at Opa-locka Airport.

The staff itself was from all military services and several government agencies (CIA, Defense, US Information Agency, and Voice of America). The military personnel were both enlisted and officer, many with Puerto Rican and Mexican American backgrounds. Very few of the interrogators had experience in intelligence, and Gleichauf had to first train them in interview strategies. Also, to ensure they were getting an accurate translation of an exile's information (taking into consideration local slang, idioms, regional dialects, and the like), they prepared a "special glossary of 'Cubanese.'" According to Gleichauf, "CIA editors worked overtime converting native Spanish phraseology into clear, concise English."[15]

The interviews were seen as an effective way to turn an immigration processing center into an intelligence collection node, a mechanism to flag potential recruits, and a shield against counterintelligence. It made sense: the US government was already interacting with immigrants through their processing, why not see if some of them were positioned to provide information on what was taking place on the island?

This collection point of human intelligence was a consistent source of first-hand information on revolutionary Cuba. And they were doing brisk business: there was no shortage of people fleeing the island to the safety of Miami. Richard Helms reported in June 1962 that 1,600 refugees a week were interrogated yielding around 250 weekly intelligence reports. In nine months, they had interviewed ten thousand refugees and produced 5,608 intelligence reports as a result.[16]

The intelligence take from these interviews was profound. First, they were able to put to rest the fundamental idea behind Lansdale's MONGOOSE plan—that internal revolt in Cuba could be instigated by American covert action (or by anything else, really). As part of the interview process, Cuban exiles were asked if they believed the conditions existed in Cuba for the possibility of a successful internal revolt against Castro. At first, the responses were quite positive: In March 1962, 66 percent of those interviewed believed conditions were ripe for a Cuban uprising. By the fall, however, those numbers had declined drastically. In September—the month before MONGOOSE was scheduled to provide regime change in Cuba—only 5 percent believed this could happen on the island.

But the major intelligence coup came in mid-September, when a new arrival at Opa-locka reported that he had observed a Soviet truck convoy leaving the Havana dock, at night, and under tight security. The trucks "towed 56- to 75-foot trailers carrying objects so large they extended over the ends of the trailers. The objects were covered, but they had large fins." The US Army lieutenant colonel conducting the interview immediately realized he had something significant. He asked the man to draw the object he had seen on the back of the truck. He compared it with photographs of known Soviet missile types, and then asked the refugee to ID the missile he had seen from a collection of intelligence photos. The man immediately picked the SS-4, a Soviet medium-range ballistic missile, out of the photo array.

On September 17, the interviewers received another report, this time from a refugee from the Pinar del Río province of Cuba, of a large convoy of Soviet trucks carrying possible missiles. Both reports were sent to Washington and played a key role in the Kennedy administration's authorization of the fateful October 14 U-2 spy plane flight that brought about the Cuban Missile Crisis.*[17]

---

*We have no plans to wade into the debate within the intelligence community regarding *what* specific intel led to Kennedy's decision to send the U-2. Multiple agencies have a right to claim it was their intel. Certainly the CIA, but also the DIA and NSA have very strong claims.

Fortress Miami

Once Soviet offensive missile installations were discovered in Cuba, Miami was put on war footing. The 82nd Airborne Division took over Opa-locka (displacing Gleichauf's team), along with the US Army's 2nd Logistical Command, whose ten thousand troops were responsible for medical, engineering, ordnance, and transportation services during the crisis.[18]

Homestead Air Force Base in southern Miami-Dade County, already a facility for both strategic aircraft (bombers under the Strategic Air Command) and tactical fighter aircraft (Tactical Air Command), provided facilities and logistical support for a slew of bombers and fighter interceptors brought in to supplement Homestead's contingent. It also served as the headquarters for the US Army Forces Atlantic Command (or USARLANT—the army forces brought together for the Cuban Missile Crisis), the command-and-control element for the more than one hundred thousand soldiers assigned to this operation, including the US Army's vaunted 1st Armored Division, who were preparing for a possible invasion of Cuba should negotiations ultimately fail.[19]

Homestead AFB was also home to the headquarters of the air defense missile batteries sent to Miami to protect the southern US from a Soviet or Cuban bombing attack. Before the Cuban Missile Crisis, this contingency wasn't considered—no one really saw the Cuban Air Force as a threat to the US. But now there were Soviet bombers in Cuba, and Soviet-made MiG aircraft. Miami was suddenly vulnerable. Secretary of Defense Robert McNamara was concerned: "We have a serious air defense problem. . . . I think we must assume that the Cuban air force is definitely capable of penetrating, in small numbers, our coastal air defense by coming in low over the water."

In response, the Pentagon deployed several air defense battalions to Miami, consisting of both Hawk medium-range missiles and Nike Hercules high-altitude long-range missiles. Now if anyone tried to attack the United States from the southeast, they would have a rude welcome waiting for them.

When the crisis ended, the vast majority of the military might brought together in Miami for those thirteen days in October was redeployed out of the city and back to its home bases. The air defense missiles stayed, however. Washington had decided that Castro and his Soviet benefactors posed too great a risk to leave an open back door into the heart of America. For almost the next two decades, the Hawk and Nike Hercules missile batteries would give Miami an all-altitude air defense system to protect it, and the United States, from an attack from the south.[20]

US military units were not the only combat forces in Miami readying for an invasion of Cuba (should that eventuality come to pass). JMWAVE had formed twenty infiltration teams of Cuban exiles, which would have joined the US-led invasion as special operations and paramilitary units. They had been essentially sequestered during the crisis, under conditions of maximum security, waiting for the call to press ahead and begin the liberation of the island. But, of course, that didn't happen, and JMWAVE needed guidance from Washington about what to do with these teams.

And time was not on their side. Ted Shackley, Miami's CIA station chief, sent a message to Lansdale in Washington, desperate for guidance:

> Human psychology and stamina being what they are, this high peak of proficiency cannot be maintained indefinitely because fighters of all types go stale as is so well documented in pugilistic annals and all other competitive fields where combat readiness is required. *This particularly true with Cubans who [are] volatile, emotional, expressive people.* While this all well known Headquarters believes fluctuations in go and stop orders over past seven days have been such that prudent judgment dictates that you be personally apprised that we are sitting on [an] *explosive human situation which could blow at any time within next forty-eight hours.* Wish assure you that while full gamut of leadership tradecraft psychology and discipline will be harnessed to prevent any human explosion we cannot guarantee that it will not happen. Believe positive or negative action is only guarantee which will ensure our retaining control over these human resources to extent that flap will be avoided. There is in my judgment no middle ground on this issue.[21]

Put more simply, the message said: For the love of all things holy, please get your s*** together and tell us what to do.

The next day word finally came down from on high—the president had spoken. The CIA was ordered to "do everything possible to insure no refugee or emigre provocative actions against Cuba are undertaken with or without our knowledge during the next several days. The Miami station and the MONGOOSE Task Force should be alerted to exercise every precaution to see that no unauthorized attempts are made. This should be done without discussion or disclosure to the refugee groups."

Also from the president: "The activities of Operation MONGOOSE are to be stopped during the next several days and therefore all prior approvals for sabotage, infiltrations, guerrilla activities, caching of arms are to be temporarily suspended."[22]

The temporary suspension would soon become permanent, and Operation MONGOOSE ended without accomplishing most of its stated benchmarks. To be honest, Operation MONGOOSE ended without accomplishing much of anything. Covert and overt action against Castro and the Cuban government was far from over (see . . . well, the rest of the book), but these activities would no longer be part of some grandiose plan hatched in Washington.

They would be grandiose plans hatched in Miami.

Part II

4

The Ocho

The Cuban influx of the early 1960s into South Florida, a steady flow of people fleeing the fruits of the triumph of Castro's revolution, was a potent reflection of two powerful American precepts. One was timeless: the pride of continuing the tradition of welcoming immigrants and maintaining the narrative of the shining "city on the hill." The other was a uniquely modern product of the times: the duty to defend freedom and democracy in the Cold War's diametrical battle of ideas. Both were being tested, not halfway around the globe, but on American soil by a crisis developing less than a hundred miles from the United States. This combination of factors made Miami—and the Cubans that were arriving—unique players on the global stage in a never-before-seen version of a classic drama.

This situation was also a unique one from a practical, procedural standpoint. The United States was well versed in coordinating refugees' acceptance into the country. In the wake of World War II, the Displaced Persons Act of 1948 allowed for over two hundred thousand persons displaced or made homeless in the conflict to resettle in the US and was later amended to allow double that number.[1] Another 205,000 resettled as a result of the Refugee Relief Act of 1953.[2] The crisis in Hungary in 1956 prompted another three thousand to relocate to the United States.[3] But the Cuban situation presented a fundamentally different challenge, and none of these populations triggered a large-scale federal program like the one Cubans inspired.

Elsewhere refugees fled to neighboring countries, where screening and immigration processing took place far from American shores. Voluntary agencies also could coordinate arrangements for housing and employment to ensure the refugees had both ready for them upon arrival to the United States. This was not the case this time: the luxury of distance was not a factor. Cubans were arriving directly to an American city in large numbers and without the preparations that the system was accustomed to.

Senator Philip A. Hart, a respected lawmaker known as the "Conscience of the Senate," and whose name graces one of the Senate office buildings, was the chair of a special subcommittee of the Judiciary Committee focused on problems arising from refugee populations. Creatively named the "Subcommittee to Investigate Problems Connected with Refugees and Escapees," the subcommittee held a series of hearings focused on addressing issues arising from the equally creatively phrased "Cuban Refugee Problem."

Senator Hart opened the first session with remarks in which he lamented, "Every day we learn more of what it means to be a country of first asylum. It not only casts a spotlight on our foreign policy with relation to these refugees, but creates many problems in morality and economics."[4] It was no longer just a question of coordinating assistance and being the "good guy." Decisions on the status of and aid to these refugees had significant external implications on the international stage. The internal politics created by humanitarian programs and the disparities they can create—competition for jobs, and tensions with newcomers as a potential threat—were all a part of a far more complex problem set.

And Miami was center stage.

Operation Pedro Pan

Cuba was changing and changing quickly. Land ownership was fundamentally transformed in 1959 with the Agrarian Reform Act, which was focused on breaking up large estates. The year 1960 saw the nationalization of foreign-owned property, as well as the Urban Reform Law, which prohibited landlords from renting out urban properties. Rumors swirled in Cuban circles about revolutionary intentions regarding children. There were concerns that children were to be sent to the Soviet Union to special work camps.

One rumor surfaced in late 1960 that alleged that children would not be allowed to leave the island as of January 1, 1961. Another—which was particularly concerning among Cuban parents—circulated an alleged copy of a revolutionary law that struck at parental control, a legal concept known as *patria potestad*. It declared that children would become wards of the state after age three.[5] That never came to pass, but as crazy as it may sound to modern ears, the changes taking place around them, particularly in the education of their children, made anything seem possible.

In Cuba, 1961 was dubbed the "Year of Education," and one of the main revolutionary goals was the eradication of illiteracy. A worthy goal, to be sure. The Cuban government mobilized volunteer educators and armed them with a teaching manual to standardize training. Called *Alfabeticemos*, or roughly "Let's Teach Literacy," it had a companion manual for students called *Venceremos*, the revolutionary rallying cry of "We Shall Prevail." It was clear that this was no ordinary literacy curriculum.

Alfabeticemos had twenty-four themes that were designed to support the student workbook, including such classics of basic literacy fundamentals as "Fidel Is Our Leader," and "International Commerce." And who can forget the riveting "The Revolution Wins All Its Battles"?* This was a campaign to help eradicate illiteracy on the island, primarily in rural areas. It was also clearly an opportunity to mold and shape a captive and receptive audience.

Teachers using *Alfabeticemos* were reminded that "we Cubans respect and love the leader that helped the people take up arms against tyranny and foreign domination. . . . Together with the great leader of the Revolution, we also respect and love those leaders that share in his responsibilities, such as President Dorticós, Raúl Castro, Che Guevara . . . and others."[6]

Also included in the manual designed to teach rural populations the basics of reading and writing were several very helpful discussions of international alliances and global power struggles, to help the average Cuban farmer make informed choices about their geopolitical alignment:

Goodnight Moon this most certainly was not.

We consider friends those populations that have achieved their absolute liberty and honestly and selflessly help other nations fight against the colonialist yoke that imperialism imposed upon them. This includes the Soviet Union, People's Republic of China and the other socialist states.[7]

And:

"The Cuban people . . . are on the side of those countries that proclaim a policy of peace and understanding between nations; the policy of the USSR and socialist countries known as 'peaceful coexistence.'"[8]

The vocabulary list was also full of interesting choices that the Ministry of Education felt were "convenient to clarify," words that don't show up in your average literacy book. Military terms like "entrenchment," "counterattack," "rearguard," and "combatant" were included. Just to be clear who the other side was, terms like "lackey" and "mercenary" were listed as well. This was also back when *ch* was still a separate letter in Spanish, so "China" made the list, whose definition of course was "Asian country that has created a social revolution which has allowed it to—in ten years—become one of the most developed countries on that continent." The Soviet Prime Minister was listed under *N*, although the Ministry of Education likely regretted listing him as "Nikita Jruchov."[9]

There were a number of vocabulary words focused on the neighbors to the north, including the FBI, or the "North American institution dedicated to criminal investigation and also political persecution." The State Department, listed in English, was defined as a department "charged with relations with other countries, relations based on imposing will due to their military and economic power." And despite clarifying for teachers that the workbook does not include the letters *K* or *W* due to their limited use in the Spanish language, the vocabulary list had a *K* section for one term: the Ku Klux Klan. It's unclear how often the average rural Cuban ended up discussing federal agencies or racist networks in the US, but there was one US-related vocabulary word that was likely used on a regular basis, defined as "the name given to North Americans:" *Yanqui*.[10]

Urban families were noticing significant changes as well. The schools were closed for months in 1961 in order to recruit the literacy teachers who would use *Alfabeticemos* in the field. Another pillar of youth activity, the Scouts, was eliminated and replaced with Los Pioneros, a government-run youth organization that instilled revolutionary doctrine.* And at a time when other youth learning to read were exploring the brand-new release by Dr. Seuss, a book entitled *Green Eggs and Ham,* a story centered around Sam-I-Am and his lesson about being open-minded and less susceptible to unfounded prejudice, Cuban children were reciting this poem about a different Sam:

> *I swear to you, Uncle Sam*
> *That one day in Algiers or Siam,*
> *We will bury close together*
> *The dollar and the Ku Klux Klan.*[11]

With all this swirling around them, many Cuban parents felt that getting their children out of the country was the best course of action. An Irish-born priest in Miami, Father Bryan Walsh, seemed an unlikely person to play a key role in any of this. He had spent a few months the summer before at an intercultural studies program at the Catholic University in Puerto Rico, where he picked up basic Spanish. It would come in handy in ways he never imagined.

Father Walsh was hearing from the Catholic community and private school network in Cuba that there was likely going to be a huge demand to help minors get out of Cuba. Faced with the potential looming deadline of the rumored prohibition of children leaving the island as of January 1, 1961, Father Walsh and others in Miami prepared to receive a wave of unaccompanied children.

The day after Christmas in 1960, a brother and sister were the first two to arrive. In a matter of days, however, the situation changed dramatically. In the back-and-forth between Cuba and the US in the early days of the Revolution, Castro demanded the staff at the US embassy in Havana be reduced from 120 to 15 personnel to mirror the Cuban staff allowed in Washington. The Eisenhower administration responded by severing diplomatic relations and closed the embassy in Havana on January 3, 1961. A visa was still required

---

*Their motto "Pioneers—Always Ready!" was changed in 1968 after a certain revolutionary leader's demise to "Pioneers for Communism! We will be like Che!" which is how it remains to this day.

for entry into the United States, and upon its abrupt closure, the embassy had fifty thousand pending visa applications.[12]

Father Walsh and others working the issue in Miami helped secure visa waivers from the State Department and were given wide concessions: they had blanket authority for children between the ages of six and sixteen; children sixteen to eighteen had an extra administrative security hurdle; those under six or over eighteen were not authorized.

Thousands ended up taking advantage of the opportunity. The program ran quietly, and due to fears of repercussions for parents and children in Cuba, Father Walsh and others requested it be kept secret. The media cooperated and largely agreed not to divulge how it was done. A Miami journalist accompanied a few of the minors who were continuing from Miami to Illinois in March 1962 and gave a glimpse into the experience. While most thought the separation—and, to be honest, the Revolution itself—would only last several months, parents tried their best to send their children with what they could. As a result, it was often easy to tell the Cuban children from others: they were the ones with multiple shirts on. Stewardesses told the reporter that one child that month had nine shirts on and three pairs of pants. The reporter kept quiet about the details but mentioned the "underground railway in the sky—Operation Peter Pan." He tossed in a throwaway line: "Maybe it should be called Operation Pedro Pan."[13] Little did he know that name would stick, and by the time it was ended due to the suspension of flights between Cuba and the United States following the Cuban Missile Crisis, more than fourteen thousand children had fled Cuba.

Operation Pedro Pan was a watershed experience for a generation of Cubans, many of whom ended up shaping their new home. A musician considered one of the bards of the exile experience, Willy Chirino, arrived when he was fourteen years old through Pedro Pan. The city of Miami has been literally shaped by another who became one of South Florida's most prolific developers. Another served in the United States Senate. One sixteen-year-old boy who arrived through Pedro Pan was wearing a jacket made from cleaning cloths, which was all the family had available. He made it to the United States, became an engineer, got married, and adopted his bride's four-year-old son. That sixteen-year-old's name was Miguel Bezos, and his adopted son was named Jeff. He ended up starting a company you may have heard of.

On February 1, 1961, then under President Kennedy, the Department of Health, Education, and Welfare (HEW) was charged with coordinating a Cuban Refugee Program guided by nine points:

1. Render all possible assistance to voluntary relief agencies in providing daily necessities for needy refugees, for resettling as many as possible, and for securing jobs for them
2. Obtain the assistance of both private and governmental agencies to provide useful employment opportunities for displaced Cubans, consistent with the overall employment situation in Florida
3. Provide funds for the resettlement of refugees to other areas
4. Furnish financial assistance to meet basic maintenance requirements of needy Cuban refugees in the Miami area and, as required, in communities of resettlement
5. Provide for essential health services
6. Furnish federal assistance for local public school operating costs in the Miami area
7. Initiate measures to augment training and educational opportunities for Cuban refugees
8. Provide financial aid for the care and protection of unaccompanied children—the most defenseless and troubled group among the refugee population
9. Undertake surplus food distribution to needy refugees[14]

Interestingly, in light of how Miami's eventual demographics developed, one of Washington's main priorities was actually the third one: resettlement of Cubans out of Miami to other regions of the country. In an effort to try to limit the impact on the local economy, it was the policy of the Cuban Refugee Program not to actively provide any job referrals to refugees in Miami. Caseworkers who helped families on public assistance would visit homes to provide guidance and counseling, most importantly counseling these families on the benefits and necessity of resettlement to other parts of the United States.

Four organizations would be essentially subcontracted by the federal government for providing services to families. Many of those services were associated with resettlement, from helping find new communities, to housing and employment: Catholic Relief Services, a humanitarian organization affiliated with the Catholic Church; Church World Service, a Protestant umbrella agency; the International Rescue Committee, a migration-focused NGO; and the United Hebrew Immigrant Aid Society. This system and these organizations also depended upon Americans themselves providing sponsorship or job opportunities. One informational flyer from the effort provided a slogan that encapsulated the moment and the ethos that has made the United States unlike any other: "Sponsor Cuban Refugees: Fulfill Their Faith in Freedom."[15]

There were concerns, particularly as the flow continued over time, that the Miami area would not be able to absorb all these refugees. In a 1965 letter from President Johnson to the Secretary of Health, Education, and Welfare, LBJ made this prioritization very clear: "We must continue," he wrote, "to place prime emphasis on swift resettlement outside the Miami area."[16] It's a good thing that was a priority, because Castro was about to test the system.

On September 28, 1965, as per usual, Fidel Castro spoke publicly and made sure to lambast the Yankee government. No surprises there. However, that day was markedly different. His words weren't just the same old boring jabs at capitalism. They were a very direct challenge to the US government. And the weapon of choice was his own people.

In response to the Cuban Missile Crisis, the US had cut off organized flights to and from the island. The demand to leave Cuba, however, continued unabated. This led to large numbers of people leaving the island clandestinely, which was trumpeted by the West and irksome to Castro. Perhaps he had had enough, or maybe he was being politically opportunistic, or maybe both. Whatever his rationale, he chose his speech that day to drop a significant surprise.

Not that Fidel ever needed an actual reason to speak publicly for hours on end, but the speech was to commemorate the fifth anniversary of the Committees for the Defense of the Revolution, a watchdog organization that plants government informants in every neighborhood in Cuba, a mechanism that exists to this day. Near the end of his marathon remarks, he asked the crowd rhetorically how to stop the Yankee propaganda about migration and told them that they may have a good solution: he proposed opening Cuban ports, allowing anyone with a family member in the United States to go there freely.

"It is not we who are opposed to the departure of those who want to go, but the imperialists, and since this is the case, we are even ready to fix up a little place somewhere so that all who have relatives here will not have to run any risks." It quickly became clear this was not him simply thinking aloud, as he continued with this not-so-hypothetical scenario: "We could, for example, fix up the port of Camarioca, one of the closest points, so that to all who have relatives we could give a permit to come by ship . . . to come get them and take them by a safe means."

As if he was making this up as he went along, he casually threw out a day: "I will even set a date—say 10 October," and then, the gauntlet was thrown. "So, it is not we who have to be watching. Now it will be seen if it is we who do not wish or if it is the imperialists. If it is we, we are to blame for anyone's drowning in trying to reach . . . the Yankee paradise. . . . This is our policy. Now the imperialists have the word. We are going to see what they do or say."[17]

This was an interesting play, albeit a callous and heartless one. It forced the Americans to either publicly deny these people entry, which would not be a good look, or accept them and the administrative and societal impacts they would bring. Not to mention the fact that Cuba could abdicate responsibility for any loss of life in the Florida Straits to the authorities up north running the Yankee paradise. All this while ridding the island of potential troublemakers who clearly didn't want to be a part of the experiment being forced upon the people of Cuba. It seemed like a pretty strong move. One could imagine Castro waiting with a wry smile for which route the *yanquis* would take.

He wouldn't have to wait long. Days later, on October 3, President Lyndon Johnson signed the Immigration and Nationality Act of 1965, a major piece of legislation that introduced significant changes to the American immigration system. Johnson spoke about the legislation, its impact, and thanked those congressional members who were instrumental in getting it passed. He also chose the moment to announce that those Cubans fleeing the island would be welcomed: "I declare this afternoon to the people of Cuba that those who seek refuge here in America will find it. The dedication of America to our traditions as an asylum for the oppressed is going to be upheld."[18] Johnson did not waste the opportunity to characterize the migration as a clear choice of freedom over oppression, the free world over communism:

> The lesson of our times is sharp and clear in this movement of people from one land to another. Once again, it stamps the mark of

failure on a regime when many of its citizens voluntarily choose to leave the land of their birth for a more hopeful home in America. The future holds little hope for any government where the present holds no hope for the people.

And so we Americans will welcome these Cuban people. For the tides of history run strong, and in another day they can return to their homeland to find it cleansed of terror and free from fear.[19]

Challenge accepted.

But Johnson was keenly aware that the most dramatic message that day wouldn't come from him, or from any politician present that day, but from who stood behind him. Sometimes the strong, silent types can make a statement no one else can, and President Johnson was counting on it. He wasn't in Washington. He was at Ellis Island and chose to speak in front of the most recognizable symbol of America as a refuge from oppression: the Statue of Liberty.

That dramatic and symbolic backdrop was of course strategic: Lady Liberty was chosen to silently emphasize a powerful message to Castro, Cuba, and the world. The United States was already committed in Vietnam, and the opportunity to highlight individuals with firsthand experience of communism making drastic, life-changing decisions to choose the West was pure Cold War gold. The fact that they were coming from the sole Communist eyesore in the hemisphere was an added bonus. The world had heard of daring escapes and clandestine crossings to freedom from East Berlin. It was important that the same narrative of the innate human desire for freedom ring true at America's doorstep, and that the public imagination embrace Miami as the West Berlin of the Western Hemisphere. And so yet again, through the machinations of the global conflict between competing models of society, Miami took center stage.

Once word of the alleged offer reached Miami, a few Cubans decided to test Castro's word and made the journey to Camarioca to see if there truly was a chance to bring people out. What they found were adequate quarters constructed for people waiting to leave, and even playgrounds for children awaiting passage. Apparently this was real. The message spread like wildfire and soon hundreds of boats began heading down to pick up their relatives. Many of them were in dubious condition and definitely were not in any shape to cross the Florida Straits and return with packed decks. The Coast Guard was primarily tasked with monitoring the explosion in maritime traffic and assisting the numerous vessels in distress. This was a Herculean effort that ballooned very quickly. The Coast Guard air station in Miami, which at the time accounted for only 5 percent of the service's aviation strength, flew more than 13 percent of the Coast Guard's total mileage just monitoring and responding to the exodus: an estimated one million miles.[20]

On October 28, the Cuban Ministry of the Interior announced that starting at midnight, they would no longer allow southbound boats to arrive at Camarioca to pick up those wishing to leave. The approximately three hundred small boats already anchored there were still allowed to bring people out.

Several days later, on November 4, another abrupt announcement: as of noon that day, the Cuban government would no longer allow any departures from Camarioca. To deal with the thousands left behind by the abrupt closure, the US State Department chartered three boats and in what was dubbed "Operation Sealift," ferried 4,598 Cubans to the United States from November 13 through 22.[21]

In all, thousands of Cubans fled the island through Camarioca in little more than a month, but it could have been far more. It became clear very early on that a flotilla of private vessels crisscrossing the Florida Straits was an untenable, unsafe situation, and negotiations between the US and Cuba started shortly after the exodus began. The State Department had been negotiating a safer and more orderly flow. Interestingly, while the US position was to accept around three thousand refugees a month, Cuba preferred something closer to twelve thousand. The agreement that was reached created an air bridge that would span from an airport serving the famed beaches of Varadero to the United States. It began on December 1, 1965, and operated two daily flights, five days a week, carrying an average of around four thousand people from Varadero to Miami. Known as the "Freedom Flights," this airlift continued through 1973, by which time a total of 260,737 refugees had landed in the United States, the vast majority of whom would settle in Miami.[22]

Camarioca would be eclipsed by larger mass migrations, but it was a critical teachable moment for the governments on both sides of the Florida Straits. For the United States, it was a lesson that winning the ideological Cold War was going to require some willingness to accept a larger refugee footprint in the homeland. This conflict was at their doorstep, and the world was watching. For Castro, Camarioca had a much different lesson. It was an introduction to a powerful tool at his disposal: the weapon of mass migration.

It was not lost on him how his flippant words at the end of an otherwise pedestrian speech had triggered a swift and sweeping response from the *yanqui* government. Nor did he ignore the utility of being rid of citizens opposed to or uninterested in his autocratic vision for Cuban society. It is interesting that the speech that triggered it all was commemorating the anniversary of the neighborhood snitch network that informed the government of revolutionary malcontents. Perhaps it became clear: Why go through all that trouble of monitoring a troublesome population if you could just get rid of them and make them someone else's problem? These were lessons that Castro learned very well, and would use multiple times during his dictatorship as a safety valve when pressure on the island was building.

While the decision to accept Cuban immigrants was a big messaging opportunity in the larger struggle between Washington and Moscow, it also introduced a potential risk. What if the Cuban immigrants floundered in the United States? Would their struggles be turned against the West by their adversaries, underlining one of their key messages, that of the cold, heartless capitalist system that leaves the less fortunate behind?

In the lens of the Cold War, where everything could be turned into a virtue or a damnation of one system or another, the Cuban story was a uniquely important one to get right. John Hugh Crimmins, the director of the Miami Office of the Coordinator for Cuban Affairs, addressed this concern before a congressional field hearing held in Miami. He spoke of American openness and how the "democratic humanitarian tradition of this country which has led it to welcome the victims of oppression has been one of its greatest strengths." He warned, however, "We may all be sure that the way in which we carry out that tradition with respect to our Cuban friends and guests is being watched from abroad, most intensely, undoubtedly, by our enemies, and particularly by the Castro regime, avid for grist for his propaganda mill."[23] It seems that Congress agreed.

A Humane Postscript

Most Cubans arriving in the early stages technically had an immigration status known as "indefinite voluntary departure" or "parolee." Under those denominations, they could not apply for citizenship or change their classification. The severing of diplomatic relations with Cuba in January 1961 made it impossible to issue permanent resident visas to Cuban refugees.[24] Their only real option upon arriving in the United States was to leave the country and apply for a visa at an American consulate, usually in Mexico or Canada. This was impractical for both the Cubans themselves and the American government receiving them. There was the inescapable reality of the prohibitive cost to the refugees. Most were forced to leave virtually everything behind in Cuba and were in essence starting over; they did not have the means to travel to Monterrey or Montreal only to then return to the US. This situation also proved difficult for the US government: these consulates were not staffed to process such a huge influx of requests and it threatened to severely overtax the system.

In August 1966, there were a series of congressional hearings to discuss the merits and concerns of a bill that was winding its way through Congress to address this Cuban conundrum: How should the government legally characterize these hundreds of thousands of migrants? In addition to the practical impediments mentioned above that Cubans faced to get visas, the issue was discussed from multiple angles. Points were made from the humanitarian perspective: that there was an obligation to assist and leaving them in legal limbo was detrimental. There were economic arguments: significant numbers of professional and educated Cubans could not practice in the United States due to their ambiguous legal status. Furthermore, recognizing Cubans legally would lower dependence on public assistance and facilitate their resettlement.

US Attorney General Nicholas Katzenbach, in support of the bill, harked back to Johnson's remarks the year before on Ellis Island. "Such legislation would be a humane postscript to the message formulated by our government and voiced by the President when he said to the people of Cuba: 'those who seek refuge here in America will find it.'"[25]

That "postscript" was a bill to "adjust the status of Cuban refugees to that of lawful permanent residents of the United States." Its primary sponsor was Senator Edward Kennedy, and it directly addressed this legal issue facing Cubans, providing a fast track for legal permanent residence and eventual citizenship. It did this by shortening the period required for Cubans to reside in the United States before applying for permanent residency—the "green card."

A green card holder can usually apply for citizenship after five years, but the law provided Cubans with another advantage: while usually the date of lawful permanent residence is when one's case is completed and approved, Cubans received an up-to-thirty-month "rollback," in essence giving credit for time in the US and allowing them to apply for citizenship earlier. The bill was signed into law later that year and became known as the Cuban Adjustment Act.[26] This law became arguably one of the most significant policies affecting the trajectory of Cubans in the United States, as well as the future of the city of Miami.

One other major component of the Cuban shift toward settling down in Miami wasn't a federal policy, but a simple human predisposition toward the familiar.

Many who arrived in Miami were established professionals in Cuba, but had no credentials, no certifications, no proof of their past lives, and had to start over. One Miami story perfectly encapsulates this. A man heard a knock on the door and opened it to find someone offering to cut his grass. It took a minute to recognize him out of context, but when it dawned on him, he was almost brought to tears. The landscaper, a few short years ago and a hundred or so miles from where they were standing, had been a high-ranking officer in the Cuban Navy—the director of the Cuban Naval Academy during World War II—and a person who was an important part of his personal and professional formation.*

This experience was being replicated all over Miami. There were individuals who were professionals, small-business owners, entrepreneurs in Cuba, but due to the difficult circumstances of their departure, had no documented proof of their former experience. This made one aspect of starting over particularly difficult: access to capital. One of the more prominent Cuban bankers in town, Luis Botifoll, recalled that again and again, exiles desperate to access funds to start an enterprise in Miami came to the bank with the family jewelry they had been able to keep out of the hands of revolutionary police on their way out of Cuba. Brooches, lockets, pearl earrings, a diamond, any number of family heirlooms or keepsakes they were willing to part with for a chance to start over. Again and again, the only accepted collateral was a handshake.[27]

Not surprisingly, this wasn't the norm. Banks in Miami at the time were understandably hesitant to provide the loans required to start small

---

*He was also an important part of the formation of one of the coauthors: he was Eric's grandfather.

businesses. As a few key Cuban individuals rose in the ranks of financial institutions, things started to change. Their personal knowledge of many of the other Cuban arrivals, or the network of interpersonal relationships within the exile community, often gave them insight into potential loan recipients' past successes and reputations back on the island. This was a way to help their countrymen in a tough spot, but it also gave them an advantage over competitors.

The growing Cuban diaspora represented a huge potential market, but those with this "insider information" had a way of discerning those individuals who were good investments. The practice of providing these "character loans," based on fundamental trust in lieu of credit scores, was a critical piece in the process of helping Cubans in Miami become part of the local economy and establish small businesses. With this growing market and a number of exiles who themselves had banking experience back in Cuba, it wasn't long before there were Cubans at the very top of bank administration, which facilitated growth even more rapidly. Republic National Bank of Miami was founded in 1965, and within two years had a majority of Cuban stockholders. Banks wholly owned by Cubans themselves also began opening. By 1971, there were four Cuban bank presidents and over two hundred Cubans in various levels of bank management. Three years later, one-third of all bank employees in the county were Cubans.

As Miami's influx of Cuban exiles settled in, they were being recognized as the engines of a "genuine economic boom." In 1959, Miami had the highest rate of Federal Housing Administration and Veterans Affairs mortgage foreclosures in the country. The unemployment rate, at 10.5 percent, was above the national average. Fifteen years later, county officials estimated that the Cuban community had created at least one hundred thousand jobs that didn't exist when they began arriving in large numbers in the early sixties.[28] And the evidence was in plain sight all over the city. Cuban-run businesses were everywhere. Ten years after their arrival, three out of every five gas stations in the city were operated by Cubans. There were 230 restaurants, 45 bakeries, 30 furniture stores, 12 private schools, 10 garment factories, and (perhaps staying on brand) 20 cigar manufacturers.[29] By 1977, there were 7,333 Cuban-owned businesses in the city.[30] Twenty-five percent of all construction in Miami was Cuban-owned. Across the board, it seemed, Cubans were getting a taste of the American Dream. The annual median income of Cuban families in Miami was

$5,244 in 1967. Just three years later in 1970, it had risen to $8,091.[31] Nine out of ten Cuban families owned a car, and in what is now a quaint measure of economic attainment, more than half had the luxury of being able to watch their television programs at home in color.[32]

It wasn't just the little guys who were looking to get ahead. This economic expansion was getting attention in boardrooms across the United States. Larger American firms were recognizing the value of a city with a large population of bilingual professionals, one that could be used to coordinate and manage operations throughout Latin America. Dow Chemical, International Harvester, Eastman Kodak, Pfizer, and over twenty-five other major companies established Latin American headquarters in Miami.[33]

As has been the story of so many immigrant communities, as the number of Cubans in Miami expanded, it was only natural that they gravitated toward the familiar in unfamiliar territory. Parts of the city were increasingly shaped in the likeness of the place they left behind. Networks were reestablished and new ones created in the shared experience of exile. One of the clearest reflections of the changing landscape was on a street that begins in Miami's center. It is the end of a long road that leads through the swamps of the Everglades to the west coast of Florida before turning north toward Tampa: the Tamiami Trail. Before the Cuban population boom, the Miami end had little going for it—a nondescript line of storefronts on Eighth Street in a seemingly forgotten part of the city. It would be transformed into the cultural epicenter of the area increasingly known as "Little Havana," a bustling area of family-run restaurants, small businesses, and open-air windows selling dark, sweet Cuban coffee. A domino park in the center of the area gave it a further touch of home: the clickety-clack of dominoes on wooden tables and the deep, earthy waft of cigar smoke became, and remains, an indelible part of the neighborhood. This once-sleepy stretch of road would undergo a permanent name change; virtually everyone, whether English- or Spanish-speaking, would eventually and irreversibly refer to it as "Calle Ocho."

The combination of an expanding Cuban community, access to capital, and a growing understanding that this might be home for a while was powerful. It began to shape the city of Miami, not just as a headquarters for international business, but also as one for the Cuban diaspora itself. The broad success of Cubans in Miami was obviously great news, and a positive development for the city. The Cuban community was settling down and establishing themselves as a permanent part of the fabric of Miami. This shift would prove absolutely critical for laying the economic and political foundations of what was to come. A group that was growing in power and influence, one with a keen interest in foreign policy and the defeat of communism, was building. In time, Miami would again become one of the main fronts of the Cold War. The city would also punch far above its weight, playing a major role in shaping the policies implemented in the struggle itself.

There was also—clearly—another storyline. One of the Cuban bank presidents in Miami interviewed about this made sure to mention a key point: "It is very interesting to note that the per capita income of Cuban refugees here is almost three times the per capita income of any country in Central or South America." He didn't mention Cuba, but he didn't really have to. It was clear what he was doing. Miami was an important and powerful natural experiment highlighting one of the fundamental conflicts of the Cold War: the liberal open market versus government-run economies. Cubans in Miami were thriving mere miles from Cuba geographically, but worlds apart in terms of freedoms, opportunities, and future prospects. It was a stark contrast, and a powerful one. Berlin was another such experiment where the same population was artificially split by two systems, and lives took radically different turns. There was one fundamental difference here, though. This experiment wasn't taking place on another continent across an ocean. It was unfolding in an American city.

5

Raiders of the Lost Archipelago

After the Bay of Pigs fiasco, and the subsequent counterintelligence sweeps across Cuba, organizations with presence and activities on island shriveled. Those groups were rounded up and their members executed or imprisoned. One organization, Unidad Revolucionaria, which pulled off the brewery heist in Chapter 1 and had a relatively sizeable footprint in Cuba, suffered devastating losses and was a representative case of the aftermath of the invasion on the island. Eight coordinators who were based in Cuba fled to the US, three were arrested and later executed, two were given decades-long jail sentences, and one was killed along with his wife in a gun battle with Cuban intelligence agents.[1]

This changed the dynamic of Miami's role in the conflict. While the dream of a large-scale military invasion of Cuba still existed and would motivate exiles for years to come, that reality was fading. Miami's main role would be as a logistics hub for pockets of resistance within Cuba. And as those pockets became smaller and smaller, hit-and-run raids became an increasingly utilized weapon of choice.

It is difficult to quantify how many incursions and raids took place, but if one vessel is any indication, the Florida Straits were being constantly and clandestinely crisscrossed by boats. The *Susan Ann* was a seventy-two-foot converted World War II PT boat purchased by the Bacardí family (yes ... those

Bacardís; the rum is originally from Santiago de Cuba, and the bat on their logo is an homage to the nocturnal visitors from nearby caves in the region) and operated out of Miami by the Agrupación Montecristi, one of the main organizations that formed the FRD. In her time in this service, the *Susan Ann* reportedly took part in over forty clandestine incursions into Cuba. One of these infiltrations, trumpeted as the "first naval victory by anti-Castro forces" by a local Miami newspaper, led to a firefight with a Cuban patrol vessel, the SV-28. Three Cuban sailors were killed and five wounded in the exchange. None of the crew on the *Susan Ann* sustained injuries.[2]

Her existence and efforts were far from secret: it was publicly reported that the *Susan Ann* was based out of Newfound Harbor near Big Pine Key. Newfound Harbor must have been an ideal habitat for a World War II PT boat. In an ironic Cold War twist, she was forced to relocate when a movie crew decided to use the harbor as the backdrop for a film on then president Kennedy's wartime adventures. Kennedy's real-world, real-time efforts to undermine communist influence in the hemisphere, hindered by Hollywood.

Perhaps the *Susan Ann*'s most brazen incursion was escort duty, assisting another organization, the Revolutionary Student Directorate (DRE). Their target was a modern waterfront hotel in the swanky Miramar district of Havana. On a small peninsula across from Havana's renowned Malecón promenade, the Rosita de Hornedo hotel had a clear view of the sea to the north. One August day in 1962, two vessels entered that view: the *Susan Ann* and the DRE's *Juanin*. They opened fire on the hotel and eventually sped off. No one was injured.[3]

But the *Susan Ann* was by no means the only player in these efforts. Two weeks after the attack on the hotel in Miramar, a five-man crew from another exile organization, Alpha 66, fired upon two vessels—one Cuban and one British—off the north coast of Cuba. Alpha 66 followed up less than a month later with a raid on a shoreside installation at a small port town on the central coast. Another Cuban vessel was attacked and reportedly sunk by machine-gun fire that same week. And in December 1962, the Cuban port of Caibarién was attacked by raiders in two small boats that fired on installations and fled.[4]

By December 1962, however, the Kennedy administration had endured a string of failures and struggles. The disastrous Bay of Pigs invasion would have been enough of a challenge for any administration. But two months earlier, they had also dealt with a little bout of brinksmanship that sent humankind closer than ever to global nuclear conflict.

And Miami was right smack in the middle of both events, ideologically and geographically. In Washington's lens of the broader ideological conflict, the stakes were getting far too high to not have situational awareness on activities in Miami; it was fresh in everyone's mind that a miscommunication could have far-reaching and catastrophic repercussions. As one senator observed, "It requires no vivid imagination or academic degree in history to recognize the potential for world conflict from one person's getting involved with one vessel and one gun."[5]

While Cuban organizations felt the most immediate impact of the Bay of Pigs invasion, the Cuban Missile Crisis changed the calculus significantly for the United States. They could no longer afford to have Cuban exiles freelancing attacks on Cuba that would threaten a fragile—and vital—peace. Perhaps it was time for a bit more control over goings-on in South Florida.

The Price of Peace: Pawns in a Larger Game

The Kennedy administration recognized that there was a severe lack of coordination within the government on the issue of Cuba, even though there was a constellation of agencies involved. In order to increase coordination and information sharing on Cuba-related efforts, in January 1963 the day-to-day operations were taken over by a Coordinator of Cuban Affairs. The coordinator chaired a Coordinating Committee of Cuban Affairs, which included a number of involved departments, including Defense; the CIA; State; Justice; Health, Education, and Welfare (precursor to today's HHS); and the US Information Agency.

Due to the central importance of Miami in all these efforts, a branch office of the coordinator was established in the city. Led by John Hugh Crimmins, a career Foreign Service officer, the office was intended to serve as a US government liaison to the Cuban exile community and to coordinate federal programs in the city.

It was a massive job, both in terms of the coordination between federal agencies and liaison with the local community. On the federal side, the enforcement effort alone to curb freelance incursions into Cuba involved Customs, Immigration, the Coast Guard, the FBI, and Border Patrol. The Cuban Refugee Program—not surprisingly also a considerable operation—was under Health, Education, and Welfare. The Labor Department also had a significant presence as they coordinated unemployment benefits for Cuban exiles. The office also worked with state and local governments, and of course, with the Cuban exile community. This sounds like a logical thing to do, which it was. But it was also something of significance: Crimmins reported that this was the first time in American history that a State Department office was established in the United States outside Washington, DC.

While this was an effort to get a better understanding of the issues on the ground, there was deep suspicion from the Cuban exiles involved in armed activity. Some exile leaders had access to the highest levels of the American government, and this was seen as a step to sever that line of communication. They were right. Crimmins reported years later that he was sent down to Miami with instructions to "hold the exiles' hand, make very clear that we would tolerate no freelance activity that would, in effect, threaten the Kennedy-Khrushchev agreement following the Missile Crisis, that we would not attack Cuba." Crimmins explained that he was in Miami "trying to really play down, or participate in a transition from a highly activist period in the Kennedy Administration, with respect to Cuba—I mean all sorts of covert actions and that sort of thing—to a less active period, which put specific clamps, specific visible clamps, on the exile community."[6] This was a delicate and pivotal time. Washington wanted to make clear that the rules were changing.

Not surprisingly, these "clamps" and rule changes were not universally welcomed. Many Cuban immigrants saw them as further proof of a reversal of Washington's commitment to a free Cuba. Efforts in Miami since the rise of Castro's regime were largely focused on the collection of intelligence, and the recruiting, training, and logistical support of armed counterrevolutionary forces. Armed incursions were what they had planned and trained for—how this nightmare was supposed to end. The CIA footprint in the city and their investment in the exile community was significant. Kennedy's deal struck with the Soviet Union that essentially forbade those kinds of operations threatened all of that.

To many, it stripped them of their unofficial letters of marque and made them undesirables, pirates. For some, the dreams of following in Martí's footsteps, of helping to liberate the country by force, seemed to disappear. For others, this was a call to arms, with or without the assistance of the American government. If you thought that this meant that the Cuban exile groups working toward armed liberation of Cuba laid their weapons down, you would be sorely mistaken.

One raid, in particular, made a notable impact. In March 1963, an exile organization named Comandos L, a splinter group from Alpha 66, planned to attack Soviet shipping to try to scuttle the growing US-USSR détente. Off the coast of Cuba, a group of raiders departed their mother ship on a twenty-two-foot speedboat named the *Phoenix*. Their destination was the port of Caibarién, on the north coast of Cuba almost at the midsection of the island. After finding a suitable hiding place near the port, they settled in and waited for the cover of darkness.

After nightfall, the raiding party made their way toward the harbor. As they advanced, they readied the armaments they had recovered days before from a secret underwater stash hidden among one of the countless reefs in the crystal-clear aquamarine waters of the Bahamas. Their arsenal included some standard-issue equipment: a twenty-millimeter cannon, carbine rifles, a few hand grenades. They also brought along some stuff straight out of an *A-Team* episode: some garage napalm made from gasoline and soap flakes, and a homemade torpedo. When the resident Cuban MacGyver on the team realized that the torpedo's motor wouldn't work, he retooled it into a magnetic mine.

They slowly, quietly moved toward the pier. A lone Cuban patrol boat was making its rounds, piercing the humid, tropical darkness with a powerful searchlight—looking for nothing in particular. Looming ahead was a seven-thousand-ton Soviet freighter, the *Baku*, in port to load up sugar from a nearby mill. The *Phoenix* glided silently closer and closer. From their vantage point nearly at the water's surface, the hull of the freighter grew larger, a towering steel wall that increasingly blocked out the rest of the port. Without warning, the calm was interrupted by thunderous cracks of the cannon.

The *Phoenix*, now within thirty yards, had opened fire at the bridge of the freighter to cover their sprint to come alongside. With confused shouting aboard the ship mixing with the crack of covering fire above them, they dropped the mine as close as they could to the hull and sped off into the night. Their escape was punctuated by a dull, thudding boom, followed by a towering geyser of water next to the *Baku*. The attack left a gaping thirteen-foot hole in the *Baku*'s hull.

The men aboard the *Phoenix* fled Cuban waters and were giddy with excitement. So was the reporter from *Life* magazine that they had aboard. With the counterrevolutionary need for funds for these raids on one hand, and the drive to sell magazines bursting with riveting adventure stories on the other, arrangements were made on a number of occasions for reporters to provide funds in exchange for exclusive access to a real-life clandestine raid. *Life* billed this one as "a wild fighting ride on the old Spanish Main," and portrayed the incident as a heroic adventure of "buccaneers attack[ing] Soviet prey."[7] Not surprisingly, the Soviets didn't see it that way.

The raid achieved its tactical goal, but the intended impact was more far-reaching than stopping a shipment of Cuban sugar to Soviet tables. It seems to have had the desired short-term effect of inconveniencing high-level government officials in the US and the USSR; it was definitely effective in getting their attention. A telegram was sent that same day by Foy David Kohler, the US ambassador in Moscow, back to Washington. The communication revealed that news of the small pinprick raid had gone all the way up to the Soviet minister of foreign affairs, Andrei Gromyko.

Kohler had been named the ambassador to the Soviet Union only weeks before the Cuban Missile Crisis, and he and Gromyko had worked the negotiations from their respective sides, so discussions regarding Cuba, exiles, and subterfuge were not new to either of them. Gromyko, for his part, had previously earned the moniker "Mr. Nyet" in the American press during his tenure as the Soviet representative to the United Nations for his trigger-happy use of the Soviet Union's Security Council veto. He would go on to serve as foreign minister for twenty-eight years.

According to the communiqué, Gromyko had received word of the attack just before their meeting, which was not the first "provocative action against Cuba and Soviet ships." He emphasized the severity of these actions, and the apparent American underestimation of them. "If the US correctly estimated [the] gravity of such actions," he warned in veiled diplomatic-speak, the United States "would not permit them to take place."[8]

Kohler responded with the official American stance: that these raids did not originate in the United States, that the US government did not believe such raids served any useful purpose, and that those who conducted them had no ties to the government of the United States. Gromyko relayed his government's complete disbelief, asking, "Can [the US government] really hope to find serious people who can believe that it is not involved, when this exile scum was sitting under US wing? These groups only acted with the knowledge and connivance of the US Government." Kohler reiterated that the raiders had not come from US territory (this is technically true, since their last destination prior to the incursion was the Bahamas). He also checked the lowbrow reference to Cuban exiles in a manner befitting a classic freedom-loving Hollywood script: "With regard to 'scum,' we have a different understanding from Soviets of who are scum and who are honest people." He did, however, state that the US was "opposed to these raids and would do everything it could to discourage them."[9]

One aspect of the meeting was particularly interesting. Gromyko stated that all of this was a result of American threatening of Cuba, and that they should just leave the island in peace, a course of action in the best interests of the US and the world. He was met with the rebuttal that the opposite was true: Soviet meddling in Cuba was poisoning the US-USSR relationship and the best way to repair it was to remove the poison. They parried back and forth regarding what the "poison" was—whether it referred to these raids or to the Soviet presence in Cuba.[10] Perhaps this verbal fencing is what all these diplomatic meetings are like: scoring points through ideological lunges and parries. The most striking fact, however, is that the senior member of the Soviet Ministry of Foreign Affairs and the ambassador of the United States in the USSR were talking about this insignificant raid as a touch point of the entire geopolitical struggle. Not bad for a handful of raiders, a homemade torpedo, and a twenty-two-foot boat.

Beyond attracting attention, the Comandos L had also hoped to force the American government to change their stance in relation to Cuba. In this, they would also be successful—but not in the way they intended.

When Ambassador Kohler told his Soviet counterpart that the US government was opposed to raids into Cuba and would do all it could to discourage them, he meant what he said. These incursions put the United States in an awkward position: they were only clinging to the most technical of truths regarding the origins of these raids. More importantly from Washington's standpoint, the cost-benefit analysis of letting them continue was clearly not in their favor. Potentially undermining the fragile détente crafted from the brinksmanship of October 1962 and the Cuban Missile Crisis for some erratic acts of sabotage understandably wasn't worth it. As a result, Miami again played a central role in the geopolitical struggle enveloping the entire globe, this time as a proving ground to the Soviet Union that the United States was serious about peace.

Clamping Down

The Kennedy administration did not wait long to signal to the Soviets that peace forged from crisis was a higher priority than these Cuban exile incursions. On March 30, 1963, a joint press release from the State and Justice Departments clarified their position in no uncertain terms:

> The position of the United States Government regarding hit-and-run attacks by Cuban refugee groups against Soviet ships and other targets in Cuba have been made perfectly clear by the President and Secretary of State. These attacks are neither supported nor condoned by this Government. The President has pointed out that they may have effects opposite to those presumably intended by those who carry them out; that is, they may strengthen the Soviet position in Cuba rather than weaken it, tighten Communist controls rather than loosen them. . . . We intend to take every step necessary to ensure that such raids are not launched, manned, or equipped on United States territory.[11]

The administration tried to thread the needle between supporting the cause of these freedom-loving democratic exiles and showing the Soviets that the Americans would not condone these clandestine raids, nor be willing to risk resulting misunderstandings that could involve conventional forces:

> The sympathy of this Government and the American people is with those Cubans who hope to see their country freed from Communist control. We understand that these raids reflect the deep frustration

of men who want to get back to their homeland, to a Cuba that is independent.

But this understanding does not mean that we are prepared to see our own laws violated with impunity or to tolerate activities which might provoke armed reprisals, the brunt of which would be borne by the Armed Forces of the United States.[12]

This was obviously not welcome news in Miami among those who had been involved in those very activities. Nor was the action that accompanied the release. That same day, Robert Kennedy's Justice Department served a number of known Cuban raiders with a Notice Not to Depart, a restriction-of-movement order that confined some to US territory and forbade others from even leaving the land limits of Dade County.* Violation of the order was potentially punishable by imprisonment or deportation. A week later, the Coast Guard significantly increased its patrol presence in the waters off South Florida, adding six aircraft and twelve boats to forces dedicated to interdicting "Cuba-bound raiding vessels" and to "apprehend persons suspected of aggressive intentions against Cuba."[13]

Washington requested international assistance in shutting down these operations as well. The Bahamas, then still a British colony, were a well-known logistical hub for a number of these freelance raids. This chain of islands is not only an ideal smuggler's paradise—with countless coves and ungoverned territory—it is also closer to Miami than Orlando is. Perhaps understanding the larger international implications, the British agreed to be on the lookout for potential clandestine efforts in Bahamian waters.

Clearly the "clamps" that the Office of the Coordinator of Cuban Affairs was sent to implement were being applied. While the message to the Soviets may have been the intended one—that the United States was committed to avoiding another potentially catastrophic flare-up in the Caribbean—the one received by Cuban Miami may not have been. Disillusionment spread as many believed that American commitment to Cuban liberty was waning.

---

* "Dade County"—named after an Army Major ambushed and killed in the Second Seminole War—was changed to the current "Miami-Dade County" in 1997 to better capitalize on international recognition of Miami.

In early April 1963, weary from infighting and convinced that the United States was no longer prioritizing efforts to liberate Cuba, Miró Cardona, the leader of the Cuban Revolutionary Council, submitted a detailed letter of resignation. He specifically cited a number of recent actions, and the speed of their implementation, as proof of American indifference: the government's public condemnation of recent Cuban exile raids; the geographic confinement of certain exiles to South Florida; the immobilization of certain vessels to depart Miami.

He also included what he saw as the most disconcerting of all: the recruitment of the British in enforcing these restrictions in the Bahamas, ensuring that "Khrushchev's most sinister designs [are] protected by the most efficient maritime police of the two most democratic powers in the world."[14] After attempting to explain these measures by other theories, he came to what he saw as the only logical explanation: "Faced with all the arguments the force of events leads to this conclusion: the Cuban struggle is in the process of being liquidated by the government [of the United States]."[15]

This was coming from the exile leader who had met personally with both the president and the attorney general regarding Cuban issues, who was onstage with the president at the event commemorating the return of the Bay of Pigs combatants as a representative of the exile organizations under the council's umbrella. It was significant. The Cuban Revolutionary Council had been one of the main conduits between the exile community and Washington. US government funding for the Cuban Revolutionary Council, a $90,000-a-month subsidy, was cut off on May 1, 1963.[16] Faced with this stark turn of events, and concerned about being eclipsed by other groups, the new leadership of the council would attempt to regain support and recognition the best way they knew how.

The Last Straw

On the morning of June 20, 1963, the Cuban Revolutionary Council issued a press release:

> Commandos of the Cuban Revolutionary Council have landed in different parts of Cuba, continuing the actions which will definitely lead to the liberation of our country. The first reports sent by our

forces reveal that the landings were effected without any difficulty and had the utmost cooperation of the peasants in the surrounding zones. These commandos, perfectly armed, have entered Cuban territory. Tomorrow at 1:00 pm, the general headquarters of these forces will offer a radio transmission, from Cuba, to the exiles, in the forty meter band, 7018 kilocycles.[17]

At around ten that morning, four CRC representatives were featured on a Miami television program verifying that commandos had landed in Cuba. A late edition of the *Miami News* that day ran an article entitled "500 Refugee Commandos Land in Cuba, Exiles Say." The article cited other exile sources who reported that as many as five hundred men using several beachheads had successfully landed on the island and proclaimed this as "the beginning of the liberation of Cuba." Congressman Paul Rogers of Florida reported that he had been informed that *three thousand* well-armed exiles had landed at three separate beachheads. This caused jubilation among Cubans in Miami: news of hope for the beginning of the end of their nightmare.

Official channels were eerily quiet, however. Cuban radio had no broadcasts regarding hordes of imperialist troops on revolutionary soil. Both the State and Defense Departments claimed no knowledge of such an invasion. Neither Havana nor Washington—or Moscow for that matter—had any official response to these reports. The media was quick to pick up on this anomaly. The following day, the UPI wire service released an article that highlighted the official silence, as well as rumblings from sources close to the CRC that only a few men were actually involved.[18]

One day later, the *Miami Herald* published an article which reported that experts in Washington doubted any more than fifty counterrevolutionaries could have been landed in the previous few weeks. On June 23, roughly seventy-two hours after the initial announcement, the *Miami News* laid bare the reality of the alleged invasion with a hard-hitting headline of their own: "Raid a Hoax: Cuban Exile Boss Quits." It reported that the CRC was focused on raising its visibility. While the council itself did not provide the inflated numbers, "the proposed landing of up to 3,000 commandos was a fraud that ballooned with the tacit consent of other publicity minded CRC members." The CRC president resigned as a result of the fiasco.

The CRC attempted to limit the damage by releasing a statement, which rejected any responsibility for false external interpretations of their original statement and reinforcing its veracity (commandos did infiltrate Cuban territory and radio broadcasts were made from the island). They also denounced an alleged "campaign of defamation against the Council, orchestrated by individuals who postpone the supreme interests of Cuba to their own ambitions and hatreds."

Not surprisingly, this was ineffective. The damage had been done. A report completed months later by the Office of the Coordinator of Cuban Affairs in Miami on the political prospects of varying exile groups mentions that the "incredibly stupid performance in June blowing up a minor infiltration attempt into a reported 'invasion' of Cuba has left the organization little more than a hollow shell" and that it had been "utterly discredited and ineffective as an anti-Castro group."[19]

The CRC's fall from grace from the highest profile and most well-connected Cuban exile organization to a "hollow shell" was the most dramatic result among exile groups of the US policy shift. But Washington's need to signal to the Soviet Union that the Neutrality Act could work, and that raids into Cuba from American soil were not permitted, affected all the exile organizations in Miami. This was a different reality that felt much more like Martí's experience in Fernandina: the need to continue efforts to free Cuba remained, but with an increased risk of government interference.

Comandos L, the organization whose raids in March 1963 caught the attention of both Washington and Moscow and precipitated the policy shift, had a representative experience. They continued plans for clandestine raids, including sabotage operations on oil refineries and sugar warehouses in eastern Cuba slated for late September 1963. The organization was making preparations in Miami, including assembling explosive devices for the upcoming operations.

They had even secured a freelance reporter to accompany them on the raid and document their efforts, a field journalist by the name of Georgette Meyer. On September 21, the house they were using as the bomb-making compound was raided by Customs agents and local police. They confiscated twenty homemade bombs, sixteen sticks of dynamite, ten pounds of black powder, napalm, three rifles, a machine gun, and a twenty-millimeter cannon. Meyer was in the house but was not detained by authorities.[20]

The following day, Comandos L issued a public statement in response to the confiscation of what they considered "war matériel." They saw the shift in US policy as an infringement on their right to fight for their country's freedom and took aim at it in no uncertain terms. "We are devoted to the interest of Cuba and to the dignity of men above all things and do not accept that our cause be subjected to the interest of other countries and to the complexities of international politics. We are opposed to seeing Cuba used in the bargaining that is taking place with the Kremlin."[21] The statement closed with a message of defiance in all caps: "TO TAKE OUR ARMS DOES NOT DISARM US," calling this episode a "decided inconvenience" that would not impede them from ultimately achieving the objective of a free Cuba.

They would face more decided inconveniences a month later, when federal authorities seized their entire "expeditionary force" of four boats, including weapons, ammunition, and supplies in violation of the Neutrality Act, a loss estimated at $40,000. They followed very closely in Martí's footsteps, but unfortunately down the path he took as an author of a plan frustrated by US authorities, not as the author of their country's liberation as they had envisioned.*

Without direct US funding, a vicious cycle began to emerge. Organizations interested in continuing clandestine operations needed to get external funding, largely from the Cuban exile community itself. The best way to garner that support? Successful clandestine operations. Those were the best, most popular and well-received way to show the capability and willingness to strike against the Castro regime. This created a pressure not only to continue the fight, but to publicize any successes in order to increase their prestige and probability of future funding.

A few months after the high-profile seizures and retaliatory statement, the Women's Auxiliary of Comandos L was planning a variety show to help raise funds to replace the equipment confiscated in the struggle to liberate Cuba. It was going to be held in an old Pan Am Airways seaplane hangar on the waters of Biscayne Bay that had been converted into a convention

---

*Ironically, the one who most closely mirrored Martí in this whole episode was one of its most tangential players. Meyer, who was slated to cover the aborted raid, was a hardened battlefield reporter better known as Dickey Chappelle. She had covered Iwo Jima and Okinawa in WWII and had been covering another front of that time subject to the "complexities of international politics," Vietnam. She, like Martí, was a writer destined to lose their life on the battlefield. She was killed by a booby trap while on patrol in Vietnam with the Marines in 1965.

center (and remains one to this day). While guests were enjoying the event, they were going to hear an announcement: Comandos L were on a mission to attack a ship close to Cuba at that very moment![22] What better time to donate than when you're reminded by your hosts that they have people in harm's way on behalf of a cause you hold dear? A very clever public relations stunt, to be sure. And one that revealed the need to get creative in order to survive.

Many exiles recognized that the fall of the Cuban Revolutionary Council left an important strategic gap. While it had its difficulties, the CRC was the closest the exile community had to a unifying force among those actively working toward the reinstitution of democratic rule in Cuba. One Cuban exile who was uniquely positioned both in terms of role and resources spearheaded an effort to fill that void and establish an entity that could represent and speak on behalf of the exile community, and coordinate the cause of Cuban liberation from communist control.

José Pepin Bosch was the chairman of the board of the Bacardi Corporation, the rum company originally from Santiago de Cuba. Right around the time that the CRC was losing its financial support from Washington, Bosch was concerned about the gap this would create, and organized a group of twenty-one prominent Cuban exiles to execute an ambitious plan. Perhaps understanding the chaotic nature of exile organizations up to that point, the group, the Pro-Referendum Committee, was formed to organize a referendum by which all Cubans in exile all over the world could vote for members of a five-member representative board.[23] This would in theory create, through a democratic vote, the critical element that had eluded the exile community to that point: a group empowered to promote unity of action in the effort to liberate Cuba.

This was a massive undertaking. It required a census of Cubans in exile, as well as the resources to print, mail, collect, and count all the ballots. Luckily for the Pro-Referendum Committee, people really like rum and drink a lot of it. And Bosch was willing to put the resources of the rum powerhouse behind the effort. By early May 1964, the committee reportedly had received registrations from over seventy-five thousand Cubans in exile across the world, as well as the support of thirty-three exile organizations. On May 23, 1964, the votes were in. Thanks again to rum proceeds, the effort was able to contract top-notch technology, and votes were tabulated by a subsidiary of IBM. The results: 40,905 in favor of the slate of candidates for the five-member committee, 979 against. The group included Ernesto Freyre, a lawyer who was the coordinator and foreign relations chief; Vincente Rubeira, former labor union leader, as the liaison to exile organizations; another labor leader, Aurelio Fernández, who was responsible for delegations throughout the hemisphere; Erneido Oliva, the former second-in-command of the 2506 Brigade at the Bay of Pigs,* as military coordinator; and another Brigade veteran and student leader named Jorge Mas Canosa as the head of public affairs.[24] Four days later, the newly elected board held their first meeting in Washington, DC, and established themselves as the Cuban Representation in Exile (RECE).[25]

Their first action as an organization was to demand that the Organization of American States impose sanctions on Cuba. RECE had big plans. The military coordinator, Erneido Oliva, was convinced that internal resistance in Cuba was insufficient to overthrow Castro, as were disjointed external actions. "People who think [Castro] can be overthrown from within are making a mistake. . . . We cannot overthrow Castro by separate actions," he said.[26] He believed that a large-scale united exile force, one that united all the disparate armed efforts, was the only answer. One of their main tasks to this end was a census to gather information on the military capabilities and experience of exiles over the age of eighteen, in order to compile a roster of those "willing and physically able" to aid in an armed struggle against Castro.[27] The recent election gave them a head start on how to reach thousands of them.

Among their stated objectives were to not "interfere with any plan of any existing organization. On the contrary, [RECE] will cooperate in every patriotic, serious, useful, and feasible endeavor which deserves to receive financial assistance and advice."[28] This apparently included funding raids into Cuba, particularly after resources and support for the larger initiatives, such as the large exile armed force, didn't materialize. For example, RECE provided funding for sporadic attempts to try to effect change, such as the attempt to assassinate Castro in Havana in 1966. Six exiles on a twenty-three-foot fiberglass boat were planning to do what no one else had been able to. Two were put ashore and planted two rockets aimed at the Comodoro Hotel in Havana. Unfortunately for them, a student attending a school at the hotel saw the landing party and alerted the authorities, which resulted in eleven Cuban

---

*Or, more precisely, "The Battle of Triggerfish Bay . . ."

patrol boats converging on the team. The landing party, as well as the two crew of the inflatable boat that put them ashore, were killed. One of the two who stayed back reportedly lost a hand when a grenade exploded in the boat.[29]

Had RECE emerged earlier, perhaps things could have gone differently. But times were changing. The response from the military census was tepid, and most of the respondents were already known entities: 2506 veterans, commandos, and individuals who had joined the US Army and responded from Fort Jackson.[30] The vision of a grand Cuban liberation force was also a very expensive proposition. The drying up of resources from Washington, forcing a reliance on donations and other unreliable sources of income, was devastating. Another Caribbean Normandy, this time with a larger force founded and funded exclusively by Cuban exiles and coordinated from Miami, wasn't meant to be.

AMOZON Prime: Special Deliveries

Although the US was shying away from overt support for exiles' anti-Castro efforts—largely to maintain a semblance of order and balance with the Soviet Union—there was still a global ideological struggle going on. And having a Soviet satellite state ninety miles from American shores was still an undesirable prospect. The United States agreed not to invade Cuba overtly, but there were many activities below that threshold that could be done to help nudge the island toward the desired outcome of Castro's downfall. Support for counter-revolutionaries on the island was one. Another was sabotage, efforts designed to both cause damage to key infrastructure and economic assets as well as inspire uprisings in-country. JMWAVE and its significant presence in Miami were used to continue maritime incursions into Cuba far after the US government had publicly cracked down on exile organizations doing the same thing.

They had several vessels at their disposal. Two 175-foot patrol craft, the *Rex* and *Leda*, were the largest in the fleet and were primarily used as support vessels. Due to their size, they could carry more fuel and supplies, but were less than stealthy. As a result, they would usually stay farther offshore and serve as mother ships for smaller craft that would enter Cuban waters. The *Riptide* was a dark-blue-hulled 159-foot craft, a bit smaller, but rounded out the support vessels and often would serve in that function. Due to their size, seakeeping capabilities, and longer endurance, they were often used for missions on Cuba's south coast, which required much longer transits.

The smaller boats went deeper into Cuban waters and sometimes (for northern coast incursions where distances from South Florida were significantly shorter) would function largely independently, although a support ship was usually at sea for any contingencies. There were two thirty-five-foot Prowlers, which were shallow-draft wooden-hulled boats popular with sportfishermen: the dark-green-and-gray *Bee*, and the *Twilight*, with a maroon hull and beige superstructure. There was also a dark-green-hulled fifty-four-foot boat named *Neptune*, which in JMWAVE's service was engaging in far more interesting work than her original function as a water taxi.

These vessels were busy. One December alone they had eleven operations planned. Missions varied: some were movement of people, either infiltration of operational personnel or exfiltration of the same personnel or collaborators in Cuba in danger of discovery or arrest. These missions often were code-named COBRA, and subsequent infiltration/exfiltration operations were COBRA XI, COBRA XIV, and so on. Others, such as CHALICE, were cache missions, specifically for hiding weapons, ammunition, equipment, and other necessary materials for use by assets on island. One such stash comprised twenty-eight containers: the first contained cash; containers two through nine held grenades and explosives; ten held maps; eleven to fourteen held medicine and other equipment; fifteen to twenty-two had rifles; twenty-three contained food; twenty-four to twenty-six were ammunition; twenty-seven had car parts; and the last contained detonator caps.[31]

These caches were important to the efforts on the island. One mission, which called for operatives to access one of these caches, was a reminder of just how unpredictable and dangerous these missions could be. Operation CLEOPATRA took place in December 1963, and planned for infiltration of a five-man team. They were to approach the Cuban coast on their converted water taxi, the dark-green-hulled *Neptune*, and make landfall using a small craft with a silent outboard engine. The team landed without incident, but as they began crossing a mangrove swamp in order to use a known cache, they came across four locals.

Two were laborers cutting wood for a nearby cooperative. The other two were armed militiamen. The militia opened fire and the team returned it. In the confusion, the two laborers were reportedly killed, and one of the militiamen was wounded. Both militiamen escaped.[32] The threat of more militia returning to investigate was bad enough. It was compounded by the fact that they were in a swamp with thick mud—it didn't require a bloodhound to track the team's footprints directly to their hidden small craft, their only means of escape. The team would make it back to the *Neptune* and safety, but it could easily have turned out very differently.

There were missions focused on sabotage as well. Some were infiltrations targeting infrastructure. DIAMANTE was one such operation focused on destroying bridges. Others, like CUSHION, looked to attack electrical plants or transformers, and initial plans requested scouting of ideal mortar positions to hit a known electrical plant. Operation DUCK was one that spoke to some of the more sophisticated training being provided by the CIA. It was a sabotage operation aimed at limiting Cuban authorities' capability to monitor coastal waters by crippling their patrol boats stationed on the Isle of Pines, the island off Cuba's southern coast that the Castro regime has since renamed the Isle of Youth. This strike utilized a seven-man underwater-demolition team (UDT), capable of silent infiltration, placing of explosives, and extrication without detection.

Personnel and Training

These capabilities: navigation, use of small arms, demolition and use of explosives, underwater demolition—and the personnel trained in them—were no accident. A significant part of JMWAVE's efforts in Miami was focused on the recruitment of exiles suitable for these types of missions. The geography of South Florida, which offers an entire archipelago of small islands, provided the perfect training grounds. There was a maritime training site in Flamingo, a remote site in the Everglades swamp, as well as a nearby firing range. Survival training was on Plantation Key in the upper Florida Keys. Big Pine Key, in the lower Keys closer to Key West and the end of the island chain, was the site of a special operations training area.[33] These personnel received a minimum of three months of intensive training in a number of skills ranging from field photography, tradecraft, and communications equipment to boat handling, sabotage, and use of weapons up to and including 4.2-inch mortars. The teams were all named with the same convention: AMADDER, AMANCHOR, AMBEACH, AMLILAC, and others—even the unintentional foreshadowing of a delivery team named AMOZON—provided weapons, personnel, and matériel to efforts in Cuba to topple the Castro regime.

Knowledge and Assistance from USCG and USN

While this may have been taking place shielded from the prying eyes of the public (and, of course, in direct conflict with stated official US policy), these operations were conducted with the knowledge and assistance of other federal entities. Due to the use of smaller vessels, the frequent transiting of both South Florida waters and international waters, and the potential for any number of contingencies, JMWAVE reached out to two of the most important partners with the highest federal presence in those waters: the US Navy and the Coast Guard.

In internal CIA communications, Coast Guard Rear Admiral Irvin J. Stephens, the commander of the Coast Guard Seventh District, was singled out for his cooperation. The Seventh District, based in Miami, oversees all Coast Guard operations in the southeastern United States and the Caribbean, from South Carolina through Georgia and Florida, Puerto Rico, the US Virgin Islands, and the Caribbean Basin. This wasn't the first time his Coast Guard career had brought him to Miami; during World War II, between a tour on the Greenland Patrol and taking command of a destroyer escorting convoys in the Atlantic and Mediterranean, he served as the Coast Guard liaison to the US Navy's Submarine Chaser Training Center based in Miami. He had taken command of the district in July 1962, meaning just a few months into his tenure he had to deal with the Cuban Missile Crisis. That was one event with robust intelligence and maritime components, so he likely built some relationships through that experience.

But the fact that Admiral Stephens's regular day-to-day operations required liaison and relations with Bahamian authorities was of particular interest. It allowed him to be a key secret interlocutor with the Bahamas on behalf of JMWAVE's operations. Stephens could and did easily inquire about certain vessels of interest, deconflict areas of concern, and ensure that vessels in the JMWAVE fleet met with minimal interference. This was a significant contribution: the Bahamians were publicly pursuing a policy against these very same kinds of raids. Having a high-ranking officer who could in essence flag vessels to leave alone was invaluable and avoided potentially messy misunderstandings. As a result, JMWAVE would keep Admiral Stephens regularly apprised of certain aspects of their operations, in case his assistance with Bahamian authorities was required.

The US Navy had a major presence in Key West, a few hours south of Miami at the end of the Florida Keys, including a Naval Air Station, which is still in operation. The commanding officer at the time was Rear Admiral Louis Kirn, a decorated naval aviator who had earned two Distinguished Flying Crosses, a Navy Cross, and an Air Medal for his service at Guadalcanal and the Solomon Islands in 1942.

JMWAVE met with both admirals to address one issue of concern for CIA planners: the rules of engagement in the event that their vessels engaged in clandestine operations against Cuba came under attack. The discussion yielded a detailed plan of how this information would be passed on. If a vessel came under attack, they would obviously alert their JMWAVE handlers and any other JMWAVE vessels operating in the area via their clandestine radio channel and provide basic information on the situation.

However, they would also simultaneously put out a call on frequency 2182, the established frequency for distress calls constantly monitored by the Coast Guard, stating their vessel's name, general position, and relaying that it was in distress with engines stopped and taking on water. JMWAVE handlers would then contact the Coast Guard to clarify that this was one of theirs under attack. In those days, particularly in the wake of the Cuban Missile Crisis, it was standard operating procedure for the Coast Guard to request US Navy air cover for any distress call close to Cuban waters. However, under this plan, Coast Guard watch standers would contact the Navy in Key West and let them know that this was a condition "ZEBRA," meaning this was air cover for a JMWAVE boat under attack.

This made sense for operations off Cuba's north coast and closer to US waters. Operations off Cuba's south coast presented unique challenges. They were conducted out of range of the 2182 distress frequency. They also usually involved JMWAVE's larger vessels, like the *Leda*, *Rex*, and *Riptide*. These vessels were foreign-flagged to provide plausible deniability and make them easier to crew. That, however, made it more difficult to justify US air cover if they came under Cuban fire. The standing guidance for air cover was that it be provided to vessels in distress that were "not clearly identified as of non–United States registry." Not the clearest guidance in grammatical terms, but basically vessels with evident foreign registry weren't authorized that level of response. The usual merchant shipping frequency used for distress was constantly monitored by the Coast Guard, but it was deemed too risky.

By law and convention, the closest vessel to a distress call is required to render assistance. In those waters, that could be merchant shipping from a friendly country, a British or Dutch freighter, or it could just as easily be a Soviet merchant ship. To avoid this, it was proposed that they broadcast their distress call on an alternate distress frequency used by merchant shipping. To check the ambiguous nationality box required for air cover, the agreed-upon broadcast for identification was "This is *Riptide* (or *Leda* or *Rex*) operating out of Miami," which in planners' minds was ambiguous enough to not clearly identify their foreign flag status.[34]

It seems as if, at least in the Coast Guard, the guidance regarding collaboration with JMWAVE filtered all the way down to the boat crews. This makes sense from a practical standpoint in that there was a higher likelihood of more frequent interaction between JMWAVE vessels and the Coast Guard due to law enforcement and other duties that put them in regular contact with public boaters. A JMWAVE Operational Plan (OPLAN) for an operation code-named ZORRO, an incursion to replenish a weapons cache near Playa Morrillo in northwest Cuba, included information on the cover stories provided to operatives if intercepted by the US Navy or the Coast Guard. If they were stopped by the Navy or any other friendly vessels, they were to provide the true name of their boat—in this case another small vessel named *Marlin*—hailing from Miami, and state that they were on a research project when they developed some mechanical trouble. However, if they were intercepted by the Coast Guard, their guidance was far simpler. It was a one-word reply, the agreed-upon recognition signal: "Sesame."[35]

The JMWAVE planners had reason to prepare for contingencies. This was dangerous business and Cuban authorities would obviously not stand idly by if these operations were discovered. Team AMOZON ran into this very scenario and benefited from some of these discussions with the Navy and Coast Guard. They were on an operation named SALLY XIV, and departed their operational vessel code-named JADE at approximately 10:25 p.m., a few miles offshore of the Dromedarios island chain off Cuba's north central coast. Upon reaching a bend in a narrow channel, one of the crew heard the sound of a gun bolt chambering a round. He immediately opened fire at a Cuban boat hidden in the mangroves only ten to twelve feet to their right, and the hidden boat fired back almost simultaneously. The AMOZON team also took fire from another boat on their left. One engine was hit and stopped functioning. Fortunately, they managed to get to a wider part of the channel, turn around, and resume firing at both boats to head toward open water. The entire firefight lasted about ten minutes.

The Cuban boats launched white flares to try to locate them before they escaped. Once they had made it to open water, the AMOZON team reported two red flares sent up by the Cuban boats but didn't see any signs of pursuit. Once at a safe distance, the team came to a dead stop: the lone remaining outboard was straining under the load. They jettisoned some equipment to lighten the boat and slowly made their way to their rendezvous point three hundred miles away in the northern Bahamas, arriving almost fourteen hours later. They noticed a Coast Guard aircraft was circling the area.[36]

Their boat had around twenty bullet holes in it, and several had struck their destroyed engine. A few members were slightly injured, one of them miraculously so. Upon inspection, the bullet that ended up hitting him in the upper left arm had passed through his jacket from one side of his body to the other without hitting him anywhere else. Another member wasn't so lucky. In the firefight, he was struck and fell into the water without making a sound. He was a well-respected radio operator with AMOZON for almost three years and SALLY XIV was his seventeenth mission to Cuba.[37]

This AMOZON mission, which involved an exchange of gunfire, took place in 1966. By then, Cuban exile groups were largely out of the infiltration game: it was far more difficult to maintain without consistent financial support. As it became increasingly clear that these hit-and-run raids weren't going to achieve the exile community's longed-for goal of regime change, interest dwindled. The view from Washington had changed significantly as well. The Cold War priorities and focus of the United States government had shifted from Cuba toward an ever-increasing conflict of communist containment in Southeast Asia. Miami as a clandestine-operations hub for incursions into Cuba was winding down, but the experience would shape the region for years to come.

6

A Rogues' Gallery

The US government's shift in its attitude toward clandestine raids changed the dynamics of armed incursions significantly. Miami was no longer completely open for those kinds of operations, and concerted efforts were made by federal authorities to dissuade and stop them. While Miami had at least in theory ceased to be a permissive environment, some very dangerous seeds had been sown. Miami was crawling with men possessing various levels of training in guerrilla tactics: clandestine warfare, small arms, explosives, small-craft handling, and other specialties. Many of these individuals were frustrated by the turn of events and by the US government's perceived abandonment. They felt that their dedication to the liberation of Cuba had been betrayed, and that it was no longer a priority to the American government. For some, all that meant was that the struggle would have to continue: with the resources at their disposal, and against any available targets that could advance the cause.

This led to some eyebrow-raising attacks in the name of the counterrevolutionary movement. In December 1964, Che Guevara, the famous Argentinian allegedly responsible for numerous executions in Cuba and untold posthumous T-shirt sales, was the Cuban Minister of Industries despite having virtually no knowledge of Cuba or industry. He was on a much-publicized visit to New York, where he was making the case for better relations with Cuba. Protestors crowded every stop he made. Upon his arrival at a television studio, he was greeted by 150 screaming protestors, one of whom hurled a cigarette lighter at him, which harmlessly bounced off the pavement several feet away.[1] This wasn't the only projectile launched at him during his visit to New York.

Two days earlier, Guevara was scheduled to speak before the United Nations. He was, not surprisingly, greeted by throngs of protestors, many of whom took up the chant "Guevara *carnicero!*"—"Guevara the butcher!"[2] He took the podium, his green fatigues echoing the green marble backdrop of the General Assembly's dais. A few minutes after noon, with Guevara midway through his speech railing against the United States and global imperialism, a dull boom rattled the windows of the building. Many inside likely assumed that there had been an attack by the angry protestors in front of the building. The reality was far more colorful than that.

A bazooka shell had been fired from the far side of the East River at the United Nations headquarters. The shell missed the building, falling into the water around two hundred yards short of the glass structure, sending up a geyser of water off West Forty-Third Street. A tugboat captain who was transiting the area of the river at the time recalled seeing a puff of smoke across from the UN headquarters but didn't see anyone at the spot where the smoke appeared, or anyone flee the area. A few railroad workers found the bazooka less than two hours after the attack, behind a metal-supply company.

It probably wasn't hard to find; it had a Cuban flag tied to it. There was something else attached to it: a metal rectangle the size of a cereal box. It had a timing mechanism in it, rigged to fire at 12:10 p.m. The weapon was a German-made rocket launcher manufactured in World War II that had been sawed off from its original five-foot length to less than three.[3]

As crazy as this event was, according to the bomb squad that responded, it could have been far, far worse. The river is approximately nine hundred yards wide at the site of the incident, and this weapon had enough range to actually hit the United Nations headquarters. The weapon was propped up at a twenty-degree angle; had it been at a steeper angle it could have struck the building. The bomb squad on scene also reported that the projectile may have contained just under two pounds of a high explosive known as "Composition B."[4] With a number of world leaders and representatives of multiple governments among the almost five thousand people inside the headquarters at the time, one can imagine how catastrophic a direct hit on the building could have been.

Two weeks later, on Christmas Eve, media reported on three individuals identified as the perpetrators. One lived in the Bronx, one in Manhattan, and one in New Jersey. Two of them were brothers. Despite their New York ties, they were linked to a Miami-based exile organization, the Cuban Nationalist Association. All three were adamant that they intended to miss the UN building, and that their intent was to draw attention away from Guevara's speech and steal the day's headlines.[5]

Boomtown

Around this time, Miami was starting to see a transformation. Since the rise of the Castro regime, it had been the tip of the spear for the counter-revolution, a launching point for raids and the main recruiting grounds for anti-Castro efforts. But as those windows began to close and opportunities to strike against the island itself dwindled, some in the struggle had to look for other ways to effect change. And there were open rumors for years that the Castro regime itself had a significant presence in the city, infiltrating groups and sowing division and discord. Cuban intelligence had already done an effective job virtually eliminating the underground on the island. Increasingly, the conflict began playing out on the streets of Miami.

Many groups in Miami had received US paramilitary training with the specific goal of helping to overthrow the Castro regime and were looking for ways to stay in the fight. If they couldn't directly attack Cuba, there were still opportunities to advance the cause. Companies that did business with Cuba had offices in Miami. Consulates and representatives of governments that tacitly or openly supported the Castro regime did too. Some organizations began seeing these as legitimate targets and saw the placing of small bombs as an attention-grabbing form of protest.

In early 1968, the Mexican consul in Miami found a surprise when he walked into his garage to drive to work. A quarter of a stick of dynamite had detonated during the night near his car.[6] Mexico had close diplomatic relations with Cuba. He would be the target of at least four attacks before the end of the year, including a hand grenade being lobbed into his home.[7]

A week after the car bomb at the Mexican consul's house, a local Spanish-language newspaper ran an article alleging that the British government was going to start selling weapons to Cuba. While this wasn't true, the British consul's house was hit as well by a bomb placed outside his garage.[8] In the days following the Chilean government's decision to allow a few of Che Guevara's guerrillas to return to Cuba, a small bomb was slipped through the mail slot of the Chilean consulate in Miami. The Spanish tourist office in the city was targeted twice using the same method of a small explosive device in the mail slot: both failed to explode but nonetheless made headlines and delivered a message. By September 1968, the city of Miami had been rocked by thirty-eight of these bombings.[9] And it was an unfortunate tactic that would prove to have some staying power. From 1970 to 1978, the Dade County bomb squad responded to 130 explosive devices that were placed but didn't detonate. They also responded to the aftermath of 129 that did.[10]

There was one person in Miami who had gained a reputation as someone with both expertise with explosives and the willingness to use it. The FBI in classified reports noted that he was widely recognized by those engaging in these activities as the "Dean of Cuban Bombers."[11] His name was Orlando Bosch.

Bosch was linked to the Insurrectional Movement for Revolutionary Recovery (MIRR), one of the exile groups that was begun in Cuba in the early days of the Revolution and had established a Miami presence in support. Bosch had always been a believer in raids and attacks as an effective method to overthrow the Castro regime. He and the MIRR coordinated some high-profile raids against sugar mills and other targets in Cuba. He was consistently looking for ways to keep the pressure on: he once planned to attack a Cuban freighter but was thwarted when he was stopped in Miami rush hour towing a homemade radio-controlled torpedo.[12] He also claimed that he had attempted to assassinate Castro at a baseball stadium in Havana by bombing it with a privately owned B-26 bomber.[13] He was, not surprisingly, shunned by much of the exile community, seen as too fringe, too impractical, an extremist whose ideas likely did more to harm the cause than advance it. His next scheme was another outlandish attack that pushed even his own boundaries.

It took place in an area familiar to most who have visited Miami. The MacArthur Causeway is the road that connects the island of Miami Beach to the city of Miami itself. It also runs parallel to the port: anyone who has driven to South Beach, or waved from a cruise ship while departing it, knows this stretch of road. One night in 1968, it was the site of a most unusual event. The Polish freighter *Polanica* was docked at the Port of Miami. Poland was, of course, part of the Eastern Bloc and aligned with the Soviet Union at the time. The *Polanica* was a large four-hundred-foot vessel that had just come in to port after steaming from Portugal and was slated to leave for Mexico the following night. Among her cargo was some equipment and gear for the Polish Olympic team to be delivered prior to the Summer Games taking place in Mexico in October: these were the games that provided the international stage for the famous Black Power fist-raising on the podium. But nobody knew about her sports-related cargo. All that was apparent was that a ship flying the flag of a communist nation aligned with the Soviet Bloc was sitting in Miami. And something was going to be done about it.

It was around 2:45 in the morning. Aboard the *Polanica* there were a few junior crew members awake on watch. A US Coast Guard boat was in the channel nearby providing waterside security. All of them reported hearing the same thing: an explosion that was a few times louder than the average grenade. One coastguardsman who had been in Vietnam said that he heard what sounded like a round fired from a recoilless rifle. But nobody saw anything out of the ordinary: there were no other boats on the water, and the causeway didn't have any unusual vehicles or cars speeding away. The crew of the *Polanica* came to the side of the ship where they had heard the impact and checked the damage, aided by the spotlight of the Coast Guard boat that had come alongside. There was a dent in the side of the ship, with some paint that had been scorched or damaged. That was about it.[14]

The damage was minimal, but the action itself—firing upon a foreign vessel in a US port—was not. The FBI was called in, as was the local bomb squad. They found a half-submerged .57-millimeter recoilless rifle, with about two feet of the barrel sticking out of the water. Their investigation revealed that there were two men at the firing position that night, but lookouts could be forgiven for not seeing anything.[15] Two men had set up on the far side of the highway, one of them pretending to be fishing until the last minute. There was another car farther away that was there to watch. Inside was Orlando Bosch.

A few days after the attack on the *Polanica*, a call came in to the local Latin-news editor of Channel 7 from a man identifying himself as a member of an organization called Cuban Power. He said that an individual named "Ernesto" was going to hold a press conference and that the TV station should participate and bring a cameraman. The journalist was instructed to meet at a local Sears parking lot at 8:00 p.m. the following night. Upon arrival at Sears, joined by some writers from the *Miami Herald*, all the media were instructed to get into a waiting car and blindfold themselves. It only got weirder from there. They were driven to a residence and greeted by a man who informed them that "Ernesto was ready," and took them to a room where a few other journalists, mostly from Spanish-language radio, were already seated. They were finally in the presence of "Ernesto." "Ernesto" looked like a blob, a formless shape of a man under a dark hood or sheet that covered him entirely. He was seated behind a small table with a white tablecloth, so there were no discernible characteristics of this individual that were visible. He did not speak; the hooded form merely nodded toward a number of envelopes that each had a copy of a statement from Cuban Power. Each journalist took their copy and there must have been an incredibly awkward silence, since "Ernesto" remained silent. Their escort told them shortly afterward that it was time for them to leave, and they were sent off with "Ernesto" rising up from his chair and in a manner clearly intended to disguise his voice, said "Viva Cuba Libre—Long Live Free Cuba." The journalists were escorted to the waiting vehicle, where they were asked to blindfold themselves again, before being returned to where the entire bizarre experience began, the Sears parking lot. The journalist who received the phone call turned the press release over to the FBI.[16]

The statement reported that the organization would protect the identity of "Ernesto," for his own safety, but for the good of the cause, not out of cowardice: "Neither the fury of Fidel Castro, nor the fear of any jail will stop the triumphal advance of Cuban Power," it proclaimed.[17]

It also unequivocally claimed responsibility for the attack on the *Polanica*. The statement went on, claiming that the failures in the previous seven years of fighting the Castro regime were largely caused by the US government's lack of understanding that this was a "battle for liberation" that should be left to Cubans, and that any aid should be provided to them as an alliance of equals, not as a government dictating terms. The statement closed by announcing that Cuban Power was extending an appointment to Dr. Orlando Bosch as the political delegate of Cuban Power in Exile to serve as a representative of the alleged Cuban Power affiliates on the island.

Bosch was arrested a few weeks later for the attack on the *Polanica*. The FBI also had reason to believe he was involved in a number of explosions and attempts to bomb numerous vessels based in countries that traded with Cuba. In the span of four months, there were explosions aboard two British freighters, two Japanese vessels, a Spanish ship, and an attempt to dynamite a third British freighter named the *Lancastrian Prince*.[18] En route to the FBI office in Miami, Bosch reviewed his copy of the indictment regarding the shelling of the vessel and while in the car with two agents said, "That was a good shot." Incredulous, they asked him to repeat what he had said. One of the special agents specifically asked if he said "shot" or "charge," referring to the indictment. Bosch reaffirmed that he was talking about the shot taken at the *Polanica*, making clear that it was a Polish ship, meaning communist.[19] That distinction, in his mind, clearly made the vessel a legitimate target. He was sentenced to ten years for the attack and would end up serving four.

Orlando Bosch was a horrible cautionary tale of unintended consequences. Miami had become another Cold War Pandora's box: providing weapons and training to those that align with your interests can be helpful, but once released, the use of that knowledge and expertise can be impossible to control. The lawlessness and brazen acts during a time when the world was divided into clear ideological camps are part of the story of how the city of Miami became what it is today. Miami is a crazy place, and the story of Bosch and his friend Luis Posada Carriles may be the high-water mark of the city's craziness, which is part of why it is included here.

But there are those who would try to highlight this as the quintessential story of Cuban exile groups, the government of Cuba being chief among them.[20] That would be unfair and inaccurate. Bosch had gone to the extreme, a perversion of the true and heartfelt yearning for a free Cuba that so many held on to and worked toward. There were thousands who selflessly and legitimately showed a willingness to labor and risk themselves to help liberate their country from an oppressive system that continues to rule their homeland.

Armed insurgents infiltrating the island by boat—it's how the earliest nationalists tried to wrest the island from Spanish dominion. It is the path in which José Martí, the apostle and founding father of Cuba, chose to participate in the struggle for freedom. It's even how Fidel ousted Batista, with a ragtag band on a rickety boat called the *Granma*. And it was perfectly scripted for the Cold War. Some never let go of that vision, even as the world moved on from the struggle of dual superpowers and old age began limiting these cold warriors' capacity to execute it.

Most Miamians today, if asked about exile organizations, would mention Alpha 66. It is the last surviving organization that has been around since the beginning. Comandos L was an offshoot of the organization in the early sixties, and Alpha 66 was one of the most active exile groups, effecting incursions for decades. But many in Miami know them from their twilight: as an organization of aging ideologues that still trained out in the swamps of the Everglades near the city in the hope of being called upon one last time. Eventually they retired their paramilitary efforts, but always kept the option open. One leader mentioned that incursions were in the past, but if dissidents in Cuba rose up in arms, they were "morally obligated to rush to their aid."[21] They are tragic figures, quixotic warriors whose lives were uprooted by forces beyond their control, forever grasping for something beyond their reach. And they, more than most, are one of the most powerful and lasting distillations of the Cold War experience that has shaped Miami.

7

Exporting Counterrevolution

L ocation, location, location.

It's both the key variable in the business of real estate and also the business of where-to-place-the-headquarters-for-your-top-secret-clandestine-paramilitary-and-psychological-warfare-operations.*

Well, location *and* the availability of well-trained, military-aged men. That matters too.†

And Miami fit the bill perfectly, making it the ideal area from which to launch operations across Latin America and elsewhere.

Guatemala, 1954

In 1950, Jacobo Árbenz Guzmán became president of Guatemala through what was almost universally considered a free and fair election. More of a nationalist than a "card-carrying" communist, Árbenz still wanted to reduce the economic dominance of his country by American business interests, in particular the United Fruit Company. Guatemala is not a large country, and the United Fruit Company owned *550,000 acres* of the country's

---

* Admittedly, the first one gets more use.
† Not so much for real estate, but we suppose it could?

most arable land, and as a result, had a massive say in how Guatemala used its national resources.

Árbenz proposed a program that would redistribute some of the land owned by the American business. Not all of it, by any means. In fact, the United Fruit Company wasn't even using most of the land it owned. Instead, they had left the majority of their land fallow for years at a time. It was just sitting there, unused, instead of providing for the people of Guatemala. Why? It kept prices high. By regulating supply, they could affect the market.

The Árbenz government even offered to pay United Fruit for the land. But no dice. It wasn't long before the US government began to see Árbenz as a problem. Part of the concern was that Árbenz, in order to govern effectively, had established at least a working relationship with Guatemalan communists. This alienated him from Guatemalan Catholics, landowners, business interests, and the military (among others). A bigger part of the issue was the United Fruit Company and its power in Washington. CIA Deputy Director (and future director) Allen Dulles, and his brother, future Secretary of State John Foster Dulles, were shareholders in United Fruit. From there it was a quick transition from Árbenz was a nationalist trying to help his country, to Árbenz is a stooge of the communists working directly for Moscow.[1]

In 1952, President Truman authorized an operation code-named PBFOR-TUNE, a CIA plan to aid Guatemalan exiles in overthrowing Árbenz.* However, after a month of planning, CIA Director Walter Bedell Smith canceled the mission after he learned operational security was so bad that Árbenz and the Guatemalan military were aware of the plan.

In the fall of 1953, US political and intelligence leaders, now under the Eisenhower administration, decided to try again. This time it would be code-named PBSUCCESS.† The operation, developed and run by the CIA's Western Hemisphere Division and coordinated with the State Department, would include elements of psychological warfare and economic, diplomatic, and paramilitary actions against Árbenz. The stated objective of PBSUCCESS was "to remove covertly, and without bloodshed if possible, the menace of the present Communist-controlled government of Guatemala."[2]

---

* Sound familiar?

† Which, if you think about it, is a bravely named operation. What if it failed?

For the day-to-day management of PBSUCCESS, a temporary CIA station code-named LINCOLN was set up on December 23, 1953, on an old Marine air base in Opa-locka, Florida, the Miami suburb. LINCOLN occupied Building 67, part of a group of buildings that were built during the Second World War as barracks for US Navy aircrews. According to one local researcher, this particular building was likely chosen because it also housed a day-care center—perfect cover for clandestine CIA operations.[3]

The key component of PBSUCCESS was Radio Liberation, the covert psychological warfare operation code-named SHERWOOD. Content for SHERWOOD was created at LINCOLN, using Guatemalan exiles to record radio "programs" that would later be beamed into the country. Some of the content included:

- **Acusamos de Alta Traición** (We Accuse of High Treason), which featured talk about the "virtues of the liberation movement's cause, the evils of communism and the treason committed by Guatemala's leaders." It was always accompanied by "dramatic background music."
- **Que Somos y Adonde Vamos** (What We Are and Where We're Headed), a political program that "switched between attacking communism and explaining the goals of the liberation movement."
- **Pegando Centro** (Hitting the Bullseye), a series of two-minute quick hits that gave a warning to a specific named person, "for having hoarded illegal arms."
- **La Mujer y la Patria: Opiniones Femeninas Sobre el Problema Comunista** (Women and the Fatherland: Feminine Opinions on the Communist Problem) was believed to be "probably very effective." A segment targeted at a female audience, and always with the same female announcer speaking in the first person, the program "addressed women in their roles of the period, as Catholic wives and mothers." Containing "strong religious content," this was likely used as a counterpoint to communist ideology.
- **Miscelanea Musical del Aire** (Musical Miscellany of the Airwaves) had music and "low-brow" jokes, and probably targeted the "less-educated sectors of Guatemalan society."

Did you say jokes? Oh yes. Yes, we did.

Here is a sample:

"Oh, what a beautiful mule!"

"That's a picture of Jacobo."

Árbenz says to his wife, "I'm going to fire my driver. Today was the third time he almost gets me killed."

"Don't be that way," she responds. "Why don't you give him another chance."

Chief of staff at the palace: "Is the president drunk again?"

President's valet: "I don't know, but it is unusual to see him try to take his pants off over his head."

Mrs. Árbenz is chatting with one of her husband's new aides, Ivan Noskapop.

"I understand you were wounded in WWII," she says.

"Yes, ma'am."

"And where were you wounded?"

"In the Dardanelles, ma'am."

"My, that must have been terribly painful!"[4]

Not exactly Mark Twain.

But the crazy thing is, it worked.

On June 16, 1954, a small force of CIA-backed exiles entered Guatemala. They didn't have enough manpower or firepower to take the country from Árbenz, but it soon became clear that the top Guatemalan military officers no longer supported the president. Nor did a good portion of Guatemala's population. The propaganda campaign was ... dare we say ... a SUCCESS. Árbenz resigned the presidency just eleven days later.

A CIA assessment of the psychological warfare component of the operation concluded it was "highly effective," and "energized some military personnel to resist, and influenced important sectors of Guatemalan society against communism, against the Árbenz regime, and in favor of the 'Army of Liberation.'"[5]

Not bad for a small, ad hoc CIA station in Miami.*

So what happened to Building 67 once the CIA had completed the Guatemala mission? It was put into use again as a facility to receive children sent to the United States as part of Operation Pedro Pan, and then later would be used to provide temporary shelter for children brought over during the Mariel boatlift in 1980 (which we will discuss more in a later chapter).[6]

Congo, 1964–1965

Part of the Bay of Pigs operation was a contingent of Cuban exile pilots, who sortied against aircraft and ground targets the day before the main invasion force landed at Playa Girón. The next day they prepared their aircraft again, this time to provide direct air support for the 2506 Brigade's assault on Cuba. But when it came time to take off, they learned the White House had canceled their part of the operation. They were grounded.

Sad. Angry. Feeling betrayed. The pilots looked for ways to avenge their comrades who had fallen so bravely on the beach. The CIA, to their credit, realized it would be foolish to lose all these well-trained and courageous combat pilots. Through a Miami-based front company,† the Agency rehired their exile pilots and formed a break-glass-in-case-of-emergency mini air force they could deploy anywhere it was needed—and could do so without exposing the role of the US government. True plausible deniability.

It turned out there was an emergency brewing in central Africa in 1964. Congo had just declared independence from Belgium, and the new government was doing its best to keep the country together. There was an insurgency force, who called themselves Simbas and were supported by the Soviets and the Chinese. Why would the Soviets and Chinese care about Congo? Why would the US? Because it was, and still is, resource rich: copper, gold, cobalt,

---

* Unless you consider the civil war that erupted soon after the coup, lasting decades and killing or wounding hundreds of thousands.
† One of the many, many, many front companies we discussed earlier.

diamonds . . . and uranium. Chinese Premier Chou En-lai publicly pro-claimed that the key to controlling all of Africa was first control of Congo.[7]

The United States supported the Congolese government, but the war wasn't going well. By early 1964, the Simbas had taken almost half the country, including the provincial capital of Stanleyville. In Stanleyville, the Simbas tortured and killed thousands of Congolese civilians, and took hostage hundreds of foreign missionaries, many of them American, and US government officials. The insurgents threatened to kill the Americans unless the US withdrew its support for the Congolese government.

It was time to break the glass.

Formally, the exile Cuban air force would be called the 211th Squadron, 2nd Group, of the Congolese Air Force, but the Cubans didn't use that often. Instead, they referred to themselves as El Grupo Voluntario Cubano (Cuban Volunteer Group), or their now-famous nickname, the Makasi (which meant "strong" in Lingala, a native Bantu language of the Congo).

Operation Dragon Rouge was launched in November 1964 and consisted of multiple elements. Along with the Cuban pilots there was a small ground force of Cubans commanded by an American paramilitary officer. There was a contingent of the elite Belgian Régiment Para-Commando, and a larger ground force of three hundred mercenaries cobbled together from different British commonwealth nations, but mostly South Africa. On the day of the assault, the Belgians were brought into Stanleyville on US Air Force C-130s, while the two ground forces closed in. The Cuban pilots provided devastating air support. When the dust settled, it was one of the—if not *the*—most successful US hostage rescue missions in history.[8]

At the end of the operation, the aircrews landed their planes at the Stanleyville airport. The mercenaries, being . . . well, mercenaries, "liberated" a nearby brewery, and began passing beers out to the Cuban pilots as a thank-you/job well done. The beer was called Unibra Polar. The bottles had a logo on them: a snorting bull. The Cubans loved the image, and from then on the noses of their aircraft would be decorated with that same snorting bull, along with the word "Makasi."[9]

The battle at Stanleyville was won, and the hostages were rescued, but the war was far from over. The CIA was aware that the Simbas were bringing Soviet-supplied weapons, ammunition, and supplies from Tanzania into

Congo across Lake Tanganyika, the longest freshwater lake in the world. At 45 miles wide and nearly 450 miles long, it made an easy conduit for rebel weapons and materials, especially at night. Aircraft and land forces were useless against this kind of resupply operation. What was needed were boats, and trained boat crews to man them.

But where could boats and crews be found, especially if the US involvement needed to remain hidden? The US Navy couldn't be sent in. The mission was supposed to be a secret. The answer was sitting in Miami, waiting for something to do.

As we know, after the failure at the Bay of Pigs, the CIA sponsored a number of anti-Castro operations. One of these was based around the organization known as the Movimiento Recuperación Revolucionaria (MRR, see Chapter 1). Led by Manuel Artime, the MRR was running maritime raids against Castro's navy from a base in Central America. Many of his men were Cuban exiles from Miami, including Félix Rodríguez, who coordinated many of the missions via radio from MRR headquarters.

In September 1964, Artime's maritime force was on a nighttime patrol in the Windward Passage, looking for any Cuban vessels to attack. All of a sudden, there it was: a massive ship. They closed on it and shined a powerful marine search light on the hull. Written across the aft hull of the ship was the word "Sierra." Could it be? Could this be the infamous *Sierra Maestra*, the flagship of the Cuban merchant fleet?

The boat crew radioed back to Rodríguez at headquarters: We've found the *Sierra Maestra*, do we have permission to attack? Rodríguez, assuming they knew what they were talking about, approved the attack. In his words, the exile crew proceeded to "shoot the shit out of the boat" with fifty-seven-millimeter recoilless rifle rounds.[10] The ship was set ablaze and would eventually sink. The crew returned to base, exhilarated and proud. They'd just struck a major blow to the Cuban government. Félix Rodríguez called his higher headquarters with the good news. A short time later, they replied: "Félix, in what ocean are you operating? The *Sierra Maestra* crossed through the Panama Canal yesterday and is in the Pacific Ocean."

To the dismay of the exiles, the CIA, and the US government, the ship the crew thought was the *Sierra Maestra* was actually the *Sierra Aranzazu*, a Spanish freighter bringing toys, garlic, and cork to Havana. The attack killed its captain, second mate, and third engineer, and wounded seventeen other Spanish sailors.

Following the attack, the Johnson administration had had enough. They canceled the operation and cut off the MRR's funding. The Cuban exiles spent about another month in Central America, before packing their gear and heading back to Miami.

The CIA was waiting for them upon their return, ready to offer them another job. To maintain operation security, CIA didn't tell the boat crews of their true destination until they arrived at Miami International Airport. They assumed they were going to Vietnam but were willing to go anywhere the CIA would let them fight against communism.

So now the mission had its boat crews. But who would lead them?

Jim Hawes was a SEAL, and a good one. In the summer of 1964, he was in Vietnam, training South Vietnamese naval units, and leading them on clandestine sabotage and psyops raids into North Vietnam. He was the perfect man to organize and lead this operation in Congo.

Now working for the CIA, Hawes arrived in Congo and began immediately to put his interdiction navy into the action. He and the fifteen Cuban exile sailors mapped out a plan. They would send one boat out on patrol and keep another in reserve. That way they could rotate crews, and always (or at least a lot of the time) have coverage of the lake and its resupply routes. When they ran into a suspicious boat that might be carrying arms to the rebels, they would stop it—one way or another. If the rebels resisted, they had the firepower to sink a small navy (and that's just what they intended to do).

During one operation, they heard something strange on the radio. A transmission, in Spanish. The Cuban sailors instantly knew who they were dealing with. "The voices, the accents, the names: Lleyo, or Tico, he heard them calling each other openly by name. 'Cubans are the same, doesn't matter what side you're on' . . . 'I know for certain there are Cubans out there.'"[11]

The CIA and the national security establishment in Washington were fully aware of the Soviet and Chinese support to the Simbas, but at this point no one in DC knew there were Cuban forces on the ground (and on the water) in Congo.

The exile boat crews agreed to come to Congo to fight against global communism, but now they were going to get a chance to take the fight to their true enemy, Cubans in the service of Fidel Castro.

But who was here in the Congo to lead *them*? Could it be someone important? Could it be someone very important?

Could it be Che?

Rumors had been swirling in the media and in intelligence circles about the location of Che Guevara, who had disappeared from public life in Cuba and was thought to be moving from place to place, trying to foment proletariat revolution. There were reported sightings in Egypt and elsewhere in Africa. Sightings and rumors of Che just about anywhere potentially ready for a leftist takeover. But no one knew. Nothing was substantiated. He could be anywhere.

He could be in Congo.

The boat crews now operated with a renewed sense of purpose. On one mission, they ran into five small boats traveling together. Even though the Cuban exiles were outnumbered, they had a considerable firepower advantage over just about anyone on the water. The only chance the five smaller boats had would be to try to run away. But four of the five turned toward the larger, more heavily armed exile boat, and attacked, while the fifth boat ran for safety. It was not a fair fight, and the four small boats were chewed up in the ensuing firefight. So what could have motivated those four crews to sacrifice themselves to protect the fifth boat? Was there someone on board worth protecting?

Hawes believed there was then, and knows there was now.

"Che Guevara and his ill-fated rebel band had been out of food, money, weapons, supplies, and luck. We ran them out of the Congo."[12]

If you don't think Hawes is a reliable source, that's fine. Ask Che what he thinks.

In the opening line of Che Guevara's book, *The African Dream: The Diaries of a Revolutionary War in the Congo*, Che laments, "This is the history of a failure."

Bolivia, 1967

This is the continuation of the story of Cuban exile Félix Rodríguez, and the end of the story for Argentinian-turned-Cuban revolutionary Che Guevara. Their lives had been working in converging directions since the late 1950s, and here in Bolivia, in 1967, their paths were about to meet.

Che chose to bring his revolution to Bolivia for several reasons. First, it was far enough away from the United States that he thought the Americans might be less inclined to intervene. Experience had shown him, and the Cubans, that when revolutionary movements popped up close to the US, the *yanquis* reacted strongly and swiftly, and the revolution failed. Second, Bolivia was a poor country, and its peasant population would be more susceptible to communist ideology. Finally, Bolivia was bordered by five countries (Argentina, Chile, Brazil, Peru, and Paraguay). If Che and his rebels succeeded in Bolivia, it could be used as a jumping-off point for any, or all, of those countries.[13]

Che's forces in Bolivia included fifty-three rebels: thirty Bolivians, seventeen Cubans, three Peruvians, one Argentinian (a writer named Ciro Roberto Bustos), one East German woman (Haydée Tamara Bunke Bider, who had been assigned by the KGB to keep tabs on Che), and one French communist, the writer Jules Régis Debray.[14]

To combat this insurgency, the Bolivian government requested assistance from the United States. But President Johnson, already mired in an unpopular war in Vietnam, was not going to send American soldiers to fight in South America. On orders from the White House, the US ambassador to Bolivia said that no US citizen could participate in any combat activities in areas where Che and his guerrillas were operating. So no sending in the special forces, and no sending in a team of CIA paramilitary officers consisting of men named Bob, John, Kevin, or Dave.

But it didn't take long for the CIA to find a solution. They had a number of men who were working for them, or had worked for them in the past, and were not US citizens (at least not yet; Rodríguez would become a citizen in 1969). And when the CIA asked for volunteers to go after Che, they didn't need to ask twice.

Rodríguez was only twenty-six years old when he left Miami for Bolivia, and he had already been at war with Castro for almost a decade. His wife and two young children had no idea where he was going or what he would be doing. But he knew he had to go. This was the chance of a lifetime.

When he arrived in country, he found a confused situation. Bolivian units were not coordinating intelligence with other Bolivian units. This was one of the first things Rodríguez looked to change. Che was operating using a tactic that has now become commonplace among many insurgency movements: he "set up his base camp in an area controlled by one Bolivian unit, but he operated across a river in a nearby area controlled by another."[15] If Bolivian military forces weren't sharing information, then they stood no chance of catching Che.

After four weeks in Bolivia, Rodríguez and the Bolivians got their first big break—the capture of a guerrilla named José Castillo Chávez, who went by the nickname Paco. Rodríguez spent two weeks with Paco, debriefing him each day for several hours. Félix knew that the best way to get information from someone like this was to treat him humanely, so he sent a nurse twice a day to tend to Paco's wounds. He brought him medicine, and clothes, and things to read. Rodríguez even got him a haircut, arranged to have his laundry cleaned, and offered to get a message to his parents. Most importantly, Félix "talked to him man to man."[16]

These methods worked, and Félix gained Paco's trust. Paco provided the CIA officer with a key piece of intelligence: Che's guerrilla force operated in three groups as it moved through Bolivia, a vanguard, a main force, and a rear guard. The vanguard moved about one kilometer ahead of the main force, and the rear guard was one kilometer behind. Che would be in the main force, the strongest group and the one which would provide Che the most protection. What this meant was, if you found *any* of the sections of Che's rebel "army," you would know where Che was.

A few weeks later, the Bolivians engaged some of Che's forces and killed several rebels. One of them was a man, Miguel, whom Paco had told Félix was the head of the vanguard. Now they knew where they could find Che—at least they had the knowledge he was roughly one kilometer away. Yes, it could be one kilometer away in multiple directions, but it was the best intelligence on Che's location they'd ever had.

And it paid off. On October 8, 1967, Bolivian forces caught Che. He was wounded, but alive. Félix Rodríguez rushed to where he was being held, hoping to question Che and to convince the Bolivians not to execute him on the spot. Félix's orders from the CIA were to do all within his power to keep Che alive. The Agency wanted to take their time interrogating him. They wanted to see what intelligence he could provide about the Castros in Cuba, or other Latin American communist movements he might know about.

But the Bolivians wanted him dead. He had invaded their country and tried to foment an overthrow of their government.

Rodríguez was able to stall for time and got an opportunity to speak to Che for several hours. He had radioed back to the CIA to tell them of the capture, and hoped they could convince the Bolivian government to hand over Che, alive, to the Americans. Much in the same way he questioned Paco, Félix treated Che as a human (the Bolivians had tried to coerce him into talking about his operations, and he resisted). Rodríguez assumed Che would take this information to the grave, so instead he spoke to him about more general topics—why they were in Bolivia, communism and revolution, and Che's relationship with Fidel Castro. When asked if Félix could convey a message for Che, Guevara told him, "Tell Fidel that he will soon see a triumphant revolution in America [he meant the Americas, not the United States]. And tell my wife to get remarried and try to be happy."[17]

Unfortunately, the US government pressure on the Bolivians did not work. Félix got the message during a telephone call with higher headquarters:

> The orders had come down by telephone in the code the Bolivians predetermined. I took the call from Vallegrande myself and heard the words, "Five hundred—six hundred." Five hundred meant Che. Six hundred meant execute him. If the Bolivians had wanted him kept alive I would have heard the number seven hundred.[18]

Félix didn't conduct the execution himself; that was left to the Bolivian forces. Before Che was killed, Rodríguez asked if he could take a picture with the man who held so much responsibility for the pain and suffering of his family, and the families of tens of thousands of fellow Cuban exiles. Che agreed, and in the last picture of Che alive—in fact the only picture that survives of Che alive on the day of his execution—he is standing next to Félix Rodríguez.

But Rodríguez wasn't done in Latin America.* Just six weeks after he returned to Miami following the Bolivian operation, he was sent to Ecuador to help train an elite Ecuadorean unit in counterinsurgency and counterterrorism techniques. The CIA, and Rodríguez specifically, were there at the request of the Ecuadorean president. Later in 1968, Rodríguez was sent to Peru, to teach basic intelligence tradecraft and long-range patrol tactics to a Peruvian paratrooper unit, and one of the country's first dedicated anti-guerrilla combat units.[19]

---

* And we will see him again later too.

Part III

8

Open the Gates

Another act on the Cold War stage with South Florida in a starring role begins with a simple building in the background. It was a large, white two-story complex with wooden-slat window shutters and crowned with the curved clay-colored Spanish roof tile that is so common in the tropics. It sat on a half-acre compound shaded by royal poincianas—tropical shade trees with brilliant red flowers—mango and papaya trees, and manicured grass. It could have been any of a number of similar structures in Miami. But this one was in Havana. And technically on Peruvian soil.

Havana in 1980 was seeing a creative new way Cubans had devised to get off the island: accessing embassies to request asylum. A group forced their way into the Venezuelan embassy the previous December and were allowed to leave for Caracas. Earlier in the year, twelve Cubans used a vehicle to ram their way onto the premises of the Peruvian embassy in Havana to request asylum. The Peruvian ambassador denied their request, sent them home, and even wrote a letter of apology to the Cuban government. His decision, which apparently was taken without consultation with his own government back in Lima, was roundly criticized in Latin American diplomatic circles as a violation of a key right to request asylum. The Peruvian Foreign Ministry agreed. The ambassador's decision was rescinded by the Ministry. He was further ordered to bring all twelve Cuban asylum seekers back to the embassy, which he reportedly did personally using that most 1980s mode of transportation: his own station wagon. After wrapping up his brief diplomatic Uber service on the streets of Havana, he was recalled as Peru's ambassador to Cuba and departed the country.[1]

On April Fools' Day in 1980, perhaps emboldened by Peru's clear message in defense of the right to request asylum, a group of six Cubans took over a city bus and attempted the same thing: they barreled toward the gates of the Peruvian embassy in an attempt to gain their freedom. They weren't the only ones who remembered the previous incident. The Cuban guards posted at the gate realized what was happening and opened fire. The bus charged through the gunfire and crashed the gate into the Peruvian compound. Two of the asylum seekers were wounded by the guards' small-arms fire but had reached their objective—foreign soil and a chance at getting out of Cuba. The gate, however, wasn't the only casualty. One of the guards was shot and killed by their own cross fire.

The Cuban government's response was to retaliate by simply pulling their security personnel, leaving the entrance of the Peruvian embassy open and unguarded. They were unwilling, in their words, to "defend the impunity of common criminals."[2]

These weren't common criminals, they were people looking for a better life, and an opportunity to get out of a repressive system. And they took full advantage of the opportunity they were presented with.

The decision was broadcast on the radio and plastered on the front page of the government-run newspaper *Granma*. "As a consequence of the painful death of a guard of Peru's diplomatic location . . . the Revolutionary Government of Cuba has decided to withdraw the protection of said diplomatic location."[3]

Word spread like wildfire, and by midnight, there were three hundred Cubans on the grounds. Three hours later, the number swelled to five hundred. By the time the Cuban government intervened and barricaded the street to the Peruvian embassy, there were 10,865 people on the compound. It had been unguarded for thirty-eight hours.[4]

More than ten thousand people in a space smaller than half a football field becomes a serious issue very quickly. People were shoulder to shoulder on the grounds. So were those that had climbed up and taken shelter on the balconies or the roof. Others climbed trees and linked arms to try to ensure they didn't fall out when dozing off. Virtually every outdoor space of the Peruvian embassy's property was occupied. Fruit trees were quickly stripped bare by hungry asylum seekers. And one could imagine how the sanitary conditions deteriorated to a level that became dangerous in a very short span of time. For days there were only two toilets available. A Canadian reporter was appalled by what he saw: "Children sprawled on the floors. Many of them are naked and they lay in their own excrement, although there is an effort to keep the place clean."[5]

This was a shocking development and not surprisingly got the world's attention. Peru was understandably overwhelmed, and requested assistance, both for the immediate needs of those on the grounds and for other countries to take in some asylum seekers. Other Andean countries offered to help but pointed out the obvious: most of these people wanted to go to Miami. While it was evident that the destination of choice for virtually all of them was the United States, the US government was clear in its position that this needed to be an international solution. President Carter agreed to take 3,500 of them and applauded offers of other Latin American countries to take in some of those seeking refuge.

Castro for his part realized that a humanitarian crisis in his capital was not a good look, particularly one involving Cubans who preferred even those conditions to living under his regime.* He worked to mitigate the public relations damage, both internally and externally. The Cuban government via loudspeaker offered safe-conduct passes to those on the premises to return home. Those who did would be given documentation to leave Cuba to any country that would take them. To disincentivize future similar shenanigans, those who chose to leave were harassed by revolutionary watchdogs and regular Cuban citizens who were following the party line. Castro also made his point clear to his internal audience by making sure an upcoming event, a parade to celebrate the anniversary of the Bay of Pigs victory, turned into a massive repudiation of those "common criminals."

Realizing the Cold War implications of this, and of course understanding that this was an election year, a Republican presidential candidate weighed in on the situation. Reading from a prepared statement, he saw the movement

---

* It would also be quite bad for the actual people involved, of course, but we can't be sure that even entered into his calculations here.

of ten thousand Cubans to the Peruvian embassy as a "spontaneous break for freedom . . . not equaled since the days before the communist government in East Germany built the wall of shame." By the end of the decade, he would be a key figure in the dismantling of that wall: this candidate, of course, was Ronald Reagan. But that's a story for another day. In April 1980, the decision of thousands of Cubans to vote with their feet and storm the embassy in hopes of escape was a major Cold War opportunity, one that Reagan recognized. He called for the United States, in coordination with Latin American countries, to "allow a rescue mission of unprecedented proportions. . . . Such a rescue would be akin to the Berlin Airlift—massive and swift."[6] He was very correct about the size of what was to come. But he wasn't alone in seeing the unfolding human drama as an opportunity. Fidel did too.

The revolutionary government that was surprised by the response to the storming of the embassy gates that month had soon learned its lesson. Its decree on April 4 that had started this whole thing stated their decision to "withdraw the protection from the [Peruvian embassy]." Castro was going to turn the tables and use this crisis to his advantage. A few weeks later, the Cuban government published virtually the exact same language, but with one deeply consequential difference. On April 22, Cubans read on the front page of the government-controlled newspaper: "We have withdrawn protection from the peninsula of Florida."[7] Fidel was on the other side of the gate this time. And the gate had just been swung wide open.

Castro hadn't forgotten the lesson of Camarioca: that he could use the flow of his own citizens to force the hand of the United States, to make it react. An effort to airlift some of the asylum seekers to Costa Rica was quickly shut down. Castro claimed it was being used for propaganda purposes against his regime. He wanted to ensure that if these people were going to leave the country in a manner that made his revolution look bad, there should at least be some kind of value extracted from it. If these "criminals" were given asylum in multiple countries, their effect was atomized. But if they could be concentrated and sent to one place, they could be very disruptive. And in all the world, there was one community in one city in one country that he was interested in destabilizing.

The Cuban community in Miami started galvanizing almost immediately upon hearing word of the plight of those at the Peruvian embassy.

Thousands of dollars began pouring in to help. Food and in-kind donations were collected for those stuck on the embassy grounds.

Despite there being a State Department for such matters, Castro's government had been speaking with an exile organization in Miami. Known as the Committee of 75, they were controversial in exile Miami since they engaged in dialogue with the Cuban government. But they were successful—they had negotiated the release of thousands of political prisoners and exile family visits in years past. One of the organization's leading members, a veteran of the 2506 Brigade named Napoleon Vilaboa, got assurances from the Cuban government that exiles wanting to pick up their relatives could do so if they also took some of the embassy asylum seekers. One-for-one was the agreed-upon deal. Vilaboa began broadcasting on Miami Spanish-language radio that Mariel, a port city on the northern coast of Cuba west of Havana, was open for those who wanted to pick up family members. In less than twenty-four hours, a flotilla of forty-two boats was ready to go.[8]

The first to arrive in Mariel were the *Dos Hermanos* and the *Blanche III*, two lobster boats from Key West.[9] The following day, *Granma* reported on these pioneering boats: "Two vessels from Florida picked up forty-eight antisocial elements. Today eleven vessels from the same place will take more than three hundred to that country."[10] For the next several weeks, in *Granma*, the bottom right corner of the front page had a small box called "Mariel News," which started with the same sentence, only the numbers changed: "Yesterday [XXX] antisocial elements left the Port of Mariel for the United States. At the printing of this edition there were [XXX] boats in port from Florida." Both of those numbers eventually grew to regularly hover in the hundreds on a daily basis.

Carter got a taste of what some of his predecessors faced with the Cuban community in Miami. Kennedy with the raiders and Johnson with Camarioca. He had to strike a very delicate balance between highlighting the plight of Cubans and the failure of the communist system, while at the same time maintaining US law and general order.

Speaking at a League of Women Voters event, Carter took a question from a woman from Hays, Kansas, on behalf of the Florida delegation. She joked about shaking from nerves at asking a question to the president, and Carter retorted that he was shaking too since he knew where this question was going.

His words on the influx of Cuban refugees were heartfelt. "We as a nation," he said, "have always had our arms open to receiving refugees in accordance with American law." He closed his answer with a seemingly innocuous statement: "We'll continue to provide an open heart and open arms to refugees seeking freedom from Communist domination and from economic deprivation, brought on primarily by Fidel Castro and his government."[11]

While that statement was likely overlooked by most Americans as a mere cookie-cutter political response, Miami heard something completely different. These were words of support from the president of the United States to bring whomever you could out of communist Cuba to American shores. Southbound traffic to Cuba exploded. Cubans in South Florida bought, leased, or chartered any boat they thought could get them to the island and back. Boating supply stores struggled to keep shelves stocked: charts, buoys, ropes, fuel. Everything was being snatched up to take advantage of the opening.

It didn't take long to see that Castro did not intend to honor his "one-for-one" offer allowing people to bring a family member back for one embassy asylum seeker. Reports began arriving with the first boatloads that the Cuban officials in Mariel loaded whoever they chose. In Miami, a screening station was set up in a large city park, with the FBI, CIA, and INS among the agencies present to fingerprint, feed, medically assist, and interview incoming refugees. They were starting to see a pattern: a small but noticeable number of criminals recently released from prison were among those seeking refuge. Boat captains were reporting that some of the strangers put on their boats actually told them that they were in Cuban prison just days before and told to leave. Word started leaking out around Miami that hidden among this uncontrolled mass of humanity were hardened criminals.

The truth is that Castro had released some individuals from Cuban prisons, along with some residing in mental institutions. Homosexuals were seen as social pariahs unfit for the Revolution and were also sent away. All these "revolutionary undesirables" were in very small numbers, particularly when taken as a part of such a large movement of people. But as we all have sadly seen, logic and numbers often don't stand a chance against public fear and rumor.

A word of clarification on the Marielitos in general and "criminals" in Cuba in particular. The vast majority of those who came over on the boatlift had never seen the inside of a Cuban prison. And a majority of those who did were there for things that would never be considered a crime anywhere outside of a dictatorship: things like speaking out against the government or not being "revolutionary enough." The idea of pre-crime detention is something you watch in movies like *Minority Report* in the United States. In Cuba, the "Dangerousness Law" gives the government the right to detain someone that they think is capable of committing a crime. Article 72 of the Cuban penal code states "'dangerousness' is considered to be the special proclivity of a person to commit crimes as demonstrated by behavior that manifestly contradicts the norms of socialist morals."[12]

Cubans didn't even have to commit a crime to be imprisoned, they just had to seem (to the Castro government, at least) like the kind of person who would. That law was on the books in Cuba for decades.

To their credit, officials in Miami emphasized this nuance, and publicly stated that only a very small fraction (approximately 1 percent) of those arriving had any violent crime on their records. But that was lost on the vast majority of the public. The idea of an unchecked wave of people including an unknown number of criminals invading their city was terrifying to many. The *Miami Herald* ran a front-page article on the results of a recent poll about the Cuban refugees arriving: almost 70 percent of white residents and almost 60 percent of black residents thought that they would have a negative impact on the city. The article summed up the general feeling in one sentence: "Dade County," it said, "is the land of the free and the home of the scared."[13]

Change *is* often scary, and the city was seeing drastic change in the face of an unprecedented wave of humanity. Families took in as many as they could, but Miami was straining under the weight of so many in need. The Orange Bowl became a homeless shelter. The field that almost twenty years before had echoed with hopeful cheers erupting from President Kennedy's emphatic promises about a free Cuba became a temporary home for hundreds still waiting for that promise to be fulfilled. Many would leave the stadium looking for work during the day and spend the night on a green army cot under the bleachers or in the locker room of the Miami Dolphins. This would be home for them for several months. They would be moved as one of the most powerful forces in America edged closer: the upcoming NFL season. The refugees would be relocated to a tent city under an overpass in the heart of Miami. While it housed a small percentage of those who arrived, and only existed for a short period of time, it became a visible, tangible manifestation of the chaos unleashed by the opening of the port of Mariel.

An alarming article a few months later painted a picture of a city in the grasp of newly arrived lawless bandits. The *Miami Herald*'s front page was splashed with an analysis of a crime wave in Little Havana, and the numbers were eye-popping. Compared to the year before, there was a 775 percent increase in robberies, and a 284 percent rise in car thefts. Burglaries rose by 191 percent, and residents endured a 110 percent increase in assaults.[14] The difference between Little Havana in 1979 and 1980, of course, was the arrival of the Marielitos, which the article claimed were overwhelmingly responsible for these crimes.

This wasn't just sowing distrust between Cubans in Miami and those with no ties to the island. This was creating significant rifts within the Cuban community in Miami itself. The Cuban exile community that was now established in Miami were from the middle and upper-middle class, and prided themselves on the perception many held that they were a model group of immigrants. The Marielitos were a much different group than the ones that had arrived in previous waves and reflected the Cuba that had arisen after the departure of many of the Miami Cubans. They were far more ethnically diverse, and largely working-class. Some in the Cuban community struggled to identify with these new arrivals. Others were far less kind. The mayor of Miami at the time, the city's first Hispanic mayor, faced with rising crime, increased burdens on public services, and all the criticism those issues bring, said of the incoming refugees: "The Cuban Communist dictator flushed his toilets."[15]

All of this, of course, must have been tremendously entertaining to Fidel. He was the conductor of this symphony of chaos. After getting over the initial shock of the response at the Peruvian embassy, Castro—always the master tactician—settled down and thought about the opportunity this situation presented to him. These were people who were not satisfied with the Revolution and wanted to leave. Why spend time and effort trying to convince them, to police them, to punish them, when he can just get rid of them? And he fully realized he had control over who left, so why not get rid of "undesirables" that were a burden? The entire episode started with freedom-seeking Cubans that he had labeled "common criminals." By releasing just a few, he had sowed enough doubt in the minds of many to taint the entire group.

Mariel was classic Fidel Castro. He was a master of creating division, sowing doubt, and using it to his advantage. The entire concept of revolutionary vigilance, the neighborhood watch constantly on the lookout for the crime of insufficient government support, is built on this. You often don't really know who you're talking to, and you never know who's listening, so it becomes very difficult to organize, coalesce, and coordinate. It also creates rifts that can divide, splitting communities that otherwise would have so much in common. Castro used Mariel as an opportunity to off-load "undesirables" and make his revolutionary efforts that much easier. But he also masterfully manipulated a humanitarian mass migration to destabilize a city and export this tactic of division to the Cuban community in Miami. This wasn't just classic Fidel Castro; he had torn a page out of the *actual* classics: the Mariel boatlift was his Trojan horse.

The last boat out of Mariel was ironically a vessel named the *Hedonist*.[16] By the time the floodgates closed in September, over 125,000 Cubans had arrived in the United States. It was a godsend for those people, as well as the families that anxiously awaited being reunited with them. And the Marielitos, like the exiles that came before them, would become valuable contributors to the fabric of Miami and America. But the boatlift was also a grotesque example of Castro's willingness to weaponize his own population.

Fidel was no doubt pleased with the results. The city of Miami was filled with distrust, rising crime, and a new source of division among the Cuban exile community, scars that would take years to heal. Public perception of the Cubans in Miami began to shift as well, and not in a good direction. Previous Cuban arrivals were mostly characterized as victims of communism and model refugees. When Miami was becoming overwhelmed by those first waves, many were taken in by host families across the country and held up as success stories in the broader immigrant mythos of America. In 1980, however, thousands of refugees were placed in camps on military bases in Florida, Arkansas, Pennsylvania, and Wisconsin. Faced with the uncertainty of their future, and living in conditions that some thought worse even than what they had left behind, there were uprisings and outbreaks of violence. This made media coverage on Mariel arrivals expand beyond Miami into other communities, and the coverage was far more negative than that of earlier arrivals.

The Marielitos had a very difficult time escaping the branding that Castro had stamped them with before letting them go: social deviants, miscreants, criminals, undesirables. His messaging, combined with consistent and critical media coverage, was startlingly effective. A Gallup poll conducted in 1981 quantified just how devastating this was to public perception of Cubans after the Mariel boatlift. In a poll that would be exceedingly difficult to conduct today, Gallup asked over 1,400 Americans in more than three hundred communities across the country to look at a list of groups of people and select ones they would *not* want as neighbors. Nationwide, Cuban refugees were designated as the second-most undesirable to have next door. The only group less welcome? Members of religious cults.[17]

For the Cubans arriving, this reception was harrowing and difficult: leaving your homeland was hard enough, but being seen as social outcasts only compounded the challenge of starting over. For those exiles who had already been here, it was a shocking turn of events, and the tarnishing of a reputation they felt they had worked hard to earn and uphold.

No one embodies this perception of the undesirable Cuban refugee better than one of the most famous Cubans that never lived: Tony Montana, better known to the American public as "Scarface." Don't get us wrong: Tony Montana is an iconic, entertaining character. But bathtub chainsaw massages and terrible accents aside, he's also a perfect distillation of the bogeyman that the Castro regime was painting: corrupt, violent, power-hungry, with insatiable greed and utter lawlessness. And he and his friends are in your neighborhoods, America! Oliver Stone's screenplay latched on to all the key storylines the Cuban government was crafting about the Marielitos. Scarface, however, was the least of Miami's worries. He wasn't real, after all.

9

Up Up Down Down
Left Right Left Right B A Start

Eugene Hasenfus probably never imagined he'd see his name splashed
across the front pages of newspapers around the world.

He almost certainly didn't think his name would end up in history books
(like this one).

The ex-Marine from Wisconsin had been recruited for a top-secret operation, so covert that even the president of the United States (allegedly) didn't
know it existed.

But on October 5, 1986, that operation—and Hasenfus's anonymity—
came to an abrupt end.

By this time, Hasenfus had made at least ten flights to provide weapons,
ammunition, and supplies to the Contra rebel forces in Nicaragua. So far,
so good. But on October 5, his luck ran out. The Sandinista government had
learned from the frequent resupply missions traveling along the exact same
routes. They moved radar and anti-aircraft units into the area. A Sandinista
teenager—really just a kid—used a Soviet-made shoulder-fired anti-aircraft
missile to shoot Hasenfus's C-123 cargo plane out of the sky.

The two other Americans on the flight were killed in the attack, but Hasenfus managed to parachute safely to the ground—where he was promptly captured by government forces. Within the wreckage of the aircraft, the Sandinistas found documents linking the plane to a US State Department office, the Nicaraguan Humanitarian Assistance Program, and numerous Americans covertly working Contra resupply out of El Salvador.

At an October 9 press conference staged by the Nicaraguan government, Hasenfus publicly stated he was an American working for the CIA on a clandestine mission to provide guns and supplies to the Contras. He said he worked out of the Ilopango airfield in El Salvador, where he reported to two CIA employees, Max Gómez and Ramón Medina. Gómez and Medina ran the show for the CIA in Ilopango—they oversaw housing for the crews, transportation, fuel for the aircraft, flight plans, everything. According to Hasenfus, it was a full-scale CIA operation.

Reagan administration officials and the CIA vehemently denied this to the public and Congress. Of course they did; the CIA was not going to publicly admit it was working in El Salvador, illegally supplying the Contra rebels.

Especially when it wasn't.

It was the rare occurrence in which the CIA was (mostly) innocent. They weren't behind the operation in Ilopango.

But one can forgive Hasenfus for his confusion. He was working for two *ex-CIA* officers in El Salvador. He just assumed, pretty reasonably, that they were still active and lying to keep their cover. Max Gómez and Ramón Medina were aliases. Medina was really Luis Posada Carriles, former CIA employee-turned-international-fugitive. And Gómez?

Max Gómez was Félix Rodríguez.

The denials were working (at least well enough) until about a month later, when the wheels fell off. On November 3, a Lebanese journalist revealed the Reagan administration had secretly sold weapons to Iran. Three weeks later, on November 25, 1986, Attorney General Edwin Meese acknowledged that some of the money from the sale of weapons to Iran had been funneled to the operation to arm and supply the Contras.

The Iran-Contra scandal was on! And you'll never guess which city was at the center of it all.

OK, maybe you will.[1]

The Enterprise

For most of us born after 1975, the Iran-Contra affair is just a fleeting memory, or even just a couple of paragraphs we skimmed over in history class. It was a complicated and confusing scandal, and the only reason many of us paid any attention to it was that people kept telling us it could "bring down the president!"

But, of course, it didn't.

To ensure we are all on the same page, here is everything you *need* to know about Iran-Contra (at least for the purposes of this book).

In 1979, a coalition of rebel groups overthrew the US-sponsored government of right-wing dictator Anastasio Somoza Debayle and replaced him with a leftist government known as the Sandinistas (to be exact, they were the Frente Sandinista de Liberación Nacional, or the FSLN, which translates to Sandinista National Liberation Front). Ronald Reagan, then just a presidential candidate, was immediately critical of this new regime. He advocated cutting all aid to Nicaragua, and promised as president he would do something about this new threat in Latin America.

And he did. Reagan began providing support to the counterrevolutionary forces, the Contras (short for *la contrarrevolución*), in 1981, while using his bully pulpit to convince the American people, and the world, of the righteousness of this cause. He argued the Sandinistas were going to turn Nicaragua into another Cuba, but perhaps even more dangerous to the United States, because Nicaragua wasn't separated from the US by water. As Reagan famously warned, Nicaragua was only two days' driving time from Texas.

In 1984, the ruling junta government went for legitimacy and held an election. Daniel Ortega, one of the leaders of the coalition who ousted Somoza in 1979, was elected president of Nicaragua. Ortega's government was now internationally recognized and democratically elected. He and his supporters were also avid fans of Fidel Castro, whose government (along with the Soviets) sent material, economic, and military support to the Sandinistas. For Reagan, the dominoes were falling. And getting much closer to the United States.

It would be one thing if Ronald Reagan was supporting a peace-loving, ragtag group of free-market capitalists who idolized the ideals of the American Revolution and pushed for a Nicaragua governed by a liberal democracy.

But they weren't. Many of the Contras were former soldiers or members of the security services of Somoza's repressive dictatorship. They purposely used battlefield tactics such as rape, torture, and execution of civilians in their fight against the Sandinistas.

Making matters worse, they were not very . . . how do we say this . . . good at it?

The Sandinistas were winning, so the Reagan administration ordered more direct actions—in April 1984, it was publicly disclosed that the CIA had secretly mined Nicaraguan harbors, a dramatic escalation of what was meant to be a covert operation.

Democrats in Congress were not amused. It had been barely a decade since the end of the Vietnam War, and the emotional (and physical) scars of that conflict were still fresh in their minds. They weren't going to let Ronald Reagan lead us into another anti-communist crusade.

Plus, they didn't particularly like the Reagan administration's foreign policy, and could use their power to limit US support. In late 1984, Edward Boland, the chairman of the House Intelligence Committee, introduced an amendment to the Department of Defense Appropriations Bill.[2] It stated:

> During fiscal year 1985, no funds available to the Central Intelligence Agency, the Department of Defense, or any other agency or entity of the United States involved in intelligence activities may be obligated or expended for the purpose of which would have the effect of supporting, directly or indirectly, military or paramilitary operations in Nicaragua by any nation, group, organization, movement, or individual.[3]

In Congress-speak, this means the US government is done covertly supporting the Contras. Boland explained this during the final debate for this amendment—there were no loopholes. According to Boland, this amendment, "clearly ends US support for the war in Nicaragua. . . . There are no exceptions to the prohibitions."[4]

In response, the CIA and the Defense Department withdrew most of their personnel from Central America. But President Reagan wasn't giving up on the Contras. He ordered his National Security Advisor Robert McFarlane to keep the Contras alive "body and soul." Something else would need to fill the void left by official US government entities.

That something would become known as the "Enterprise," and it would be directed by McFarlane's NSC staffer Lieutenant Colonel Oliver North.

North had been briefed on the CIA operation in Nicaragua even before the passage of the Boland Amendment—the CIA could see the writing on the wall, and they leaped right into contingency planning in anticipation of congressional action. In the summer of 1984, CIA Director William Casey set up a number of meetings in Central America, Miami, and Washington with North and members of the Nicaraguan resistance. During these meetings, the CIA handed off responsibility for the operation to North.[5]

The Enterprise was formally launched at a secret meeting in Miami on June 28, 1985. It was attended by North; Adolfo Calero, political leader of a Contra faction known as the FDN—Fuerza Democrática Nicaragüense, or Nicaraguan Democratic Force; Enrique Bermúdez, the commander of the FDN military; Richard Secord, a former US Air Force two-star general with considerable covert-operations experience; Thomas Clines, a former CIA officer (he worked as one of Ted Shackley's top aides at JMWAVE in the sixties) who at that time was working as Secord's arms buyer; and Rafael Quintero, also a former CIA officer who was working for Secord as his point person in Honduras, El Salvador, and Costa Rica.

At the meeting, North told the group that cash payments for the Contras would no longer be sent directly to Calero and the Contra leadership. Instead, Secord (with North's approval) "would arrange for all weapons purchases and deliveries."[6]

According to the Iran-Contra report:

Secord later described the June 1985 Miami meeting as a "watershed" event for him and his involvement with the contras. North convinced Secord to take charge of a covert air-delivery system, one that would mirror earlier CIA efforts to arm the contras. Thus, in addition to his activities as an arms purchaser and supplier, Secord began hiring airplane crews, acquiring or leasing aircraft, arranging for warehouses in Central America, and gaining landing rights in the region.[7]

Contra aid had now gone private (except for North). But where would the money come from?

Mostly from the Saudis, who donated millions to the cause. Other like-minded countries chipped in too, as did concerned private citizens in the United States.

But really it was the Saudis.[8]

And, of course, Iran. But they weren't exactly "donating" money to the Contras. They were buying arms (more on this aspect a bit later).

The Enterprise used Southern Air Transport (SAT), an air-charter company out of Miami, for both of its Contra and Iran operations. In 1985 and 1986, SAT received almost $2 million for its Contra-related services. This included the purchase of a C-123 cargo plane, repair and maintenance of Enterprise aircraft, sale of spare parts, and a supply of cash for the mission in Central America. The Enterprise also paid SAT $200,000 for a JetStar aircraft that was used by Secord (and others) for Contra-related travel.

Southern Air Transport also created a cut-out company, Amalgamated Commercial Enterprises (ACE), in late 1985 to add an extra layer of security and to hide the identity of the true owners of the resupply operation. ACE disbursed about $1.5 million of Enterprise funds.[9]

The Iran-Contra independent counsel would eventually trace the movement of a total of $2.7 million in ninety-seven separate cash transactions, much of it moving to Central America via SAT/ACE. The cash itself was carried south in amounts ranging from several thousand dollars up to $50,000 by pilots and other Enterprise employees traveling from Miami to Ilopango. Once the cash arrived in El Salvador, money set aside for aircraft fuel was deposited by Posada and Rodríguez.

In December 1986, an employee for Southern Air Transport carried $6,000 in cash from SAT headquarters in Miami to Sally Hasenfus, Eugene's wife. This amounted to two months' salary for Hasenfus (who would be released from jail that month and allowed to return to the US).[10]

Aside from cold hard cash, the Enterprise used traveler's checks to run their operations—$2,691,950 worth of traveler's checks. Adolfo Calero's lawyer, Carlos Morales, purchased the blank traveler's checks from BAC International Bank in Miami. Some were sent to Honduras, some were used to pay the travel expenses of Contra leaders, some on supplies for the Contras purchased in the US, and some payments went to the families of Contras living in the United States.[11]

Speaking of Contras living in the United States . . .

Nicaragua Hoy, Cuba Mañana

By the middle of 1986, an estimated sixty thousand Nicaraguans had set up residency in Miami-Dade County since the Sandinistas took power in 1979, including Adolfo Calero. The umbrella organization for multiple Contra organizations, the United Nicaraguan Opposition (UNO), was headquartered in Miami as well. In the Everglades, Contras set up camps for paramilitary training. Cuban exiles provided money and material for the anti-communist forces, and passed along their CIA training to the Nicaraguan rebels.

All of a sudden it was the 1960s again in Miami.

Juan Perez-Franco, at the time the president of the 2506 Brigade veterans association, told the *Washington Post* in October 1986, "We would prefer to dedicate all our efforts to liberating Cuba. But the reality is there are no guerrillas there now. We have to support others who are opposing communism, and the nearest fight now is in Nicaragua."[12]

Cuban exile support for the Contras also included money. The Miami community raised (at least) $1 million through radio marathons and private funders.[13] They also sent teams of doctors and nurses, more than $1.5 million in medical supplies, food, and clothing, and other nonlethal aid, such as shoes, military uniforms, compasses, and canteens.

The fight against the Sandinistas was seen as a fight against Fidel. "This is our contribution against Castro," a Bay of Pigs veteran told the *New York Times* in 1986. "Any Communist defeat in this hemisphere is going to be a defeat for Castro."[14]

Jorge Mas Canosa, an exile politician whom you will hear (much) more about in the next chapter, coined a new saying for the Cuban exile community: "The road to Havana runs through Managua!"[15]

Contra leaders were all too happy to accept the Cuban exiles' help. Leonardo Somarriba, the UNO coordinator in Miami, told the *Washington Post* that the Miami Cuban community had "been extremely important to us in terms of material assistance and moral support because of the degree of their commitment. They help us not to make the same mistakes they made, to deal in realities."

How committed were they? Until 1986, only Cubans who fought at the Bay of Pigs could become members of the 2506 Brigade veterans association. In an "unprecedented move," membership was extended to include all "freedom fighters," including the Contras fighting the Sandinistas.[16]

The Problem with Félix

The Miami Cuban exile community wasn't just sending material goods to support the Contras, it was sending people too. More than four dozen Cuban Americans from Miami left South Florida to travel to Central America and fight alongside the Contra rebels. Some called themselves "advisors," others preferred "freedom fighters." It's all semantics, really. The Cubans just wanted the chance to stick it to Castro by killing as many communist Sandinistas as they could. What matters most is that many of these exiles spent *years* assisting rebel soldiers in southern Nicaragua.

But Félix was one of the first.

He had been intimately involved in the Cuban community's support of the Contras since the junta in 1979, helping to provide them with food, clothing, educational materials, and other humanitarian (nonlethal) assistance. But by 1981 Rodríguez felt that "more direct action was necessary." He worked on developing a counterinsurgency plan for Central America with a friend who had been a Makasi pilot in Congo and spent years trying to find the right audience for his ideas. In January 1985, Rodríguez finally got to the correct people—General Adolfo Blandon, chief of staff of the Salvadoran military, and General Juan Rafael Bustillo, commander of El Salvador's air force.[17] El Salvador at the time was in the midst of a twelve-year civil war fought between the Salvadoran government and the Farabundo Martí National Liberation Front (FMLN), a coalition of left-wing groups backed by Castro and the Soviets.[18] Rodríguez offered his help, and Bustillo gave him the use of the Ilopango military air base outside San Salvador.[19]

Later that year, Rodríguez was joined at Ilopango by Luis Posada Carilles, who had just escaped from a prison in Venezuela.[20] He went there to work

with his old friend Félix, to continue his "war to the death and without quarter against Fidel Castro," and because, well, he didn't have a lot of other places
he could go without ending up back in prison.[21]

For Oliver North and the Enterprise, Félix's operation at Ilopango was
perfectly situated to help the illicit supply of the Contras. For one, Rodríguez
and Posada were CIA-trained professionals. Also, they had a perfect setup at
Ilopango, and the support of the Salvadoran military. Finally, the two of them
were extremely committed to the mission—Félix Rodríguez took no pay for
the duration of the operation.

Perhaps, however, they were too committed. For Félix, the cause trumped
everything else, and if it looked like anyone was standing in his way, he made
a point to deal with it, and deal with it harshly.

It didn't take long for Rodríguez and North to come into conflict. North's
Enterprise was a private venture—yes, they wanted to aid the Contras, but
they also were in it to make money. A lot of money. It wasn't difficult for Félix
to realize that all the money collected for the Contra operation was not making it to the fight against the Sandinista government. According to Rodríguez, the aircraft the Enterprise bought were in terrible shape. On one C-123,
the navigation equipment was so antiquated that it caused the plane to go off
course and graze the top of a mountain. But as much as he asked—demanded,
really—requests for new equipment and safety devices "were all spurned by
Secord and his people."

One of the American contractor pilots gave Félix a letter of complaint
that Rodríguez passed along to Oliver North. It read:

> I demand respect for my life, the lives of my fellow crew mem-
> bers, and some respect for those we are supposed to be support-
> ing. I would like to think that we/you are all motivated by respect
> for life in this endeavor. How, then, can we be pressed into service
> (and, please, don't deny the pressure) without equipment listed
> above [radar, LORAN, altimeters, night vision goggles, functional
> instrumentation] without parachutes, without minimum sur-
> vival gear, without adequate communications with the DZ [drop
> zone], with inadequate (even withheld) intelligence, without secure
> communications.

Is it simply greed that drives some of you to drive the rest of us?[22]

The operation was in such bad shape that during July and August 1986, the Enterprise was only able to launch one successful mission. To Rodríguez, getting supplies to the Contras "seemed to be the least concern of those who ran it." Instead, Félix believed that "Secord and his partners were now only interested in turning a quick profit."[23]

The money for missions had dried up. In July, Rodríguez sent messages to Rafael Quintero in Miami, begging him for assistance:

7/21/86—Ilopango to Miami. Today last day to pay tel bills. We have responsibility with house owners and no cash has been received. . . . For your info we are closing all activity on this end until a serious approach is taken on your end . . .

7/21/86—Ilopango to Miami. After we had long meeting, Gen. Bustillo expressed his deep concern and disappointment at the total lack of professionalism, operational capability your organization has displayed. He believes that hundreds of thousands of dollars are being spent with almost no results. . . . A/C [aircraft] are in terrible condition. . . . If this situation is not completely resolved within a week the General will require all personnel from your organization to leave Ilopango.[24]

Rodríguez was most concerned about the possibility that the Enterprise was planning to sell off the aircraft, supplies, and other operational assets to pad their pockets.

He wasn't wrong. In midsummer 1986, the administration finally convinced Congress to approve $100 million in Contra aid. The Enterprise was out of time, but they still had the chance to milk the program for all it was worth.

Unless, of course, Félix got in the way. After threatening in the spring to move back to Miami and tell North he was on his own, in July Rodríguez posted armed guards around the planes used by the Enterprise at Ilopango. This prevented any resupply flights, but it also prevented North and Co. from selling the Ilopango planes off.[25] At the end of the month, after a trip to

Miami, Rodríguez decided to prevent the Enterprise from selling off some of the aircraft that were currently there.

So he stole one of the Miami planes. It was a C-123 full of spare parts that was set to be liquidated by the Enterprise. Rodríguez had other ideas, and he personally flew the plane from Miami to Ilopango.

Oliver North was not amused, but Félix didn't care. The mission had been compromised by North and his cronies. They were making money off brave soldiers who were fighting communism—in essence, fighting Castro. A cause to which Rodríguez had dedicated his life, and still does to this day.

Félix, too, was not amused. But he had the power to do something about it.

10

Critical Mas

The calculus in Miami was shifting. The original strategy for dislodging Castro and communism from Cuba was one seen throughout the country's history, and one the Cuban exiles were seeking to replicate: bring change to the island through armed insurgency coordinated from abroad.

The largest, most concerted effort was the Bay of Pigs, organized and funded by the US government . . . and a spectacular failure. Washington's change of heart (and policy) made this far more difficult to sustain. The attempts to continue armed struggle had resulted largely in pinprick raids, and while harassing an autocratic regime with a stranglehold on their homeland was always welcome, many were starting to realize that it wasn't an effective method of getting their country back. Add to that the unfortunate and violent misuse of some of the skills the CIA had cultivated, and the need for another path became clearer and clearer.

Many exiles felt that the overreliance on the US government was one of the biggest weaknesses of past efforts, that allowing Washington to dictate the terms of the liberation of their home country led to mistakes and miscalculations that had cost the dream dearly. Being aligned in wanting Castro gone was helpful, but not sufficient: Washington wasn't as dedicated to regime change as they were to containment. Containment, however, doesn't get you back home.

But it wasn't just the realization that armed action was insufficient to meet the need. It was the recognition that other options were available, ones that were a result of the years of establishing roots, of embracing and embodying the American Dream. Exiles in Miami were starting to see that instead of petitioning the US government for weapons, engagement in the political process could be the most potent weapon in their Cold War struggle. And that realization, as well as its far-reaching repercussions, would be largely embodied by one person.

Jorge Mas Canosa was no stranger to the cause of expelling communism from Cuba. His name had been circulating in the exile community since the 1960s. And he likely grew up with stories of past exploits on behalf of freedom: his grandfather, Florentino Mas y Mirare, was an officer in one of the wars for Cuban independence.[1] Mas Canosa had been a part of the armed phase of the struggle in a number of ways. He was a member of the ill-fated 2506 Brigade. He had also served as a part-time broadcaster for Radio Swan, a CIA-funded station that broadcasted to Cuba in the 1960s. After the collapse of the Cuban Revolutionary Council, he was part of RECE, the organization created by the nationwide Cuban exile referendum to continue the armed struggle. His role was largely support: coordinating logistics and fundraising. Again following Martí's blueprint, he helped organize fundraising committees in New York, Chicago, Los Angeles, Puerto Rico, and elsewhere. This experience of coordination and management would serve him well, preparing him for his starring role in the next act of this unfolding drama.

It was through the RECE chapter in Puerto Rico that his fortunes began to change—quite literally. The delegate there, Hector Torres, was an engineer who had experience in the telephone industry in Cuba before the Revolution. He and a partner, another engineer with similar experience by the name of Iglesias, started a company to provide telecommunications infrastructure services in Puerto Rico. Torres recognized Mas Canosa's organizational ability after having worked with him in fundraising efforts, purchasing boats for clandestine efforts, and the like. The company was in dire straits and Torres needed help. They had established a small affiliate in Miami, which was flailing and threatened to bring down the main effort in Puerto Rico. In 1968, Torres approached Mas Canosa asking him to take over operations in Miami. Despite having no engineering or telecommunications experience, he accepted.[2]

Mas Canosa proved to be a savvy businessman: not only did he turn the Miami subsidiary around, he ended up purchasing it outright a few years later in 1971. It was renamed Church and Tower, the English translation of the original owners' last names, and it gained momentum, securing major contracts in South Florida. Mas Canosa's wealth and influence increased, and he became a millionaire. But while he was expanding telecommunications networks and physically facilitating conversations all over South Florida, discussions in the exile community were unfolding that wrestled with what it meant to be an exile. Discussions that would slowly, but fundamentally, change the focus of the struggle.

Up to this point, the Cuban community had always seen their plight as temporary, and Miami as a stop on their journey back home. That mindset helped explain why the idea of military intervention was logical to so many and the preferred method to get back. It was the most direct: literally punching their ticket home.

Many Cubans were—and still are—insistent upon clarifying the distinction between refugees, who may have chosen to leave, and exiles, who were forced to leave their homeland against their will. Cubans were exiles, banished by a foreign system that had invaded and taken over their homeland. All of this was central to the Cuban community's identity and ethos, and kept the focus ever south, toward their island home. As a result, despite Cubans rewriting the map of the city, they were virtually invisible politically. Miami and the United States were seen as a temporary home. Nobody spends the time and effort to renovate their hotel room.

Although they were grateful for the reception they received and the opportunities provided, the idea of becoming an American citizen was seen by some as relinquishing their identity, or worse, surrendering to a fate of exile. A professor speaking at a panel on the issue in 1974 explained that "to maintain our culture we must become citizens and vote. But, if we become citizens, we automatically lose an important aspect of our Cuban culture, our citizenship. It is a paradox and a dilemma." At that point in time, less than half of the four hundred thousand Cubans in Miami were citizens. But people were starting to look at their situation differently. A survey conducted in 1972 found that 79 percent of Cubans polled said they would return if Castro were overthrown. Only two years later, 51 percent of those polled, all of whom were over the age of fifty-five, responded that they would *not* return.[3]

The 1970s saw Cuban naturalizations skyrocket. The decade prior had approximately thirty-eight thousand naturalizations, with 1969 having the highest at just under nine thousand naturalized. The very next year, in 1970, almost twenty-one thousand became citizens. By the end of the 1970s, more than 142,000 would join them.[4] Increasingly, the community was setting down roots. Fewer and fewer wanted to live in a community in which they had no say in how they were governed or how their children were educated.

They could have stayed in Cuba for that.

It took almost ten years for the first Cuban to run for higher office. In 1972, a man named Evelio Estrella ran for a seat in the US House of Representatives against Claude Pepper, a political institution who had already served in the US Senate for fifteen years and had been a Miami-area representative for another nine. Not surprisingly, Estrella lost. But it's fitting that the first-ever Cuban exile candidate's last name was Spanish for "star." He unlocked something incredibly powerful, and while he never achieved political office, his community's political star was poised for a meteoric rise. Those humble beginnings would forge a level of political influence that would reach far beyond what anyone would have dared to dream was possible.

Well, almost anyone.

By the dawn of the 1980s, the Cuban community was, for the first time since its arrival, primed to be a political force. And the timing was perfect: 1980 was a presidential election year. The well-intentioned, but confused, response of the Carter administration to the Mariel boatlift was fresh in the minds of Miami Cubans. So was the strong anti-communist rhetoric of his challenger, Ronald Reagan. Reagan was the one who had recommended direct and decisive assistance to the Cuban asylees in the Peruvian embassy several months prior. Reagan seemed to be just what exiles were looking for, and they demonstrated it at the polls. On election day, they overwhelmingly did what they could to win one for the Gipper: an estimated 90 percent of the community voted for the Reagan-Bush ticket.[5]

With a strong anti-communist hand in the White House, the specter of expansion of communism in the hemisphere as a serious concern, and the Cuban community as an emerging political power, the stars were aligning for the Cuban cause to make significant headway. One more critical star made its appearance and fell into position. Jorge Mas Canosa, who had by this time established himself as a wealthy and influential power player in the Miami community, was uniquely positioned to harness the opportunities this alignment created. In the summer of 1981, he and other community leaders founded the Cuban American National Foundation (CANF). Based on the highly successful model of a pro-Israel lobbying organization, AIPAC, the Foundation was a sophisticated operation focused on using the levers of political influence on behalf of freedom and democracy in Cuba. The Foundation was also the product of hard-learned lessons from years of exile. The Achilles' heel of the Cuban exile community had always been factionalism and lack of unity. Differing visions of how to reach the same goal, positioning for support, and scattered resources had hampered progress. The Cuban American National Foundation would provide something that had eluded the exile community for decades—a unified voice.

CANF was a sea change in the Cuban community's strategy on the Caribbean front of the Cold War. In the early days of exile, as self-identified temporary tenants in Miami looking to return home, leaders of the Miami exile community looked to the American government largely as their arsenal of liberty—an ally that could provide the tools and training to help them end their national nightmare. The Foundation was a manifestation of a complete shift in that relationship. Cubans in Miami were no longer simply a displaced population of foreigners; they were a growing community of American citizens. CANF was designed to harness that new dynamic, an organization created to influence the American government on behalf of a group of its constituents. The Alpha 66s and Comandos L of the world were still around, but the struggle had entered a new phase, and the tactics and weapons used had changed. Miami had matured, had recognized that political influence could be a far more powerful weapon than any rifle, and that legislation could land a blow mightier than any small maritime infiltration ever could. The fight had shifted from steering a course in the Straits of Florida to navigating the halls of Congress.

Its first order of business was an incredibly bold initiative: establishing air power in the struggle against Castro's Soviet satellite state. Just not *that* kind of air power. The Foundation wasn't lobbying for a squadron of F-14 Tomcats to enter Cuban airspace. They were looking to penetrate Cuban airwaves.

Perhaps it was his experience at Radio Swan or in the telecommunications industry that originally fueled the idea. Or maybe it was the proximity that was already allowing some intermittent, faint reception of programming on both sides of the Florida Straits. Particularly around Christmastime, call-in shows in Miami would be flooded with messages for loved ones still on the island, in the hopes that perhaps they could hear them. The converse was also true, and it was no doubt an annoyance to the exile community that Cuban government broadcasts could be heard in certain pockets of Miami, something that you can still do today.* But the established model of Radio Free Europe that had been broadcasting since 1950 to Soviet satellite countries had to be inspirational and a useful precedent. Cuba itself was a Soviet satellite country, so why not have something similar?

Radio Free Europe wasn't a venue for US government policy or education regarding American institutions and society; there was the Voice of America for that. And the VOA was already broadcasting in the area. The Cuban government's own Radio Rebelde reported at the time that many Cuban officials actually started their day listening to VOA broadcasting.[6] Yet it was not programming for Cubans per se, but more generally for the entire Latin American region. What made Radio Free Europe—and Radio Liberty, which broadcast directly into the Soviet Union—so powerful was that it was simply diverse programming that allowed for those behind the Iron Curtain to slake their thirst for information of the world outside. The Board of International Broadcasting, which oversaw Radio Free Europe and Radio Liberty, explained them this way: "They seek to create neither 'American Radio,' in the narrow national sense, nor 'exile radio,' in the sense of organized political opposition, but an international radio . . . in the breadth of its coverage, its freedom from national or sectarian bias, its dedication to the open communication of accurate information and a broad range of democratic ideas."[7] The idea was to stock the meager shelves in the marketplace of ideas available to those unfortunate enough to live under communism, and give them the opportunity to come to their own conclusions.

CANF's talking points were a savvy mix of messaging that hit several political issues. Obviously, the right of access to information and the moral

---

* Radio Reloj, or "Clock Radio," is a Cuban station that can faintly be heard in parts of Miami and is perhaps the worst idea in the history of radio. Its entire programming consists of a ticking clock in the background and the reading of news snippets that are around fifty-five seconds long. Every minute on the minute, there is a beep, followed by the announcer telling you the new time and repeating the name of this hellish Groundhog Day of a station. In certain areas of Miami, it can be heard on your car radio. Today, you have the option of hearing it online. Listen at your own peril . . .

responsibility to strike a blow against tyranny was a key tenet. As in all auto-cratic regimes, there was a tight control on information in Cuba. Cubans' access to information was limited to what the government allowed them to read about or hear. Cubans on the island were being held in a form of infor-mational captivity, and they had a right to know about the outside world.*

While the human rights aspect was a critical talking point, another was pure Cold War competition. The only country at the time with specific pro-gramming targeted to the population on the island was the Soviet Union, with the (no doubt) intensely riveting programming of Radio Moscow. Cuba itself was using the airwaves to export revolution throughout the region: Radio Havana Cuba broadcast throughout Latin America in English, French, and Portuguese, as well as several native languages spoken by indigenous popu-lations in the Andean Ridge and elsewhere.[8] The Foundation argued that the United States was losing the war over the airwaves, ceding territory in the battleground of ideas in its own neighborhood.

Other talking points focused on its role in shaping a future free Cuba. Radio Martí could help prepare Cuban civil society for a post-communist existence by providing various points of view. There was even the argument that by presenting the possibility of a post-Castro world, cultivating discus-sions of an alternate reality difficult to imagine on the island, a dedicated radio presence could possibly help stave off another mass migration.[9]

Armed with these talking points, deep pockets, and some very powerful con-nections, Mas Canosa and the Foundation hit Washington. And they hit it hard.

The original proposed effort was called "Radio Free Cuba," an homage to its decades-old inspiration. Reportedly it was the idea of supporters within the Reagan administration to honor the intellectual father of Cuban liberty and call it "Radio Martí."[10] The idea had some bipartisan support in Congress, but also had numerous detractors, many of whom felt that the idea would derail any potential progress with Cuba. Or was an unnecessary provocation, "an act of political confrontation."[11] Others were concerned at the domestic impacts of the bill, specifically how any retaliation from Cuba would affect

---

* One anecdote CANF used to illustrate the control of information on the island had an oddly familiar ring to it, in light of recent events. When an outbreak of dengue resulted from soldiers returning from foreign battlefields, the Cuban government said nothing for months. When the epidemic could no longer be ignored, it blamed the outbreak on the CIA and the *yanqui* imperialists.

the radio frequencies used by Midwest farmers. A group of Democratic senators called the proposal "an insult to the American taxpayer." Senator Dodd of Connecticut was quite clear in his feelings about the proposal, stating that "no matter how thin you slice it, Radio Martí is still baloney."[12]

The most creative opposition came from Representative Tom Harkin of Iowa, who introduced a number of amendments providing snarky additions to the name of the "Radio Broadcasting to Cuba Act," the bill moving through Congress. For fiscal hawks, he proposed the "Throwing Money at the Castro Problem through Radio Broadcasting to Cuba Act." Concerned about migration? Here's the "Refugee Recruitment through Radio Broadcasting to Cuba Act." And just to throw some shade at the anachronistic dinosaurs in the room, there's something for you too: the "John Foster Dulles Cold War Mentality Memorial Radio Broadcasting to Cuba Act."[13]

The bill was going nowhere fast. But the Foundation had an ace up their sleeve, and in a powerful display of just how far and how fast the organization had come in two years of existence, they used it.

At the invitation of the Cuban American National Foundation, on May 20, 1983, the eighty-first anniversary of Cuban independence, President Reagan, the "Great Communicator" himself, visited Miami.

The crowds that braved the scorching Miami sun for hours for the chance at a glimpse of the president were massive. Police estimated between sixty thousand and eighty thousand lined the streets in various parts of the city, with sidewalks packed ten people deep in some places. It was Cuban Independence Day, and many were in the white *guayabera* and red neckerchief that is the traditional garb worn to commemorate that day. Cuban and American flags were everywhere, as were signs communicating their interests. One of the most popular was "We Want Freedom for Cuba." Another held aloft by countless onlookers proclaimed: "We Want Radio Martí."[14]

Reagan had lunch at a Cuban restaurant named La Esquina de Tejas, where he rubbed elbows with community leaders. His host, Mas Canosa, was at the presidential table. Reagan was treated to typical Cuban fare: chicken with black beans and rice, sweet plantains, followed by American coffee and a coconut flan. No political stop in Miami is complete without a *cafecito*, the dark, thick, sweet coffee that packs a punch so strong that it's served in small white plastic cups the size of a large thimble.* The president got applause when he downed his. He scored extra points when he recognized that the lunch they'd just eaten would likely be impossible for the average person to get in Cuba.[15]

Mas Canosa, who only two years before had created the Foundation to advance a free Cuba, set the stage in Spanish, and introduced the president. But old habits do die hard, and he couldn't resist the opportunity to publicly ask Reagan to rescind Kennedy's pledge not to invade Cuba.[16] Reagan's speech was as perfectly crafted for Cuban consumption as his lunch had been. He recognized the crowd and their exile experience as a much-needed reminder to Americans of the blessings they have and the awesome responsibility that democracy demands. He reminded them that their experience was also a strong rebuke of the system that had a stranglehold on their homeland: "The Cubans in the United States with only one-tenth the number [of Cubans on the island] produce almost two times the wealth of those they left behind. So don't let anyone fool you, what's happening in Cuba is not a failure of the Cuban people, it's a failure of Fidel Castro and of communism."[17] And he made sure to hammer home one of the key messages he was sent to Miami to deliver. "The greatest threat to dictators like Fidel Castro is the truth," he said. "And that's why I'm urging the Congress to approve legislation for the establishment of Radio Martí."[18]

Reagan was in Miami for a short time—the local paper reported him being in the city for only two hours and forty-two minutes—but the effect was seismic. Locally, his visit was a massive success. La Esquina de Tejas became almost a shrine of sorts, and for years afterward, Cubans in Miami would point at the corner restaurant and reflect, in almost hushed tones: "Reagan ate there . . ." It had repercussions on the national political stage, cementing the fledgling Cuban American National Foundation as a serious player in Washington. Reagan was the first president to actively pursue the Cuban American vote, but he most certainly wouldn't be the last. An organization less than two years old had pulled off a master stroke. And, of course, Reagan's visit helped pave the way for the establishment of the newest arrow in freedom's quiver.

A tool used for decades on the doorstep of the Soviet Union was about to be introduced in the Caribbean front of the global conflict against communism.

---

* Some call this Cuban Jet Fuel, or sometimes *gasolina*.

On October 4, 1983, President Reagan signed the Radio Broadcasting to Cuba Act, which established Radio Martí. His statement on the signing of the act into law framed its mission as "an important foreign policy objective of my administration: to break Fidel Castro's monopoly on news and information within Cuba. . . . This kind of broadcasting is 25 years overdue."[19] The Foundation was ecstatic; champagne was reportedly flowing at their headquarters in Miami. Mas Canosa summed up the importance of the president's support, his visit to Miami, and of course the people behind it. "Ronald Reagan was the star. But we deserve an Oscar for best supporting role."[20] This was a potent cast. The charismatic movie-star-turned-president and the unified voice of an organization focused on harnessing the wealth and influence of a rising community for the cause of fighting communism.

On May 20, 1985, at 5:30 a.m., the new front was opened in that fight. "Good morning, Cuba, you are listening to Radio Martí, on the air today, now." The announcer followed with words that would be repeated hourly as part of the station's identification: "Radio Martí, for the right of every man to be free, to receive information and disseminate it, to find his own truth and proclaim it among others who respect it."[21]

The successful creation of Radio Martí, and the lobbying and campaign donations that fueled that success, had put the Foundation on the political map. CANF had become a major player in Washington, and the shaping of American policy toward Cuba was increasingly influenced by their members in Miami. They had learned how to curry favor and win over elected officials. In the 1988 campaigns, the Foundation donated $182,897 to fifty-six House and Senate candidates, Republican and Democrat.[22]

There was more momentum building as well. In 1989, Claude Pepper, the long-standing Miami-area legislator, who had served both in the Senate and the House, passed away while a seated member of the House of Representatives. A special election for his seat was held, one that revealed the chafing between communities that was taking place in the city.

A member of the Florida State Senate, Cuban-born Ileana Ros-Lehtinen, ran as the Republican candidate. Her opponent galvanized the entire community on one side or the other with his slogan "This is an American seat." Her election was overwhelmingly due to the high turnout of Hispanic voters, and revealed just how significant the shift of Cubans as a voting bloc could be:

despite only receiving 12 percent of the non-Hispanic white vote, and a meager 4 percent of the African American vote, her harnessing 90 percent of the Latin vote was enough to reach a new milestone. Ros-Lehtinen, who was born in Havana and left Cuba at the age of seven, was elected the first Cuban American in Congress. The victory party was a fitting reflection of the dichotomy within the community and the changes in the city itself. Celia Cruz, the legendary Cuban singer, warmed up the crowd for Ros-Lehtinen's arrival. Cruz was immediately followed by Lee Greenwood's "God Bless the USA," which gave everyone in the audience an opportunity to proclaim aloud, "I'm proud to be an American."[23] The congresswoman-elect spoke of upholding Claude Pepper's legacy, but also spoke in Spanish to address "our brothers listening in Cuba so they can see what a democracy is like." She was the face of another major success of the exile's shift to the political arena and represented a significant change. The exile community had already figured out how to effectively slide into the gateway of political influence. Now, one of their own had been given a key.

A few months later, things really started to change.

On November 9, 1989, the Berlin Wall was breached. Some bungling of bureaucratic talking points on new migratory policy led thousands to swarm to the Wall. Overwhelmed guards eventually opened the checkpoints and the world watched, stunned, as East Berliners embraced those separated from them for so long on the western side, their arrival feted with champagne and lively celebration. Countless billions of dollars in intelligence failed to predict what was unfolding before the global community's eyes—the beginning of the dismantling of the Soviet Bloc. A few weeks later, President Bush and Soviet leader Mikhail Gorbachev met in Malta for discussions that would reshuffle the world order that had dominated the globe for decades.

The Berlin Wall was the site of one of the most memorable New Year's Eve celebrations in history, and the world now stood at the dawn of a new age. One of history's most consequential moments, the ushering in of a new era of peace and freedom, would be incomplete without one critical component: David Hasselhoff. His 1988 song "Looking for Freedom" had topped the European charts that year and had deeply resonated with the feelings of the time. He cemented himself in Cold War history by performing in a potentially Mugatu-designed piano scarf and—we are not making this up—a leather jacket studded with battery-operated blinking lights.* Valid criticism of 1980s fashion aside, Hasselhoff's song tapped into something: there was an optimism and hope for the future that was palpable, the release of decades of pent-up longings and dreams finally on the verge of fulfillment.

And the optimism was justified. The changes came at a dizzying pace. Revolutions had just taken place in Romania and Czechoslovakia. The official reunification of Germany was less than a year away. Independence movements took steps to splinter the Soviet Union into independent republics. On Christmas Day in 1991, the red hammer-and-sickle flag of the Soviet Union was lowered for the last time. The red, white, and blue of the Russian flag was raised over Moscow. The president of the new Russian Federation, Boris Yeltsin, met with President Bush at Camp David shortly after, on February 1, 1992. They released a Declaration of New Relations, which ended all doubt: "Russia and the United States do not regard each other as potential adversaries. From now on, their relationship will be characterized by friendship and partnership, founded on mutual trust and respect and a common commitment to democracy and economic freedom." As if that wasn't proof enough that the world had changed, the Russian president left with a pair of cowboy boots with crossed US and Russian flags: it was Yeltsin's birthday, and as a good Texan, Bush saw a no more fitting gift.[24]

There has been some debate as to which of these moments was the true end of the Cold War. Some point to the Malta Conference. Others to Yeltsin's meeting with Bush at Camp David. But in Miami, if you mentioned "Malta," you were still just ordering a drink. All these changes were welcome, even joyously celebrated. Hope had emerged anew and with a power not seen in a generation. A whole new world of possibilities was opening up for millions of people. For them, freedom had finally been attained, and the Cold War was now in the past.

But these monumental changes were half a world away. Just as Hasselhoff's song had captured German sentiment at the fall of the Berlin Wall, another anthem arose that spoke to Miami's experience in these blissfully

---

* In all honesty, the History Gods could not have bestowed a more appropriate way to usher out the 1980s. They also may have protected the Hoff: the video of his performance, which has been unearthed and posted on the internet, includes a moment where someone in the crowd seems to throw a lit firecracker and misses Hasselhoff's head by less than an inch.

turbulent times. It was written by Willy Chirino, a Cuban musician who fled Cuba to Miami as a child. The song called "Nuestro Día (Ya Viene Llegando)," or loosely "Our Day (It's on Its Way)" was released in 1991, amid all the crumbling of the old order. It is a heartfelt retelling of the experience of exile, but this one is different: the song ends with a roll call of countries that had recently freed themselves from autocratic governments, with a chorus responding "Free!" one by one: "Poland . . . Free! Hungary . . . Free! Czechoslovakia . . . Free! Romania . . . Free! East Germany . . . Free!" The last country, passionately shouted with unbridled hope, was Cuba. Miami was still waiting.

It was with this backdrop that the Foundation redoubled its efforts. This was the moment they had all been waiting for. The dismantling of the Soviet Bloc seemed to make the end of the Castro regime inevitable. During the Malta Conference in 1989, President Bush made a point of raising the issue of Cuba to Gorbachev in no uncertain terms as "the single most disruptive factor to a relationship that is going in the right direction" and "a gigantic thorn in one shoe for our relationship." Regarding Castro, Bush focused on pulling economic levers, telling Gorbachev, "The poor guy is practically broke. The best thing would be if you gave him a signal that it would no longer be business as usual."[25] While you'd never hear Mas Canosa or the Foundation give Castro any sympathy whatsoever, they were aligned in their assessment. Castro was on the ropes. The Soviet Union had been providing billions of dollars' worth of subsidies on an annual basis. Without that assistance, and a tightening of US economic sanctions, he was sure to fall. Mas Canosa wanted to help deal the final blow that would send him and his regime to the canvas for good.

As part of their strategy, Mas Canosa and the Foundation brought their lobbying international. They took advantage of the historical moment to have discussions that would have been unthinkable a short time ago. They teamed up with University of Miami academics and established a project, Moscow-Miami Dialogue, that brought Soviet officials, journalists, and others to Miami. A Miami-Moscow Mini-Summit included Gorbachev's foreign policy advisor and a Latin American specialist of the Soviet Foreign Ministry.[26] One Soviet journalist penned an article in support of the exiles against Havana's attacks called "The Other Cuba, Which One Hears About on Meeting Emigrants in Miami," that was published, incredibly, in the Moscow News.[27] CANF sent a delegation to Moscow, to lobby Yeltsin and the Russian

Federation to halt aid to Cuba. This was extraordinary—private citizens petitioning a fledgling foreign government to influence one of its first major post-Soviet policy decisions.

While we don't know how much CANF influenced the decision, they got a favorable outcome. President Bush, in a statement on actions to promote democracy in Cuba, said, "Russia is withdrawing the former Soviet brigade and announced that as of January 1, 1992, it was ending all subsidies to Cuba. Castro is on his own."[28] Fidel was the last soldier left standing in the wreckage of the Soviet Union, and Cuba the last battlefield. It was CANF's intention to hasten the end through an economic stranglehold. They had taken care of the largest source of funds to the Castro government. There was another country they wanted to persuade, one that provided around $750 million a year in trade with Castro.

The United States.[29]

The US embargo had been loosened over the years and provided a number of loopholes that trade could, and did, flow through. CANF saw this as a vulnerability, and with the monumental changes taking place around them, increasingly as an opportunity. Senator Connie Mack of Florida, a recipient of support from the Foundation and an ally, sponsored an amendment to a trade bill that would have closed that trade opening first introduced under President Ford. The amendment would have essentially reinstituted a ban prohibiting subsidiaries of US corporations based in third countries from trading with Cuba in 1990.

But President Bush vetoed it.[30]

Enter Representative Robert Torricelli. A liberal New Jersey Democrat, he was an unlikely partner for Mas Canosa and CANF. Torricelli had visited Cuba in 1988 and didn't leave—by Miami standards—with a sufficiently negative opinion of what he saw while there. He recalled that meeting Mas Canosa was "like walking into a hurricane."[31] Over several years, the Foundation and its influence won him over.

Torricelli introduced the Cuban Democracy Act, a two-tracked piece of legislation that had both economic sanctions and humanitarian exemptions. The sanctions would reimpose the subsidiary ban vetoed by the president, as well as keep vessels that traded with Cuba from doing the same with the US for 180 days. This, combined with the loss of subsidies from the former Soviet

Union, would be a devastating combination. Late in 1991, Senator Torricelli worked on the legislation with Mas Canosa on a boat off the coast of Miami. Not surprisingly, the sticks were all Mas Canosa; Torricelli focused on the carrots.

Decades before, the same waters saw boats slipping out to sea to bring the fight to Cuba's shores. This time, it was the backdrop for the crafting of congressional legislation to keep that same fight going.

President Bush was no more supportive of the language than he had been before. But 1992 was a presidential election year, and CANF was about to prove its influence, and that of the Cuban American voting bloc in South Florida, yet again. All it took were three words. Mas Canosa reached out to Democratic presidential candidate Bill Clinton and offered entry into Cuban Miami in exchange for support on the bill. At a fundraiser in a Miami Cuban restaurant, Clinton's assessment of the Torricelli bill was those three magic words: "I like it."

Clinton walked away with $125,000 in campaign funds, and the Bush camp realized they couldn't be left behind. The bill passed through Congress and was signed into law by President Bush in Miami (of course) on October 23, in the closing days of the campaign. Torricelli, a Democrat, was not invited. But when Mas Canosa was given the pen by the president, he made sure to later get it to Torricelli, the main force behind the bill in Congress and the person whose name became associated with the Cuban Democracy Act. He sent it with a short note: "You deserve this."[32]

The passage of the bill was a demonstration of the lobbying power that CANF had achieved. It largely crafted and pushed through the legislation, courting both sides of the aisle. The organization even exerted influence on the decision-making of both presidential campaigns. The fact that the bill was signed into law reinforced all of that and one more key point: Miami was the last American outpost of the Cold War, and would have a major role, arguably *the* major role, in shaping American policy toward Cuba.

Part IV

11

Double Trouble

The Cuban security services are exceptionally good at the spy business. Sure, the Cuban Directorate of Intelligence (the DI, formerly the General Directorate of Intelligence, or the DGI) doesn't have the size, reach, and resources of some of the big boys in the intel world. They can't compete with the numbers of spooks fielded by the old Soviet Union or the Chinese today. They cannot come close to the technical dominance of American intelligence capabilities. There's no Cuban network of spy satellites in space, sensors under the world's oceans, or listening stations across the globe.

But there doesn't need to be. To borrow a metaphor from boxing, Cuban intelligence might be pound for pound the greatest intelligence service in the world. Better than the Chinese. Better than the Israelis. Better than the old KGB. And yes, better than the Americans.

You don't need to take our word for it. Just ask Dr. Brian Latell, who worked for the CIA and the National Intelligence Council advising presidents and members of Congress on Latin America. In the early 1990s, Latell was *the* National Intelligence Officer for Latin America, the highest-ranking position for the entire region in the intelligence community. He also ran the CIA's Center for the Study of Intelligence and was the editorial chairman for their journal, *Studies in Intelligence.* Latell has been a professor at Georgetown and Florida International University in Miami, and from 2006 to 2015 was a senior research associate in Cuba studies at the University of Miami.[1]

In other words, Brian Latell is *the guy*, and his book *Castro's Secrets* is the starting point for any historical conversation on Cuban intelligence.

Latell got a number of former and current intelligence professionals from the CIA and the FBI to give him their honest (and confidential) opinions on the capabilities of the Cubans. One CIA officer told him, "I believe the Cubans have the best intelligence service in the world."

Another: "Boy, did they do a job on us!"

Many counterintelligence agents in the FBI feel the same. How are they so good at getting inside some of America's most important institutions? A former agent on the Cuban intelligence beat told Latell, "They outperformed us by any objective measure."

Latell himself: "Indeed, for years they ran circles around both the Agency and the Bureau."[2]

Finally, "in most years since the early 1960s, the number of Americans assisting Cuban intelligence—moles and spies, doubles, access and influence agents, spotters, sycophants, and support assets—probably adds up to between three and five hundred."[3]

Yet great intelligence services do not just magically appear, and good intelligence professionals don't just come out of the womb ready to place a dead drop or make a covert communication. They have to be trained, molded, developed, cultivated. The same is true for a nation's intelligence apparatus. For as good as the United States Intelligence Community is today, it took decades (some might say centuries) before we could say we really knew what we were doing (at least on a consistent basis). The same is true for Cuba. They didn't necessarily know what they were doing immediately following Castro's rise to power in 1959. In fact, they had (understandably) liquidated Batista's US-trained service. At that point, they were essentially starting from scratch.

Not that they had time to waste. As we know, less than a year and a half after Fidel Castro assumes the top job in Cuba, the 2506 Brigade comes calling. According to Soviet intelligence documents, as late as May 1963—more than two years after the failed Bay of Pigs invasion—the Cuban intelligence service wasn't all that great at collecting intelligence on what was happening in Miami among the exile community. The Bay of Pigs itself was *this* close to being an unmitigated disaster for Castro. If the plan wasn't changed, if air support was provided, if more Cubans had risen up against the government. So many ifs, each of them resulting in the end of the regime. According to Aleksandr Fursenko and Timothy Naftali, "despite the cliché that everything was an 'open secret' in Miami's Little Havana, Castro's men had to admit in 1961 that there was still much that they did not know about the activities of their greatest enemies."[4]

So how, then, did the Cuban security services go from bad to good so quickly, so efficiently? There are several key reasons for their meteoric rise into the pantheon of intelligence greats:

1. The support of the KGB
2. Motivation
3. Limited targets
4. Ease of asset infiltration
5. Underestimation
6. Ease of establishing cover
7. Desperation of the enemy

Don't worry, we are going to break these down.

The Support of the KGB

After the near-disaster of the Bay of Pigs, the Cubans requested, and were given, a crash course on intelligence by the Soviet Union. Raúl Castro had already started this process in the fall of 1960, but the KGB had intentionally kept its number of advisors low. After the invasion, Raúl asked for more support, and got it. KGB officers taught the Cubans everything they knew, and transformed Cuban intelligence from its infancy to a professional, effective security service. Not all of this was done inside Cuba. At the time of the Bay of Pigs invasion, seventeen Cubans were in the Soviet Union for intelligence training. After the attack, the Cuban government asked the Soviets to increase that number to fifty. By the end of the decade, the cadre of Soviet-trained Cuban intelligence officers would make all the difference.[5]

Motivation

Much as is the case with Israel, which is surrounded by enemies that want to destroy it, Cuba was forced to get things right, and get things right quickly, in order to prevent the demise of their regime.* With Florida only ninety miles away, and thousands of Cuban exiles ready to take up arms against them, Castro's security services knew they couldn't afford the luxury of complacency.

Cuban intelligence also used information collected on the United States as a commodity. As they picked up bits and pieces of intelligence from their spies in the US, they traded this intelligence to other countries in return for needed resources (think oil, medicine, weapons). This is one of the main reasons Cuba is considered a major national security threat. They aren't invading us anytime soon. But their relationships with so many of America's adversaries—the Soviets/Russians, the Chinese, the North Koreans, the Venezuelans, etc.—mean that we HAVE to take them seriously. Any intelligence collected on the US by the Cubans was most certainly up for grabs. At least for the right price.

Limited Targets

The US intelligence community is tasked with the collection and analysis of worldwide intelligence. It is a global enterprise. The United States, as the leader of an integrated, intercontinental economic system, has potential threats to its national security, well, everywhere. It cannot afford a blind spot in intelligence coverage, so it needs to be big. Really big.

The Cuban government did not (and does not) have this problem. Fidel Castro and his successors understood that the only real threats to their regime were the (now) thirteen US presidential administrations that have shaped Cuban policy against them. To be sure, Cuban intelligence had other, minor priorities during the Cold War—support for foreign communist revolutionaries, for example—but their primary focus, to which they dedicated the vast majority of their time, effort, and resources, was just two targets: the United States government and the Cuban exile community.

---

* We understand some might balk at this comparison. But objectively they are similar.

Ease of Asset Infiltration

We don't think this one needs a lot of explanation. It is incredibly simple for Cuban intelligence to infiltrate case officers, sleeper agents, provocateurs, and illegals into the Miami exile community. Approximately *thirty thousand* Cuban émigrés have arrived in the United States each year, and most of them settle in the Miami area.

Underestimation

There's nothing more glorious for an intelligence service than to be underestimated by their main adversary, and that's exactly what happened during much of the Cold War. For almost thirty years, Cuban security services were considered "bush-league amateurs" and "lightweights," certainly compared to the CIA and the KGB. The general perception of the American counterintelligence community at the time was that "the fun-loving Cubans would not make good spies or spymasters," and that Cubans "generally constitute very poor agent material," and "do not know the meaning of security." Furthermore, "they do not take orders well, and the lonesome courage required for espionage is rarely part of their make-up. They make good fighters but poor spies."[6]

Oops.

Ease of Establishing Cover

It can take years for most sleeper agents, illegals, infiltration agents (whatever terms you want to use) to establish a cover that is legitimate (enough) to allow them to operate in a hostile area. You have to forge or illicitly acquire documentation of who you are pretending to be. Sometimes this is done by stealing the identity of some poor kid who died in infancy. From there, you hope you can work your way up to a library card or a student ID, then a driver's license, and then (if you are really good, and patient) a passport. The entire time you are worried about being exposed for who you really are, and then spending the rest of your life in prison (or worse).

Cuban intelligence officers had it easy. They could slip in with the other exiles fleeing Cuba, many of whom had to leave the island with just the clothes on their backs. Don't have paperwork to prove who you are? That's OK, a lot of people are in that situation. We will embrace you anyway, help you find a job, housing, proper documentation. If you can fake it 'til you make it for a year and a day, the Cuban Adjustment Act of 1966 granted you permanent residency in the United States. From there, becoming a citizen was only a stone's throw away.

Desperation of the Enemy

For American intelligence officers, this one stings a bit. Since Cuba is geographically located so close to the United States, thirteen different presidential administrations have made it an intelligence priority. The problem is, Cuba is also what some intelligence services refer to as a "denied area," meaning a country in which the security services and counterintelligence services are exceptionally good. In other words, it is incredibly difficult to collect worthwhile intelligence on Cuban capabilities or intentions—or alliances, like that between Cuba and the Soviet Union.

In these conditions, American spies can get desperate. Which makes American intelligence services vulnerable to what we call in the spy business a "dangle." This is essentially just what it sounds like. An intelligence agency will "dangle" a source, hoping that their adversary's spooks will take the bait and try to recruit him/her.* Not realizing they've fallen for a trap, the victimized agency will readily accept what the dangle has to report. In most cases, this information is absolute garbage, disinformation designed to confuse the adversary.

The Cubans excelled at this. And the Americans were easy marks. The result? One of the most spectacular intelligence coups in history.

In June 1987, Cuban intelligence officer Florentino Aspillaga Lombard defected to the West in Vienna. During his debriefing, he told us something so shocking it still reverberates today—from the mid-1960s until his defection in 1987, every person the CIA had thought it had recruited in Cuba was actually a double agent. All of them. More than four dozen spies, whom the CIA counted on for nearly all of its human intelligence on Castro's regime, were really working for the DGI.

This bears repeating.

Every. Single. One.

Most of these fifty or so agents had been dangled by the Cubans. They were selected for the mission "for their psychological and intellectual

---

* The Cubans called a dangle *carnada*, which translates to "bait."

suitability and the positions they held," and then sent to a special school for training. Some of these double agents "worked" for the CIA for years.[7]

Another tactic of Cuban intelligence was to watch CIA officers in third countries. Once they observed them developing an interest in or targeting a Latin American person for recruitment, the DGI would swoop in and recruit that individual before the CIA got the chance. So while the poor schlep from the Agency thought he had himself a great catch, he was actually the one on the hook.[8]

As good as this was for Castro and for Cuban intelligence, a number of high-level defections in 1987 forced the Cuban government to do some soul searching.[9] Fidel ordered a major overhaul of Cuban intelligence, starting with the DGI, which was formally renamed the Directorate of Intelligence, or the DI. With all these betrayals, it was hard to trust, well, anyone. The loyalties of many officers were challenged. In 1989, there was even more extreme "top-to-bottom purging" of the Ministry of the Interior, which controlled the DI and several other Cuban security services.[10]

But Castro rarely missed an opportunity to turn an internal crisis into a way to stick it to the United States, and specifically the CIA. The defector issue was a problem, but what they revealed about the US intelligence community was, to be objective, pretty damn awesome. If defectors are going to blow the double agent program anyway, why not go out in a blaze of glory?

On July 6, 1987, Cuban television broadcast the first episode in a series they called *The CIA War Against Cuba*. Episode 1 centered on the American diplomatic mission in Havana and claimed dozens of US diplomats were actually case officers for CIA. True or not, it didn't really matter. This broad-brush tactic was sufficient to create enough doubt about the US diplomatic corps, which, not incidentally, probably *did* include a number of CIA officers using a diplomatic posting as cover.

Episodes 2 and 3 centered on the double agent program, and featured Cuban intelligence officers who claimed they had "penetrated" the CIA. They, as we know, had plenty to crow about.

Episode 4 highlighted the sophisticated communications equipment they said had been, and was being, used by the CIA in Cuba. Episode 5 accused the Americans of economic sabotage, and 6 claimed the CIA had used chemical warfare against the island.[11]

The most entertaining part of the series—from Fidel Castro's perspective, at least—must have been the secretly recorded footage purporting to show American "diplomats" acting extremely suspicious.* Wandering around the woods outside Havana; making what appears to be dead drops; making signal marks on benches; picking up bags and briefcases; dropping off what looked like electronics equipment. The entire time they clearly had no idea they were being surveilled.[12]

La Red Avispa

In September 1998, the FBI arrested ten members of what can safely be called one of Cuban intelligence's most ambitious operations against the United States: the Wasp Network. Over several years in the early nineties, the Cuban intelligence services were able to set up an intelligence network in Miami and the Florida Keys that consisted of an estimated forty-two spies, one of the—if not the—largest espionage rings ever to have operated in the US.† The Wasp Network was run out of Cuba through a partnership between the DI and Cuban military intelligence, the DIM (Directorate of Military Intelligence, for those keeping score). Its objectives were to infiltrate the Miami exile community, to collect intelligence on its work against Castro, to disrupt that (if possible), to find (or manufacture) dirt on the exile community, and then use that information to discredit it, especially the Cuban American National Foundation.[13]

But they had another mission, and some experts on Cuban intelligence believe this was their primary goal: collect information on the United States military. Members of the Wasp Network were tasked with targeting the headquarters of United States Southern Command (SOUTHCOM), located in Miami and responsible for US military operations in the Americas; United States Central Command (CENTCOM), located at MacDill Air Force Base in Tampa, which focuses on operations in the Middle East; and United States Special Operations Command (SOCOM), also at MacDill, which has the responsibility for special operations worldwide.[14]

Were they any good? Well, the results are mixed. They really didn't manage to collect much in the way of actionable intelligence against the American military targets, although in their defense, there wasn't much there to collect (there were no active military operations being planned against Cuba anyway).

---

* Or "sus," as I'm told the kids are saying.
† At least that we know of . . .

Members of the network got close to SOUTHCOM and the US Naval Air Station at Boca Chica, in Key West, but as far as we can tell nothing of any significance (secret documents, classified information, etc.) was compromised.[15] The FBI actually tracked the Cuban spies for years, but never worried all that much about what they might be sending to Havana. It made more sense for law enforcement to just wait and watch. Maybe they'll eventually do *something* of consequence.

So why did we say the results of the Wasp Network were mixed and not, instead, that they were an utter failure? Because some of the Wasp members did an exceptionally good job of infiltrating the Cuban exile community.

In particular, the Cuban intelligence officers were able to infiltrate the Cuban exile organization Brothers to the Rescue (Hermanos al Rescate), which helped to search for rafters fleeing Cuba to the United States and provide them with supplies to keep them alive until the Coast Guard arrived to assist. Two of the Wasps were trained pilots and got jobs with the humanitarian organization flying missions over the Florida Straits. They used this access to pass information on Hermanos to Cuba—intelligence that would later lead to the deaths of four Brothers to the Rescue pilots in 1996, when Cuban MiGs shot them down over international waters.[16]

After the arrests (which were followed by several more over the next few years), most of the network agreed to provide information on Cuban intelligence to the FBI in return for reduced sentences. But five of the arrested refused to talk. The so-called Cuban Five, Gerardo Hernández, Antonio Guerrero, Ramón Labañino, Fernando González, René González, would go on trial in late 2000, charged with a myriad of offenses (twenty-five counts). The most serious was lodged against the Wasp Network's leader, Hernández, who was on trial for conspiracy to commit murder in the deaths of the four pilots.

Evidence used against him at his trial included coded messages he sent to René González, one of the network's pilots who had infiltrated Hermanos al Rescate. One of these, sent just eleven days before the shootdown, warned him not to fly with Brothers. If he did, he was supposed to use a special code to let the Cubans know he was on the flight:

If they ask you to fly at the last minute without being scheduled, find an excuse and do not do it. If you cannot avoid it, transmit over the airplane's radio the slogan for the July 13 martyrs and Viva Cuba. If you are not able to call, say over the radio, 'Long live Brothers to the Rescue and Democracia.' That is all.[17]

In June 2001, the jury returned the verdict of guilty on all counts, including the murder charge against Hernández. He was sentenced to two life terms, to be served consecutively. Guerrero and Labañino got life, Fernando González received nineteen years, and René González fifteen.

Fidel Castro, never missing the chance to turn a crisis into an opportunity, launched an international public relations campaign to praise the five "Heroes of the Republic." The spies were portrayed as doing nothing "more sinister than trying to prevent acts of terrorism on the island by militant Miami exiles."[18] They were being treated unjustly by the United States. Los Cinco Héroes became darlings to many international organizations. The UN Commission on Human Rights, Amnesty International, multiple Nobel laureates, foreign nations (even allies), and others called for their release. There was also outcry from within the United States. Twenty US cities formed their own chapter of the National Committee to Free the Cuban Five. Robert Pastor, the national security advisor for Latin America under President Jimmy Carter, quipped, "Holding a trial for five Cuban intelligence agents in Miami is about as fair as a trial for an Israeli agent in Tehran. You'd need a lot more than a good lawyer to be taken seriously."[19]

You can still see remnants of the "Free the Five" campaign around Cuba even today, even though all of them have since been released from prison.[20] There are billboards along the highways, and the intelligence officers were frequent guests on Cuban television shows for months after their return to Cuba. Most of a generation of Cuban children "has grown up memorizing their names and biographies."[21]

The PR campaign continues even today. In 2011, Brazilian author Fernando Morais wrote a book about the Cuban Five, *The Last Soldiers of the Cold War*. In 2019, Netflix released the movie *Wasp Network*, based on Morais's book and directed by French filmmaker Olivier Assayas. It has quite an impressive cast—Penélope Cruz, Édgar Ramírez, Gael García Bernal, Wagner Moura (who played Pablo Escobar in *Narcos*), and Ana de Armas.

But is it any good? And is it even remotely historically accurate?

We watched it, so you don't have to. Because the answers to the above questions are:

1) It's best not to assume everyone's movie taste is the same as ours. Maybe you'll like it?

2) No.

In their defense, how many movies are completely historically accurate? Not many. But *Wasp Network* was clearly made with a political goal. The Cuban spies are three-dimensional, human. The Cuban exiles portrayed in the film are almost caricatures—Jorge Mas Canosa appears in the film as an almost Don Corleone–like figure, a mob boss. In the first scene with José Basulto, the founder of Brothers to the Rescue, the film has him saying he was trained by the CIA as a "terrorist" (not true), and that Brothers to the Rescue is a "militant organization" (also not true). It also shows Brothers to the Rescue scouting tourist areas in Cuba ahead of attacks by exile militants. And it portrays the Brothers aircraft being shot down *inside* Cuban airspace, when in reality they were unmistakably fired upon in international waters.

Parts of the movie were filmed in Cuba, so it's no surprise the portrayal is this one-sided. The film even ends with a taped interview of Fidel discussing the arrests of the Cuban Five.

It was interesting to see so many actors of this caliber involved in a movie that was, in so many ways, essentially just Cuban government propaganda. The real story *is* nuanced. Why not play it that way?

We hope the checks for the actors had a lot of zeros on them.

One of the things the film does well (at least compared to the rest) is show one aspect of the Wasp Network that didn't get as much press in the United States because the spy at the center of the story wasn't one of the arrested Cuban intelligence officers. Juan Pablo Roque arrived in the US in 1992, after swimming from Cuban territory to the US Naval Base at Guantánamo Bay and requesting political asylum. A major in the Cuban Air Force, Roque was the perfect defector—handsome, courageous, and passionately anti-Castro, criticizing the Cuban government every chance he got. He was treated like a hero in the Cuban exile community, and joined Hermanos al Rescate as a pilot.

But, of course, this was a ruse. Roque was a member of the Wasp Network.

To solidify his cover, Roque would marry Ana Margarita Martínez in 1995. He met her at church. She was deeply religious and very active in her parish. When she first met him, in 1992, she says, "I was still innocent, very trusting, and

I am sure he saw that." They dated, and she fell in love. "He was serious, intense and seemed sincere. He wanted to settle down. He told me he was a pilot who had deserted and, given his high profile, I had no reason to doubt him."

From what Martínez says, Roque played the role of doting husband exceptionally well. "He went everywhere with me. He did the dishes, he cleaned the house. He was very protective, very attentive to me. He told me he loved me and I believed him. He was, I see now, the best actor of all time."

Even when he suddenly disappeared one day in 1996, just eleven months after the wedding, Martínez thought he had gone off to agitate against the Castro regime. The next day, the two Brothers to the Rescue planes were shot down.

Three days after he left, Martínez finally found her husband. He was on CNN, back in Cuba, telling the world he had been working the whole time as a Cuban intelligence agent. He denounced Brothers to the Rescue as a terrorist organization and said that he had married Ana on orders from his handlers in Havana. To make matters worse, the Cuban exile community turned on her—they couldn't believe she didn't know what he was and what he was doing. She was accused of being complicit on Spanish-language radio and television, and ostracized in the neighborhood. She was even forced to leave the memorial service for one of the Brothers to the Rescue pilots. She was unwelcome in the only community she knew, in the community she loved.

Then she ran out of money. She had to sell her house and cars.

But what was the solution to the problem? She couldn't really sue Roque, what good would that do?

So she sued Cuba. For rape.

In what was likely the first time a sovereign nation was charged with rape, Martínez and her lawyers alleged that every time the couple had sex, it was sexual battery. "Sex cannot be consensual if it is derived by fraud and concealment."[22]

And she won.

In March 2001, Miami-Dade Circuit Court Judge Alan Postman awarded Martínez $7.175 million in compensatory damages, paid out in $175,000 annual payments until Martínez turns eighty-one.

So how do you collect money from Cuba? Cuban assets have been frozen in the United States for decades. Since Cuba had been designated a state sponsor of terrorism, US law allowed for compensation payments to be paid out of frozen funds. This isn't the first time this has been applied to the Cuban government. Earlier in 2001, the US government transferred about $93 million in frozen Cuban bank accounts to the families of those Brothers to the Rescue pilots killed in 1996.[23]

Speaking of lawsuits, in the summer of 2022, Brothers to the Rescue founder José Basulto decided to sue Netflix for defamation.

According to the lawsuit, Netflix defamed Basulto by depicting him as a terrorist and drug trafficker, a puppet of the US government, and one of the villains of the film. The complaint states, "The Film is an obvious attempt to rewrite and whitewash history in favor of the communist Cuban regime and is factually inaccurate. The Film portrays the Cuban Five as courageous heroes who were simply defending their homeland. In reality, the Cuban Five were a spy network that produced actionable intelligence enabling the Cuban government to commit extrajudicial killings."

Basulto's suit also argued that Cuba interfered with the making of the film to ensure it told their version of the story. The Cuban government's film office requires advanced approval of any script hoping to film in Cuba and will refuse to allow anything "detrimental to the image of the country and people of Cuba."

As of the writing of this book, this case is still pending, but Netflix did provide a response to the lawsuit: "Modern day audiences of docudramas understand that they are watching dramatizations, not exacting recreations of events."

Burrowing In

No chapter on Cuban intelligence would be complete without a discussion of Cuban attempts, some successful, some not, to recruit agents from inside the United States government. According to defector Florentino Aspillaga (as told to Brian Latell), Cuban intelligence had recruited multiple spies inside the State Department and the US Congress—including two unnamed *members* of Congress, who were able to visit Cuba through third countries and leave behind no trace of their trip. The US Senate was also a key Cuban intelligence focus. And this isn't just about the members themselves—the hundreds of congressional staffers, many of whom have access to not only classified government documents but also the most secret conversations of their bosses, make Capitol Hill a target-rich environment.[24]

Aspillaga told Latell about Cuban intelligence's most valuable recruit, a mole in the highest levels of government, so well-connected and important that only Fidel Castro and a single Cuban intelligence case officer ever knew who he was. Unless the FBI has kept his arrest secret, this person could still be working in Washington today.[25]

But the best of the best was a woman who spied for the Cubans for seventeen years and burrowed her way into the highest echelons of the US intelligence community. In the end, Ana Belén Montes will go down as one of the most damaging spies in US history.[26]

Montes was born on a US Army base in West Germany. Her father was a respected army doctor. Ana was incredibly smart and got almost straight As in school. This got her into the University of Virginia, where, as a junior, she enrolled in a study-abroad program in Spain. There, she met a handsome Argentinian leftist, who was deeply involved in the anti-American protests that were taking place that summer. Smitten, young, and susceptible to influence, Ana began to embrace political radicalism. According to one of her friends she'd met in Spain, "After every protest, Ana used to explain to me the 'atrocities' that the USA government used to do to other countries. She was already so torn. She did not want to be an American but was."[27]

Shortly after graduating from UVA, she took a job as a clerk typist for the US Department of Justice's Privacy and Information Appeals Office. Why would someone who hated American policy work for the US government? It doesn't seem like at this point Ana was doing anything nefarious. She needed money. And she was quite good at her job.

Less than a year after starting at DOJ, Ana was granted Top Secret security clearance—apparently the FBI didn't detect anything untoward during her clearance interviews or polygraph. At the same time, she began to work on a master's degree at the Johns Hopkins School of Advanced International Studies (SAIS) in Washington. It was then that she was recruited.

Cuba uses American universities as a source for recruitment. They place or recruit faculty and staff to headhunt for Cuban intelligence, to keep on the lookout for students who might, one day, work their way up to the highest levels of American government. This was something they must have learned from the KGB, who played the long game in their recruitment of spies. The Cambridge Five is a case in point. Harold "Kim" Philby and the rest of the five were recruited while in college with the hopes that they would eventually be someone important in the British government. That system worked quite well for the Soviets. It worked just as well for the Cubans and Ana Montes.

It wouldn't have been too hard for the recruiter to spot a potential asset in Ana. Her political views had gotten even more radical. She hated the Reagan administration's policies in Latin America, particularly its support for the Contras in Nicaragua. She was propositioned by Cuban intelligence in 1984, and accepted.

Montes secretly visited Cuba in 1995, where her handlers instructed her to start applying for government positions that would allow her to see classified information relevant to Cuban security. The Defense Intelligence Agency (DIA) was hiring at the time, and Montes accepted a job as an entry-level research specialist. Once she was on the inside, Cuban intelligence got to work, feeding her information that would make her look like an analytical savant, as she could "predict" their actions with uncanny ability. Soon she became the DIA's chief analyst for El Salvador and Nicaragua, and then . . .

She was promoted to be the DIA's top political and military analyst for Cuba. They even nicknamed her the "Queen of Cuba," because of her analytical "skills." The Cuban spy found herself briefing the Joint Chiefs of Staff and the members of the National Security Council about Cuban military capabilities.

And she was able to operate without suspicion for years, even as *four* of her close relatives *worked for the FBI*. Her brother, Alberto "Tito" Montes, was a special agent in the FBI field office in Atlanta, as was his wife. Her sister, Lucy, worked for the FBI in Miami as a Spanish-language analyst. Her now-ex-husband worked there too.

Her excellent tradecraft kept her safe. The Cubans had taught her well. She used brush passes and dead drops and disguises and communicated in code. The Cubans communicated with her via numbers stations, radio broadcasts that played coded messages throughout the day. To anyone listening, it would just sound like a disembodied voice spitting out random numbers. But for Ana, it relayed her instructions.[28]

She also never wrote anything down, avoiding the all-too-common espionage disaster of getting caught with stolen classified documents. Instead, she sat at her cubicle at work during lunch, memorizing hundreds of pages of Top Secret information. Once she got home, she would quickly type these notes into a laptop computer, copy that intelligence onto disks, and then eventually pass those disks along to her handlers, usually during clandestine meetings in DC-area Chinese restaurants.

In 1998, the FBI and the entire intelligence community got very lucky. Or perhaps Ana's sister, Lucy, just had a deeper sense of operational security than we might expect. Either way, fortune was smiling on the FBI at that time. Lucy, you see, had been working seemingly endless hours translating wire-tapped communications between Cuban spies in Miami who were trying to infiltrate US Southern Command.

Lucy was smack-dab in the middle of the investigation of the Wasp Network.

But she never told Ana what she was working on. Not because she questioned Ana's allegiances (she had no reason to). It just wasn't something they would naturally talk about.

As a result of the eventual arrests of the Wasp Network, Ana's handlers suddenly cut off all communication. They couldn't be sure who was compromised and who was still safe.

In 2000, Montes began dating Roger Corneretto, a senior intelligence officer who worked at the Pentagon and was in charge of the Cuban intelligence program for SOUTHCOM.

Now you might be thinking, Wow, the Cubans used Montes as a honey trap?*

On face, it obviously looks that way. But those who worked this case actually believe that Montes fell in love. The guy she fell in love with just so happened to be an exceptionally good potential source of intelligence information, but love nonetheless. She even tried to leave her intelligence work behind to start a family with Corneretto, but the Cubans wouldn't allow it. She was far too important to their operation.†

In September 2000, DIA counterintelligence got a lead that someone inside the Agency was working for the Cubans. They didn't know who, but they had their suspicions. Only a handful of people would have the high-level access to DIA information that was allegedly passed to the Cubans, and Montes was one of them. Eventually the FBI agreed to work with them on a "mole hunt," and the spook chasers set out to get their spy.

---

* A spy who uses sex to get information.

† Corneretto was fooled too. He called Montes "an unapologetic, highly educated, volunteer thug for a police state."

After a year of investigation, the FBI had built a considerable case against Ana Montes. But they hadn't been able to witness her doing any espionage activities—no dead drops or brush passes or meetings with her handlers. They were confident they had enough to prosecute her successfully but were worried she would be able to plea-bargain to lesser charges and would not get the sentence she deserved. The FBI strategy was to wait. To observe. To continue to collect evidence in the hopes that she would mess up and they could catch her red-handed.

But world events would interrupt this strategy. The attacks on September 11, 2001, put the entire national security establishment on war footing. Analysts from all over the intelligence enterprise were being reassigned to counterterrorism in the fight against Al Qaeda. Montes was no exception. In fact, because of her seniority at the DIA she was named an acting division chief and was in charge of processing target lists for the war in Afghanistan. If Montes got her hands on the American war plan for Afghanistan, DIA and American intelligence officials were worried she would pass it along to the Cubans.

Why would the Cubans care about what we were doing in Afghanistan, you might ask?

They really didn't, but they could potentially pass the information along (as a commodity) to the Taliban.

So Montes was arrested, without the damning evidence that would guarantee she'd never see the light of day again as a free woman.

When US traitors like Robert Hanssen and Aldrich Ames were arrested, the US government was able to charge them with violations of multiple statutes that carried the threat of the death penalty. The idea was to hit them with the death penalty charge, and then they would happily plead down to life in prison without the possibility of parole. And this worked for Hanssen and Ames.

The FBI did, in fact, have one charge they could levy against Montes that would potentially bring about a death penalty case, but the evidence for it could not be unclassified for use in a public courtroom. It was far too sensitive. So prosecutors had to start with life without parole, and then plead down to the sentence Montes eventually received, twenty-five years in federal prison.

She was released in January 2023, at the age of sixty-five.

12

All Politics Is International

"The Sea Is a Cemetery of People"

The Cuban government has used the Cuban people and mass migration as a weapon against the United States on three occasions.* The first time was at Camarioca in 1965 during the Johnson administration. Then there was Mariel in 1980. Each of the first two times, Castro forced the US government to react to his actions, as Fidel and his government dictated the course of events. Camarioca and Mariel both resulted in changes in US policy toward Cuba and altered the domestic political landscape for the president in power. In 1994, Castro did it again—this time forcing the hand of Bill Clinton.

The end of the Cold War and the collapse of the Soviet Union in 1991 put considerable pressure on the economy of Cuba. They could no longer count on the financial support of their once-mighty benefactor, and conditions in Cuba suffered as a result. Living standards dramatically deteriorated on the island, and many Cuban citizens wanted to leave for better opportunities in the United States.

---

* And it's possible we are in the midst of a fourth.

At first it was a trickle. In President Clinton's first year in office, 1993, the US Coast Guard rescued 3,656 Cubans at sea. But in the first half of 1994, more than 4,700 Cubans had escaped Cuba and set out across the Florida Straits for Miami. In just a two-month period, from June 4 to August 4, Cubans trying to leave Cuba made seven attempts to hijack seaworthy boats in the Bay of Havana, hoping they could take them to America.

On August 5, thousands of Cubans converged on Havana's long seawall, or Malecón, after (false) rumors spread through the city that a fleet of boats was on its way from Miami ready to pick up any Cuban who wanted to leave. Police arrived to break up the crowds, but the people refused to comply. Instead, the Malecón erupted into protests, as rocks and bottles were thrown at shop windows and tourist hotels, with the people shouting "Down with Fidel!" and "Freedom!" The police would eventually restore order, arresting hundreds of protestors.

The following day, Castro made his move. "If the United States fails to adopt immediate and efficient measures to stop the encouragement of illegal departures from the country, we will be duty bound to instruct our coast guards not to intercept any boat leaving Cuba."[1]

You want to leave? Fine. Go ahead.

And they did. By the thousands. On anything they could find that would float (and sadly, on some that didn't)—boats, inner tubes, pieces of old wooden boards lashed together, old vehicles floating on barrels. By the end of August, more than twenty-one thousand Cubans of all ages left Cuba in boats and rafts, heading for Florida.

President Clinton knew something needed to be done, both to stem the tide of rafters who were leaving Cuba and to prevent the immigration system in South Florida from being completely overwhelmed. So Clinton did something that hadn't been done in decades: he shut the door. On August 19, the White House announced that any Cubans intercepted by the US Coast Guard at sea would not be brought to the United States. Instead, they would be taken to the US Naval Base at Guantánamo. Any Cubans who avoided the Coast Guard and made it to American soil would be detained by INS while their cases were reviewed.[2]

More than thirty thousand Cubans were detained during what became known as the Balsero Crisis (or rafter crisis). In May 1995, the crisis finally ended, when secret negotiations between the US and Cuba reached an agreement on policies to try to better control Cuban immigration to the United States.

Under the deal, both the US and Cuba agreed to take steps to promote "safe, legal, and orderly" migration. The United States agreed to admit no less than twenty thousand Cuban immigrants annually (excluding the immediate relatives of US citizens, who could enter the US in unlimited numbers). To make this work, the US created the Special Cuban Migration Lottery, through which lottery winners, randomly selected, would be first in line.[3]

Most importantly, however, these agreements established the so-called wet foot/dry foot policy. In short, wet foot/dry foot said that if you made it safely to the shore, you could stay. But if you were interdicted while still at sea—and could not provide evidence of a well-founded fear of persecution (in which case you were considered for resettlement in a third country)—you were sent back to Cuba. The Cuban government promised, as part of the agreement, that none of those sent back would face reprisals for trying to leave.* If they still wanted to immigrate to the US, they could apply for one of the annual visas at the US Interests Section in Havana.

The Clinton administration thought it had a winning deal. The crisis was ended, and (perhaps) future crises like it could be avoided. But critics from both sides of the issue immediately pounced on the president. Some said they felt lied to by the White House, which had promised to keep the thousands of rafters at Gitmo. Cuban Americans were happy those immigrants were allowed to leave Guantánamo for the United States, but couldn't believe the Clinton administration had just reversed decades of US policy and would return back to Cuba those trying to escape Castro's repressive regime.[4]

Miami Congresswoman Ileana Ros-Lehtinen said, "It's another prime example of the softening and the warming up of relations between the US and Castro," and called the new policy "very lamentable."

Senator Jesse Helms, a Republican from North Carolina, despised the agreement: wet foot/dry foot was "a sign that the United States will now work in partnership with Castro's brutal security apparatus by intercepting and capturing escaping Cuban refugees, and turning them over directly to Castro's thugs."

---

* Well, they said this, at least.

The Cuban American National Foundation was so incensed that it withdrew its pledge to spend millions of dollars to help resettle the refugees now entering from Guantánamo. Jorge Mas Canosa, angry that he had not been consulted by the administration, said, "They made this policy alone. Let them now solve the problems of Guantánamo alone."[5]

Once again, Castro had used refugees as a political weapon, and in doing so transformed his own domestic problems (protests, hijackings) into domestic political problems for the American president.

And President Bill Clinton certainly had his share of political problems. In November 1994, in the middle of the rafter crisis, the Democrats got walloped at the polls. The midterm elections are usually bad for the party of the president in power, but this was beyond that. Sometimes described as the "Republican Revolution," the GOP picked up eight seats in the Senate and fifty-four in the House. For the first time in more than four decades, the Republicans had unified control of Congress. The Republican win also made Jesse Helms the chair of the Senate Foreign Relations Committee, and conservative Indiana representative Dan Burton the chair of the House Foreign Affairs Committee's Western Hemisphere Affairs Subcommittee. Together they would craft legislation called the Cuban Liberty and Democratic Solidarity (Libertad) Act, but more commonly known as the Helms-Burton Act.

Helms-Burton, if passed, would take the unusual step of eliminating most of the president's executive authority to make foreign policy toward Cuba. It fixed the embargo as a permanent policy that could not be removed by any president, unless a specific set of conditions is first met by Cuba, including:

- Legalize all political activity
- Release political prisoners
- Allow international human rights investigations
- Dissolve the Department of State Security
- Commit to free and fair elections
- Ensure no Castro, Fidel, or Raúl in government[6]

Helms-Burton would also attempt to expand the American embargo into a more global one by coercing other countries into stopping any business with Cuba. Proponents of the bill believed that the international community had propped up Castro's regime after the fall of the Soviet Union. Each year since 1992, every United Nations member except the US, the Israelis, and occasionally one other member state had voted for a UN resolution condemning the US embargo on Cuba. Helms-Burton set out to reverse that trend.[7]

But Helms-Burton didn't stop there. Title III of the Libertad Act allowed American companies and Cuban exiles whose properties were seized by Castro to file federal lawsuits against any foreign companies that they believed were profiting from that seizure. Title IV allowed the US government to punish the executives of those foreign companies who were believed to be "trafficking" in those properties by barring them (and members of their families) from entering the United States.[8]

The Clinton administration preemptively threatened to veto the bill, but the House voted 294–130 to pass it anyway. Republicans, holding a much slimmer majority in the Senate, couldn't get the required votes to push it through, and the bill bogged down even before it cleared the Senate Foreign Relations Committee.[9]

Unless something happened to change the political dynamic in the Senate (and in the White House), the bill looked doomed to fail.

An "Unjustified, Unlawful Attack"

José Basulto has lived an extraordinary life. Trained by the CIA, he infiltrated Cuba before the Bay of Pigs invasion, his cover as a physics student at the University of Santiago. He later went back into Cuba to fire a cannon at a hotel full of Soviets. In the 1980s, Basulto helped to raise money for the Contras, outfitting field medical hospitals and airlifting medical supplies to the rebel forces in Nicaragua and El Salvador. In 1991, he and a fellow Bay of Pigs veteran, Billy Schuss, founded Brothers to the Rescue, a humanitarian organization formed to help rafters survive the arduous voyage from Cuba to the United States.[10]

Taking off from the Opa-locka airport in Miami, Brothers to the Rescue aircraft would sweep the Florida Straits, looking for any rafters who might be in trouble. Once they found them, they would radio the US Coast Guard the rafter's location, and drop water, food, and other supplies so that they could survive until the USCG arrived.

The wet foot/dry foot policy changed much of that. Now rafters didn't necessarily want the Coast Guard alerted to their location. Brothers to the Rescue would still fly missions looking for rafters they could help, but Basulto expanded his operations. In November 1994, Basulto and Schuss flew over Oriente Province in Cuba and dropped anti-Castro bumper stickers out of the plane. In July 1995, Basulto flew his plane over *Havana*, and dropped hundreds of leaflets and religious medals.

He wasn't dropping bombs, or hurting anyone, but he *was* infiltrating Cuban airspace. The Cuban government, half-angry and half-embarrassed that he had breached their air defenses so easily, threatened to shoot down any pilot who entered Cuban airspace again without authorization.[11]

On Saturday, February 24, 1996, Brothers to the Rescue left Opa-locka in three Cessnas on a mission to search for rafters in distress. On one plane were pilot Carlos Costa and spotter Pablo Morales. The second had pilot Mario de la Peña and Armando Alejandre Jr. Basulto piloted the third. In his plane were four Cubans, Arnaldo Iglesias, Sylvia Iriondo, Andrés Iriondo, and Basulto.

Just after 3:00 p.m., two Cuban MiG-23 fighter aircraft took off to intercept the Cessnas. It wasn't a fair fight. It wasn't really a fight at all. Within minutes, two of the Brothers to the Rescue planes had been destroyed, and their crews killed. Basulto's plane was the only one to escape.

The Cuban government tried to claim that the Brothers to the Rescue planes had violated Cuban territorial airspace, but this was, as the saying goes, total bullshit. An international inquiry would determine that one of the Cessnas had been shot down nine miles outside Cuban airspace. The other? Ten miles outside.

According to the *Miami Herald*, Anthony Lake, President Clinton's National Security Advisor, asked the Pentagon for possible retaliatory actions, but was told that there were no military options that made sense. Instead, the United States responded by suspending charter air travel to Cuba, asking the United Nations to condemn the shootdown, and authorize the use of frozen Cuban assets to compensate the families of the killed pilots.[12]

The administration also indicated it would now support Helms-Burton.

Congress quickly moved to pass the bill, and President Clinton signed the Cuban Liberty and Democratic Solidarity (Libertad) Act into law on March 12, 1996. At the signing ceremony for the bill, Clinton said:

This act is a justified response to the Cuban government's unjusti-
fied, unlawful attack on two unarmed U.S. civilian aircraft that left
three U.S. citizens and one U.S. resident dead. . . .

By acting swiftly—just 17 days after the attack—we are sending a powerful message to the Cuban regime that we do not and
will not tolerate such conduct. The Act also reaffirms our common
goal of promoting a peaceful transition to democracy in Cuba by
tightening the existing embargo while reaching out to the Cuban
people. . . .

Today, I sign it with the certainty that it will send a powerful,
unified message from the United States to Havana that the yearning
of the Cuban people for freedom must not be denied.

Jorge Mas Canosa attended the ceremony, as did the families of the Brothers to the Rescue pilots along with fifty or so Cuban exiles. Helms-Burton was
now law.[13]

"Jesus, That F#$@ing Kid Again. That's All They Show on the News"

In November 1999, two fishermen pulled five-year-old Elián González out of
the Atlantic Ocean three miles off the coast of Fort Lauderdale. At first, they
hesitated in handing him over to authorities, fearing since he was plucked
out of the ocean, he would be sent back to Cuba under the wet foot/dry foot
policy. The Coast Guard, however, assured them the child would not immediately be sent back, since he required medical attention, which he received at a
local hospital. It was soon learned that Elián's mother and his stepfather had
died on the voyage from Cuba.

A staffer from the Immigration and Naturalization Service had been in
contact with Elián's family back in Cuba, and was aware that his biological
father, Juan Miguel González, was still alive—and wanted Elián back. Yet on
November 26, the Friday of Thanksgiving weekend, INS officials released Elián
into the temporary custody of his great-uncle, Lázaro González, a Miami-based
Cuban exile. INS would later argue that, since they were understaffed over the
holiday weekend, they thought they were operating in the best interests of the

child by handing him over to local relatives. They never imagined (according to INS) that Elián's family would refuse to return him to his father.

Of course, that's exactly what they refused to do. The next day, November 27, Juan Miguel spoke to American authorities in Cuba and told them he "expected his son to be returned to him immediately." On November 28, he formally petitioned the United States government, demanding his son's return to Cuba.[14]

That's when things went a bit sideways.

The same day Juan Miguel submitted his formal petition, CANF released a poster of Elián portraying him as a "child victim" of Fidel Castro and the Cuban regime. The Miami Cuban exile community rallied to his side. This was a cause they could get behind.

And get behind it they did. With gusto. All the passions of the exile community and their decades-long battle with communist Cuba seemingly now coalesced around a scared child, still grieving the loss of his mother.

Demonstrations in support of keeping Elián in the United States occurred daily throughout Little Havana and other Miami neighborhoods. One sign at one of the protests read (in Spanish), "3 Kings, 3 Children—Moses, Jesus & Elián."[15]

Others claimed that the Virgin Mary herself had weighed in on the situation. The first (yes, there were several) sighting of Mary was in the window of the TotalBank in Little Havana (NW Twenty-Seventh Avenue), just a few blocks from where Elián was staying. There was even one appearance of the Virgin in a mirror inside the home itself.[16]

To the outside observer, the explosion seemed illogical: Why was this one kid such a big deal?

Elián González struck a nerve in Miami like almost nothing else in the last fifty years. All over the city, decades-long friendships were severed or seriously shaken: water coolers and break rooms were divided, and shouting matches were common. This was a place with thousands who had made a similar voyage to flee repression, full of people with firsthand knowledge of a life that made Elian's mother take such a dangerous risk on the open sea. To them, the idea of sending a child back to live under such a system was simply unthinkable. It wasn't about whether the father was sincere; he was largely immaterial. To many in Miami, the question was "How can we send a child from a place that provides endless opportunities back to a system that will deny him some of the most basic freedoms?"

Keep in mind, many of these people were sent unaccompanied by their parents precisely because of the belief that the opportunities the United States offered were more important than either parent. And their lives had been proof of that belief. There were concerns that Elián would be forced to live a life where he was unable to speak or think freely—like everyone that was left on the island.

Fidel Castro, never missing an opportunity to stick it to the Miami exile community, made the Elián González affair his pet project. Elián's hometown of Cárdenas got an extreme makeover. "The entire block on Cossio Street where Elián lived was completely repainted, as was his schoolhouse. Even a hole in his desk had been repaired."[17]

And to the (non-Cuban) American public, Juan Miguel came across as a good dad, and a solid man.

On the other hand . . .

As we've discussed many times already, the success story that is the Cuban American exile community is extraordinary. There are Cuban American senators and members of Congress, CEOs, American military commanders, local and state politicians, and pillars of the community. This is the legacy of the majority of the Cuban exile community.

But not the Miami family of Elián González:

- Two of the family members had long-running battles with alcoholism. Both had multiple drunk-driving convictions, and had had their licenses suspended, multiple times.

- Luis and José Cid, who were frequently seen in the house, had significant criminal records. José had been arrested more than five times since 1986. And not just for petty crimes. He received felony charges, including robbery with force and grand theft, and had been sentenced to two years' probation for burglary. Luis was arrested in September 1999 for the assault and robbery of a tourist in Little Havana. In 1994, he had been sentenced to six months' probation for carrying a concealed weapon, and his ex-wife filed a restraining order against him, claiming domestic violence. The year before the Elián saga, 1998, he was arrested (again) for firearms possession and for prowling.[18]

Fidel, always a public-relations savant, recognized this as an opportunity. Much like in years past when the government decided a cause was worth bringing attention to, there were huge demonstrations in Cuba clamoring for Elián's return. And it seemed to have been effective. Not only did an overwhelming majority of Americans (outside Miami) support the immediate return of Elián to his father, but a Gallup poll taken at the time showed that a whopping 70 percent of Americans now supported lifting the embargo on Cuba, with only 28 percent opposed.[19]

The Elián González saga came to a head on April 22, 2000, when a team of federal agents dressed in full tactical gear pulled up outside the home of Lázaro González in four nondescript white vans with blacked-out windows. Six Border Patrol agents and a female INS officer knocked on the door and demanded entry. After thirty seconds, they breached the door and rushed inside. Other law enforcement officers controlled the crowd outside with pepper spray. Photojournalist Alan Diaz then took one of the most famous pictures in history, which won him a Pulitzer Prize and sealed the fate of the presidential aspirations of Al Gore (more on this in a moment).

Criticism of the raid, mainly based on this picture, was swift and pronounced. Why in the world did the Border Patrol think it needed military force to grab a five-year-old? It seemed like overkill.

But the government argued it was necessary, especially considering that armed and militant anti-Castro groups were entrenched around the house. Mario Miranda, a former bodyguard of Jorge Mas Canosa who frequently visited the home, carried a pistol strapped to his ankle. Five members of Alpha 66, including three men the FBI suspected were behind an attack in 1995 on a hotel in Cuba, were seen at the home and mingling with the crowd of demonstrators outside. All five had publicly expressed their willingness to resort to violence in the case of a raid. Finally, fifteen to twenty supporters of the González family had moved into the house behind them. This included "seven identified convicted felons with records for armed robbery, burglary, firearms charges and assault as well as five bodyguards for the González family, who had concealed weapons permits."[20]

The event was deeply personal to so many in Miami, since Elián's fate could so easily have been their own. And sadly, many of the concerns voiced back in 2000 regarding Elián's future have come to pass. The father was rewarded with an appointment to the National Assembly, which tainted the narrative that the Cuban government wasn't involved in a family matter. The concern that Elián would be brainwashed and/or become a political pawn? Well, let's just say there was only one little boy in Cuba who had very special appearances from a very special autocratic ruler at a number of his birthday parties. And the unique treatment seems to have had its desired effect. In a 2013 interview, Elián stated, "I don't profess to have any religion, but if I did my God would be Fidel Castro."[21] He was recently nominated to serve in the National Assembly, a one-party body that is largely a rubber stamp for the Cuban Communist Party.

There is perhaps no story (or person) that personifies the ideological struggle of the Cold War more than Elián. It was a seminal moment that had significant impacts on both Cuba and the United States. It's also a story that's still being written: Elián's place in history may prove more consequential. And it's hard to envision this story taking place anywhere other than the last outpost of the Cold War.

The raid itself came at a problematic time for the Democratic Party—right in the midst of the 2000 presidential election. While President Clinton might never want to hear the name Elián González again, it would be no surprise if Vice President Al Gore sees him in his nightmares. Although Gore split with Clinton's decision for the raid (he called for the matter to be settled in family court), he was tarnished by his proximity to the White House.

Why did it matter? In 1996, Bill Clinton carried 27 percent of the Cuban American vote, and an estimated 35 percent of the Cuban American vote in Florida. While that might not sound like a lot, it was significantly better than how Jimmy Carter did in 1980 (15 percent) and Michael Dukakis did in 1988 (13 percent). In 2000, however, George W. Bush won 82 percent of the Cuban American vote, and earned *fifty thousand* more Cuban American votes than Bob Dole did in 1996.

Fifty thousand. Al Gore lost the 2000 presidency by 537 votes.

José Basulto weighed in on the election: "It's time for pay back. Not just for those of us activists, but also for many who were watching at home. To them it was personal."[22]

13

Schrödinger's Castro

Black Friday

Thanksgiving in Miami, 2016. It was a warm one, with people outside frying their turkeys or roasting *lechón* under palm trees. Families welcomed back members living elsewhere, happily getting ready for a weekend together. As with all families and all Thanksgiving gatherings, there are always topics best left untouched. This year in particular had people dreading the week-end: one of the most contentious and divisive elections in modern history was still fresh on everyone's minds. There was an absolute deluge of "How to Survive Thanksgiving" articles online and in newspapers working to preemptively broker peace in homes across America, recommending how to navigate (or avoid) talking politics throughout the weekend. And while in 2016 open discussions about a reality-TV-star-turned-president or Hillary Clinton's emails were new entrants into the "do not bring up" category for many Miami households, there was one individual who had topped that Thanksgiving list for years: el Barbudo himself, Fidel Castro. But 2016 would be very, very different.

Fake News on Radio Bemba

That's not to say that Fidel wasn't usually a topic of conversation for most of the year. There are a constellation of radio stations in Miami that exist largely to discuss him, usually in loud and bombastic conversation. Cuban slang is one of the more colorful uses of language anywhere, and the term for the "rumor mill" is Radio Bemba, or "Lips Radio": everyone's mouths become transmitters. There were few subjects that would activate Radio Bemba more quickly and more vigorously than rumors of Fidel Castro's death. And over the years there had been plenty. Every so often, some nugget of information would be twisted into the possibility of the demise of the dictator. He was virtually always in the public eye, and when he was, he was often rambling for hours on end. Any absence from public view longer than several days would start people asking: Why would he be missing? This would play out over and over again: conjecture that Fidel was gone, disseminated over Radio Bemba, only to be proven false.

For instance, when reports circulated that Castro, the legendary cigar lover, had decided to quit smoking, speculation began about potential health concerns. That decision, combined with his absence from usual early January festivities, got the ball rolling. Word began spreading that he had died, perhaps had been dead since Christmas. One early January, a Miami-based Spanish-language radio station reported rumors that Fidel had died on December 26; a TV station put out a similar broadcast later that day.[1] Close, but literally, no cigar. Just a rumor. The Beard was still alive.

Another rumor reverberated all the way to Washington and across the Atlantic. A broadcast of Radio Reloj, the droning Cuban news station with twenty-four hours of reading, time updates every minute, and the incessant tick-tock of a clock in the background, reported on the death of a Rene Orley Sanchez Castro, describing him as an "outstanding revolutionary comrade" who died "as a result of a sudden disease." According to a State Department official, somewhere a foreign media service garbled the message and thought the report wasn't about just any Castro, but *the* Castro. Miami was electric with people looking for details and confirmation, and the word spread to the capital and European countries that had close relations with Cuba. Nope. Still false.

These were largely sporadic, until Castro got older, and signs were starting to show that his health may be deteriorating. In June 2001, he seemed to almost faint during a live speech. Who knows how many Cubans, forced to stand and listen to his notoriously hours-long discourses did the same—but it had never happened to him. What was equally shocking was that it was on live television, and was one of the first signs of Castro's physical vulnerability that anyone had seen. A few years later, after giving a graduation speech, he misjudged a small step coming down from the podium and fractured his knee. Speculation was beginning to percolate about Castro's physical and mental state.

The first sign that Castro was in significant decline was in July 2006, when he underwent surgery for an intestinal ailment and temporarily ceded power to his brother Raúl. When it was revealed that he had undergone three failed operations and that his prognosis was "very serious," rumors started kicking into overdrive.[2] Some in Miami, upon hearing that Fidel had handed over power to his brother, converged on Calle Ocho thinking that Fidel had died. This one was actually really close: leaked US embassy cables revealed that it was believed that Fidel was on death's doorstep and that his condition was severe. Almost, but no. Radio Bemba reporting: false.

For three weeks in a row in 2007, rumors that Fidel was on his deathbed swirled around Miami, along with speculation that his death was soon to be announced. One Cuban who was asked about the situation revealed just how active the rumor mill had become, reporting that "some people say he's already cremated, and others say they have him preserved in wax somewhere, but nobody really knows anything."[3] He was partially right. Not about Fidel getting the wax treatment. About not knowing anything. Yet again Radio Bemba, proven false, false, and once more, false.

Fidel was, at this point, in serious physical decline.* He required significant medical care and was no longer suited for public life. In February 2008, he formally ceded power to his brother Raúl. Fidel would regularly release musings in *Granma*, the government-controlled newspaper, which he called "Reflections" to keep in the public eye. Of course, without videos or photos, there was speculation that those were ghostwritten anyway. As usual, he was prolific and wrote frequently, often multiple times a week.[4] Then suddenly, they stopped. Over a month had passed without any "Reflections," and two

---

* Discussions involving Castro increasingly saw *el Comandante,* the Revolutionary Commander-in-Chief, being referred to irreverently as *el Coma-Andante,* "the Walking Coma."

presidents that visited the island came and went without seeing him. Could it be . . . ? Hugo Chávez, his latest protégé, added fuel to the fire when he mused on Venezuelan television in the same time frame "that Fidel in uniform, who walked the streets and towns at daybreak, embracing the people, will not return. That will remain a memory."[5] Radio Bemba did its thing: questions swirled, Miami phone lines lit up. Then Argentina's president Cristina Kirchner reported after meeting with Castro: "I was with Fidel about an hour or more. We were chatting and conversing. He looked good."[6] Fidel's demise? *No señor.* False.

Radio Bemba kicked up again in October 2012 when Hugo Chávez was reelected, and there was no word of congratulations from Fidel. It really picked up when a Venezuelan journalist reported that Juanita Castro, Fidel's sister who had been living in exile for decades, was called back to Cuba for "an important family announcement."[7] Castro had last been seen in public in March, when Pope Benedict visited Cuba. His "Reflections" had become as much of a proof of life as anything, and the government-run newspaper had not run one since June. Adding to the uncertainty, *ABC* of Spain published an article citing a Venezuelan doctor who claimed that Castro had suffered a massive embolism and was dying, characterizing his health as "precarious."[8] A few days later, Castro penned his latest "Reflection" in response. It was entitled "Fidel Is Dying," a mocking retort to the *ABC* article, and, showing a clear understanding of exactly what his column had become, included some actual "proof of life" pictures of him holding the latest *Granma* newspaper.[9] The rumor, yet again, was false.

At this point, there was a significant level of "rumor fatigue," and skepticism grew with each false report. Just as importantly, Castro had retired and was pretty much a nonfactor in the developments of the day. The pictures of Fidel submitted as his proof of existence were of him outdoors in a straw hat, a red-and-gray plaid shirt, and a wispy gray beard. He looked more like a retired farmhand than a dictator who had held a country hostage for decades. People were tired of riding the emotional roller coaster of rumors. Someday, that rumor would *have* to be true.

After surviving their respective political minefields at their family Thanksgiving tables and morning-after digestive woes, Miamians were enjoying the long 2016 weekend: shopping the big deals of the day, at home with family, or out catching up with friends. Countless revelers, taking advantage of the warm weather and the long weekend, headed out after dark to take in the legendary nightlife. Across the Florida Straits, Cuban television cut to the octogenarian Raúl Castro in his usual military uniform. He was seated on a leather chair in a room with dark wood paneling, the wall behind him displaying portraits of heroes of Cuban independence—José Martí's taking center stage—and framed black-and-white pictures of past exploits and friends. The entire scene, like the Revolution he now led and the entire island of Cuba itself, seemed trapped in time. Raúl read directly from a piece of paper, like newsmen did in the days before teleprompters: "With deep sadness, I regret to inform our people, friends from our America and the world, that today, November 25, 2016, at 10:29 p.m., the Commander in Chief of the Cuban Revolution Fidel Castro Ruz passed away." He ended the brief broadcast with "Hasta la Victoria Siempre!" or "Ever Onward to Victory!"—a typical revolutionary slogan. But it was different this time. It had never been uttered in a world without Fidel Castro.

Messages from world leaders began pouring in. Some gushed over him: Xi Jinping of China highlighted his "immortal contributions to the development of socialism around the world." Lula of Brazil hailed him as the "greatest of all Latin Americans." The Guyanese prime minister called him "an international gift to humanity." Hezbollah put out a release calling Castro "a historic symbol whose life was a lighthouse to all revolutionaries around the world." Not many leaders inspire messages from both Hezbollah and the pope, but Fidel Castro did: Pope Francis, who met with Castro during a visit to Cuba in 2015, sent a telegram to Raúl expressing "my condolences to your excellency and your family." In a break from usual protocol, he signed it himself. Former president Obama was measured in his response, stating in calculatedly broad terms that "history will record and judge the enormous impact of this singular figure on the people and world around him." President Trump was characteristically eloquent and stayed well below his 140-character limit: "Fidel Castro is dead!"[10]

Beautiful Madness

Miami simply exploded with joy. Little Havana was overrun with three generations of people whose lives had been irreparably changed by this one person, the one central to the loss so many felt: loss of home, of country, of basic rights. Cuban and American flags were everywhere. Pots and pans were banged with wooden spoons in a quintessentially Miami form of celebration. There were spontaneous renditions of the Cuban national anthem. Couples dancing salsa in the streets. Champagne flowing freely, fireworks lighting up the night sky. All the years of longing for what was left behind, of toil to start anew, of honoring those who made sacrifices so they could live in a place where freedom reigned, all of it came thundering out in a chaotic expression of celebration and hope. Some were so determined not to miss the moment that they showed up in pajamas. "Beautiful madness," one reveler explained. A son of an exiled mother was still incredulous. "I find it hard to believe," he said in the midst of the jubilant crowd. "We've been out here so many times when it wasn't true—and this time it is."[11] It was no longer rumor. Finally, it was fact.

Many were surprised by the emotions such a long-awaited day brought about. It was impossible to overlook the privilege of seeing that moment, and a great number of them shed tears for loved ones who never got to see that day or feel what it was like to live in a world with no Fidel. Others were ambivalent about the real impact of Fidel's passing: yes, he was gone, but the damage to their lives and their country had been done.

The death of Fidel Castro was, for decades, the moment that those in Miami hoping for a free Cuba were waiting for: the one that would be the spark that would eventually bring this most stubborn and enduring Cold War chapter to an end.

But then a shocking thing happened: absolutely nothing.

Fidel was a historic figure, one who for better or worse had played an overwhelmingly significant role in the events of the last sixty years. The story of the Cold War, and the story of Miami, could not be told without him. But by the time of his death, he had faded out of the public forum that he had lived in for so long.

In Cuba, nothing had changed. Fidel hadn't been in power for a number of years. The succession had already taken place. During one of the false alarms regarding Fidel's mortality, a Cuban on the island was asked what he thought. His answer was prescient and held true once the real thing happened: "He could be alive or he could be dead, but nobody knows and I really don't know how much difference it would make, because Fidel has raised us with one system. It's all we know, and even if he's gone the system remains."[12] The system did remain, and does to this day. Privation of basic human rights is still a part of daily life, and little has changed on the island.

Castro's death changed little in terms of his influence upon the region. His physical presence proved immaterial. He had spent a lifetime building a significant legacy, one that is currently entrenched in Latin America and elsewhere. Upon learning of his death, then Bolivian president Evo Morales tweeted that Castro was "the leader that taught us to fight for the sovereignty of the state and the dignity of the peoples of the world."[13] That lesson still permeates the political landscape of the hemisphere. Venezuela and Nicaragua are currently governed by leaders who see Castro as a philosophical and political inspiration. Brazilian President Lula da Silva considered him like an older brother and "always a voice of struggle and hope."[14] While communism is largely passé, *Fidelismo* remains a force to be reckoned with.

His death didn't change US policy either. Cuba was still run by a Castro, and the regime had been functioning without Fidel at its helm for a number of years. Representative Ileana Ros-Lehtinen, who left Cuba as a child and paved the way for Cuban Americans in Congress, was clear: "The death of a dictator will not usher a new wave of change because the rulers of Cuba, whether it's Fidel, Raúl, whatever names you give them, they just rule over Cuba with an iron fist."[15] Cuba is no longer run by a Castro, with President Díaz-Canel officially taking the reins in October 2019, but the system remains in place. As a result, US policy has largely done the same.

And so, Fidel Castro passed from the world stage, exactly sixty-one years to the day after embarking on the *Granma*, launching an expedition that would change the fate of a nation, and that would alter the lives of millions. It was also seventeen years to the day that a small boy named Elián González was rescued from the sea.

There was one final irony. The dictator who railed for decades against the evils of the *yanqui* capitalist system died on the one day on the American calendar set aside for maximum participation in that system—perhaps its purest expression:

Black Friday.

14

A Wretched Hive of Scum and Villainy

Nearly forty years ago, the *New York Times* called Miami the "New Casablanca," because it was a "city of international intrigue where foreign agents and competing ideological, political, criminal and industrial spies are as commonplace as palm trees and swimsuits."[1]

We see what they are getting at with the Casablanca reference. It makes some sense. But in the last decade (or so), we think Miami has looked less like Rick's Café and far more like the Mos Eisley cantina from the *Star Wars* universe.

Need to hide or launder some dirty money? We can help you with that.

Have some illicit cargo you need shipped to some far-off, exotic location without catching the attention of pesky law enforcement? We have lots of experience.

Want to start a coup or assassinate an uncooperative foreign leader? Step right up! We've got what you need.

Like rubbing elbows with spooks from the United States, Cuba, Russia, China, Venezuela, Israel, and, well, everywhere else? Have we got a deal for you!

¡Bienvenidos a Miami!

All we are missing is Greedo and blue milk.

Tap, Tap. "Is This Thing Even On?"

During the middle of George W. Bush's second term, the administration approved a $10 million appropriation for a system to broadcast TV Martí into Cuba. Replacing the infamous "Fat Albert, the limp blimp," which was destroyed by Hurricane Dennis in 2005, a 1960s-era turboprop twin-engine plane christened *Aero Martí* started beaming a signal into Cuba from twenty thousand feet over the Florida Straits. Four hours a day, six days a week. The idea was to get the signal higher (the blimp could only rise to ten thousand feet) so that it would be harder for the Cuban government to jam it.

Unfortunately, it didn't work. According to the *New York Times*, many Cubans still just saw snowy interference on the channels supposedly carrying the broadcast. Even if it came in perfectly clear, many Cubans understood that it was American propaganda. Although some Cubans *did want* to see programming from Miami, they were looking for Spanish-language *telenovelas*, not TV Martí.

Because Cuban exiles in Miami did most of the writing, acting, and directing for TV Martí programs, the episodes could be rather on the nose. From the same *Times* article, one TV Martí show, called *Office of the Chief*, depicted an actor playing Raúl Castro saying that when his brother Fidel died, he would wrap him in the writings of Karl Marx, then lie him in state on Havana's seaside boulevard.

Maybe it's funnier when you see it?

One communications professor at Penn State, who studies the effectiveness of Radio and TV Martí, said this about the program: "It's a litmus test for support for a certain policy on Cuba. Few right-minded politicians or government bureaucrats are willing to take that on. So essentially we've created a pork-barrel patronage system and the policy is hands-off."

José Basulto, the founder of Brothers to the Rescue and not exactly a member of the left-wing pro-Castro intelligentsia, is a strong critic of Radio and TV Martí, which he argues was just a graft for Miami exiles. "The joke goes on," according to Basulto. "They pay individuals who are instrumental in making the lives of United States politicians easier come election time."

Miami Representative Ileana Ros-Lehtinen disagreed. She was far more bullish on the prospects of TV and Radio Martí. She believed the new plane would pay real dividends: "The US has received reports from Havana and

Matanzas that it is being seen every day, and it's getting better as the equipment is being fine-tuned."

The *New York Times* sardonically responded, "The government, however, has no hard evidence of the station's popularity."

In 2005, the International Broadcasting Bureau commissioned a telephone survey of Cubans on whether they'd seen TV Martí in the past year. Of the 1,589 who responded, only thirteen answered in the affirmative. Nine in ten Cubans had never even *heard* of it.

Joe O'Connell, a spokesperson for the IBB, argued that the *real* number was probably higher. Many Cubans were probably afraid to admit they watch TV Martí.[2]

But it didn't matter anyway, because in 2013 the budget for the Office of Cuba Broadcasting was slashed, along with many other government programs during the period of sequestration. After $32 million spent from 2006 to 2013 beaming a signal into Cuba that very few people saw, *Aero Martí* would be grounded.

But not eliminated.

Aero Martí didn't have enough money to fly—the dollars weren't there for fuel, maintenance, pilots, etc. But that didn't mean the plane had to go away. The US government could just pay the costs to keep it in storage, in case the funding is granted sometime in the future to fly it again.

So the United States government, through the Office of Cuba Broadcasting, paid $79,500 a year for the plane *not* to fly.[3] It just sat there, gathering dust, a symbol of the futility of the program.*

Not that any subsequent methods of inserting US-friendly messaging have been more successful.

In 2011, TV Martí inaugurated a program, known as Piramideo (Pyramid), which sent unsolicited text messages to cell phones in Cuba. The messages themselves included Major League Baseball scores, links to join internet chat rooms, and a summation of TV Martí's news of the day. In theory, this would get information past the radio and television jamming and straight to the Cuban people. The problems with this plan, however, were clear from the start.

First, fewer than one in ten Cubans had access to cell phones, so the coverage—while better than the numbers TV Martí itself was getting—was

---

* It was finally killed for good in 2015.

not exactly universal. Second, those who *did* have cell phones tended to live in Havana and were of a much higher socioeconomic subsection of the population. Understandably, the people doing much better under the Cuban regime were less likely to be swayed by anti-Castro messaging. Not really the best way to foment counterrevolutionary sentiment among the masses. Finally, what the US government was doing was sending spam.* As the *Los Angeles Times* noted, "Spam is (not) the way to win the hearts and minds of Cubans."[4]

Perhaps the Cuban population could get their pro-America messaging the same way the rest of us get our news in the twenty-first century—the internet. Sounds logical, but Cuba has one of the lowest internet connection rates in all of Latin America. Even when Cubans can get online, the government controls what they see. The Ministry of Informatics and Communications is the gateway to access, while the Communist Party itself regulates and censors the domestic mass media.

But what if you could find a way around this? For two years, from fiscal years 2013 to 2015, the Office of Cuba Broadcasting hatched a plan to smuggle small, two-way satellite internet kits, known as Broadband Global Area Networks, or BGANs, into Cuba.† This would allow Cubans uncensored access to the internet through a link with commercial satellites, including Radio and TV Martí's digital component, martinoticias.com.

But the program was suspended in 2015 due to the negotiations between the Obama administration and the Cuban government over the reestablishment of full diplomatic relations. The Cubans, as a condition for normalization, called for an end to the entire Radio and TV Martí program. As we know, politically this ask was a nonstarter. Instead, according to "anonymous sources" within the administration and State Department, the BGAN program was the sacrificial lamb.

However, the OCB had a different excuse for the cancellation. Citing the high costs of the project, both for the hardware itself and the bandwidth costs of the satellite internet, the Office of Cuban Broadcasting claimed they no longer believed the program was "cost effective." Especially considering how

---

* Maybe it would work better if they sent robocalls for term life insurance. Or ones telling them their social security numbers had been stolen.
† This is the same device that got USAID subcontractor Alan Gross arrested in Havana in 2009.

the internet access was primarily being used in Cuba. According to André Mendes, who had been the interim director of the OCB at the time, some Cubans had been using the American-tax-dollar-funded internet access to do a very American thing—look at pornography.* Mendes remarked, "We are not in the business to give access to porn."[5] Perhaps not. But wasn't the whole point of the OCB, Radio and TV Martí, and the like, to bring a bit of America into Cuban homes, and Cuban hearts?

But what about social media? Surely that could be a vector for bringing content into Cuba, couldn't it?

The United States government has tried now on at least two occasions to use social media to get their message to the Cuban people. In 2014, USAID tried to create a fake "Cuban Twitter" platform called ZunZuneo. The intent was to push anti-Castro messaging through the service. It didn't work.[6]

The fiscal year 2019 Congressional Budget Justification for the Office of Cuba Broadcasting provides insights into a more comprehensive plan. In a subsection titled, "Dramatic Shift Within Digital to a Social Media 1st Strategy," the OCB explains that Cuba's censorship of the internet has forced OCB to shift their digital strategy "into a social media consistent with the metrics that place YouTube, Google, and Facebook among the most visited sites in Cuba." With the use of new technology, the OCB could stream its programming via Facebook Live, providing OCB "with an additional efficient and cost effective distribution outlet" for both Radio and TV Martí.

The next paragraph in the justification stands out:

In FY2018, OCB is establishing on island digital teams to create non-branded local Facebook accounts to disseminate information. Native pages increase the chances of appearing on Cuban Facebook users [sic] newsfeeds. The same strategy will be replicated on other preferred social media networks.[7]

So what does this mean? It means that the OCB is creating fake Facebook accounts to work their way around the Cuban censors. "Non-branded" and "native pages" means that, instead of having a Facebook account from the US

---

* Which is illegal in Cuba.

government, it would look like it was "Juan from Havana" posting links to cool content ("Check this out!") like TV Martí programming.

If it sounds familiar, that's because it is. The Russian Internet Research Agency did the same thing before the 2016 elections. This wasn't on the level of "Bob from Kansas" sharing an article about Hillary Clinton eating babies for brunch, and there's an argument to be made that there's a marked difference between evading state control of information and actively providing misinformation to try to influence a democratic process. But it was an attempt to use the anonymity the internet provides to foment political change.

So why does the US government keep doing this? Over and over, only to fail to gain traction with any of their media programs? It's easy to dismiss these projects as congressional pork-barrel schemes, as José Basulto does. To be sure, there is an element of pork here. Maybe a lot.

Yet some of the support for these efforts stems from the idea that access to information is a right—much in the same way as Radio Free Europe. For those who live under governments that censor information that runs contrary to the state, freedom to outside information can be very powerful. But it isn't easy, and even ardent supporters of these programs understood that they had little chance of success. There's an element of hope involved: a hope that this next time might be different. This next program might be the straw that breaks the regime's back.

History has proved them wrong.

So far.

Money, Money, and More Money

Miami has a long history of corrupt politicians and city officials. Books have been written about this, and it's mostly a local politics story, so we will skip a lot of that. But some of these cases have serious geopolitical consequences. In a single two-month span from late 2022 to early 2023, there were two news stories that shocked even those hardened by decades of experience studying Miami corruption. Both of them involving one of the US government's main adversarial relationships in the Western Hemisphere: Venezuela.*

---

* "Enemy" is too strong a word. But we certainly aren't in diplomatic lockstep.

In December 2022, former US congressman David Rivera was arrested and charged with money laundering and representing a foreign government without registering. Rivera, who represented Miami in Congress from 2011 to 2013, was hit with an eight-count indictment, alleging he was "part of a conspiracy to lobby on behalf of Venezuela to lower tensions with the US, resolve a legal dispute with a US oil company and end US sanctions against the South American nation—all without registering as a foreign agent."

Now, this might not sound like much. It certainly isn't as nefarious as stealing nuclear secrets or some other kind of espionage intrigue. And one could even argue that perhaps Rivera didn't know that what he was doing was wrong.

But coded chat and text messages sent by Rivera seem to show he was fully aware of how shady he was being. In these messages, he referred to Venezuelan president Nicolás Maduro as the "bus driver," an unnamed US congressman as "Sombrero," and millions of American dollars as "melons."[8]

Speaking of melons, in January 2023, the former chief judge of the highest court in Venezuela was indicted in Miami federal court for money laundering and granting legal favors in exchange for bribes. Maikel Moreno, from 2017 to 2022 the president of the Supreme Tribunal of Justice,* allegedly took $10 million in bribes from a slew of sleazy white-collar criminals. You might think someone with his knowledge of the criminal justice system would be better at crime, but not in this case. Although Moreno once reported that he made only $12,000 a year from his job on the court, somehow he found a way to deposit about $3 million into his Miami Bank of America account from 2012 to 2016. He also spent $1 million on private jets and pilots to whisk him away from Venezuela to Miami, $600,000 in credit card purchases at local Miami-area luxury goods stores, and even $50,000 at a luxury repair shop† in the Miami suburb of Aventura.[9]

Running dirty money through the wash-and-rinse cycle that is Miami real estate and luxury items is not new, of course. But most of the previous national groups who did it, even the cartels, were talented amateurs. Maybe the cartels were in Low-A ball. If you want the guys who play in the big leagues, you need to look to the quirky Miami neighborhood of Sunny Isles Beach, now nicknamed "Little Moscow."

---

* So he was essentially the Chief Justice of the Venezuelan Supreme Court.
† That's $50K to *repair* a watch.

Sunny Isles Beach is a one-and-a-half-mile strip of land that sits between the Atlantic on its east and the Intracoastal Waterway on its west. It's give or take about thirty minutes or so from downtown Miami. United States census data shows that the zip code that includes Sunny Isles Beach is home to an estimated 1,200 Russian-born residents, among the most for any one zip code in the US.

Experts believe that illicit financing has helped the Russians to snatch up much of this real estate. They estimate that Russia's elite have more than $1 trillion in offshore accounts, which they say is "disproportionally held in South Florida property."[10] The Russians used the 2008 recession to take advantage of falling prices in Miami. They "scooped up condos, sometimes dozens at a time, with few questions asked."[11] This continues to this day.

And they did this predominantly with cash. According to the Miami Association of Realtors, cash real-estate deals accounted for 53 percent of all Miami-Dade home sales in 2015, more than double the national average, and *90 percent* of all new construction sales.[12] The rich move money through off-shore shell companies—which in many cases do not require them to identify themselves as the buyer. The release of the so-called Panama Papers in 2016 demonstrated how easy it was to set up one of these companies. There are a handful of states and several foreign nations that make the process simple and pain-free. In Delaware, for example, setting up a shell company "is easier than getting a library card, or a gym membership, or credit card."*

Just to highlight how shady this can be, a company by the name of Rice Island Inc. that bought up at least one Miami property is an anonymous company registered in the Marshall Islands—the Pacific island nation allows shell companies to be registered there for a fee. In Florida public records, Rice Island Inc. lists their Miami address as 800 Brickell Avenue, floor 23.

The problem? 800 Brickell Avenue only has sixteen floors.[13]

The Russian elite have used this process to invest in Miami, and in partic-ular, in properties owned by former US president Donald Trump.† According to a Reuters review, at least sixty-three people with Russian passports or home addresses had bought at least $98.4 million worth of property in seven differ-ent Trump-branded luxury condo towers in the Miami area. And it's likely

---

* Cash deals are generally unregulated. Mortgage-based home purchases have strict reporting requirements.
† We are casting no aspersions. We are just telling it like it is.

this is a major undercount. The analysis found that about one-third (at least 703) of the owners of the more than two thousand units in the seven Trump buildings are owned by limited liability companies (shell companies), which (as we now know) have the ability to hide the true identity of the owner.[14]
Some of the identified owners of these properties include:

- Anatoly Golubchik and Michael Sall, members of a Russian-American organized crime group convicted in the US for their role in an illegal high-stakes sports-betting ring. The operation was focused almost exclusively on Russian and former-Soviet oligarchs. One of the leaders of their operation was Alimzhan Tokhtakhounov, a Russian accused of rigging events at the 2002 Winter Olympics in Salt Lake City. Golubchik and Sall owned two homes in Trump Towers valued at $2.3 million.[15]
- Alexander Yuzvik, who bought unit 3901 of Trump Palace in Sunny Isles for $1.3 million in 2010. From 2013 to 2016, Yurvik was a senior executive at a state-owned Russian company called Spetstroi. Spetstroi is a construction company that worked projects at the Moscow training academy for the FSB (one of the successor agencies to the KGB) and in the administration building of the general staff of the GRU, Russian military intelligence.[16]
- Dmitry Rybolovlev, the Russian billionaire who bought a Miami-area mansion from Trump in 2008 for $60 million *more* than the asking price.[17]
- Pavel Uglanov, a Russian businessman who served as a deputy minister for industry and energy in central Russia from 2010 to 2011. He ran for local government in 2011 as a member of Vladimir Putin's United Russia party.[18]
- Lev Parnas and Igor Fruman, while not Russian, have deep Russian ties. Both associates of Rudy Giuliani, they were prosecuted for playing key roles in efforts to try to find information in Ukraine to use against the campaign of Joe Biden in 2020 (which led to Donald Trump's impeachment*).[19]

---

* The first one, to be clear.

This Russian real-estate boom was fantastic for the Miami construction industry and for local tax revenue, but it hammered local residents who wanted to live the American Dream and own a home. Foreign investment drove values through the roof, and priced out most working-, middle-, and even upper-middle-class families. Even when the local buyer had a strong financial footing, anyone trying to buy a house in Miami with a mortgage was outcompeted by cash buyers who were willing to pay far over the listing price. The result? Two-thirds of Miamians rent their homes—a number higher than *any* other major city in the United States. And even this is tough for most locals. The high housing costs have driven up rent costs. According to the *Miami Herald*, this dynamic has made Miami "the least affordable city for renters in the country."[20]

You can't buy and you can't rent. Thanks, Russia.

And then there's the Russian birth tourists.

The what, you say?

Russian birth tourists.

Apparently, having a baby in Miami is a major symbol of status in Moscow. NBC News ran a report on this in 2018. They showed that wealthier Russians hire travel agencies that offer "birth-tourism packages" that can cost anywhere from $50,000 to $100,000. Why do this? Well, it gives the child automatic US citizenship. Also, according to immigration law, once the child turns twenty-one they can sponsor their parents for a green card.

The *Daily Beast* added, "For $84,000, expectant Russian mothers can get an apartment in a Trump Tower with a gold-tiled bathtub and chauffeured Mercedes-Benz."[21]

Not a bad deal, if you've got that kind of cash lying around (which they do).

The issue, as some in the US national security establishment see it, is that these children will be born in the US, but then go back to Russia. They will be raised in a Russian society, under Russian rule of law, and Russian ideologies—and Russian allegiances. Maybe they will join the Russian military, or even the Russian intelligence services.

And they will be US citizens, already with an American passport.

Of course, there's no way to tell if these kids, actual "anchor babies," will become spies for the enemy. But we can't imagine the FBI (and other American intelligence agencies responsible for counterintelligence) can be too happy about this development. They won't even need to steal the identity of some dead child. They'll already have the (legally acquired) proper documentation to live and work in the United States. As Yakov Smirnoff would say, "What a country!"

Rent-a-Coup

As the two authors of this book set out to decide on the content it would include, we thought we'd have it easy. The rich history of Miami's role in the Cold War (and beyond) gave us all the material we would ever need (and then some). We *thought* we had all we would use, but then an annoying thing started to happen: every time we thought we were done, some other major Miami-related event would be reported in the news.

There was the Russian spy caught in Miami, or Vladimir Putin calling Russians living in Miami foie-gras-and-oyster-eating traitors to the Motherland, or changes in Cuban politics, or changes in American policy toward Cuba. It was hard to keep up.[22]

But there were two events that occurred while we were prepping this book that, at first, did not seem immediately related to Miami, but that we expected *would* be before too long. The first was the attempted "coup" in Venezuela in the summer of 2020. The second, the assassination of the Haitian president in the summer of 2021. In both cases, one of the authors of this book texted the other, saying: "Ten bucks says this thing was planned in Miami."

That is a sucker's bet. Of *course* they were planned in Miami.

The Haitian assassination is not, by any means, a fun story. People died. The Haitian government has not recovered. The citizens of Haiti are suffering every day. It's not something we are going to make light of. The fact is two dozen retired members of Colombian special forces, who had been hired as contractors by a Miami-based private security firm, may have been complicit in the assassination of Haitian president Jovenel Moïse. The firm, CTU Security (which stands for Counter Terrorist Unit), based in the Miami suburb of Doral, was tasked with providing protection for the Haitian leader. Instead, it has been alleged, the Colombians turned on their protectee, and joined with Haitian forces in storming the presidential residence in an operation that resulted in the president's death.

But did CTU know of the revised plans? Were they complicit in the killing? Probably. At least it seems so.

According to the US Department of Justice, Haitian police, and Colombian intelligence, CTU was laden with massive debt (evictions, bad checks, lawsuits). Apparently they discovered the presidential residence was flush with cash—between $45 million and $53 million was stashed inside the president's home. A Colombian source told the *Miami Herald*, "We believe they were going for the money."

One of the managers of CTU Security, Antonio Intriago, who lived in Miami, traveled to Haiti in the weeks before the attack and "met with some of the key Haitian suspects." Another Miami-area resident, a financier named Walter Veintemilla, funded the recruitment of the Colombian special-ops soldiers/mercenaries. According to Haitian police, the CTU leadership told the Colombian soldiers that Veintemilla's company had secured billions in investments that would be brought into Haiti once a new government was in place.

It strains the limits of credulity to suggest CTU was unaware of the plot.[23]

Haiti has been dealt such a bad hand over the years. Poverty, corruption, famine, natural disasters, foreign meddling, armed gangs, and now this. It's such a sad story.

The attempted "coup" against Venezuela, though, is something entirely different. It's ridiculous. It might even be funny.

One commentator called it the "Bay of Piglets." Another quipped, "It made the Bay of Pigs look like D-Day."[24]

It was named Operation Gideon, and it was planned in meetings across Miami. In the back of limousines, in restaurants around the city, and even apparently on the twelfth fairway of the Red Course of the Trump Doral golf course.[25]

The man in charge of Operation Gideon was Jordan Goudreau, a former Green Beret Sergeant First Class who was awarded three Bronze Stars for valor during service in Iraq and Afghanistan. Once out of the military in 2016, he worked security for the presidential campaign of Donald Trump and later worked in Puerto Rico providing security for the humanitarian effort after Hurricanes Irma and Maria. Then he moved to Miami, and in 2018 founded a private security firm, Silvercorp USA.

In February 2019, Goudreau was hired to provide security for a benefit concert sponsored by gajillionaire Richard Branson in Colombia. The concert was right on the border of Venezuela, and its purpose was to try to force Venezuelan president Nicolás Maduro to allow humanitarian aid into Venezuela. The Venezuelan economy was in dire straits, and violence and hunger had driven millions into Colombia. Goudreau saw the situation in Venezuela and thought he might be able to do something about it. Or he saw dollar signs. Or maybe both.

Goudreau went back to Colombia in July, and met with General Cliver Alcalá, a former top officer in Hugo Chávez's military, but who had a falling-out with Chávez's successor, Maduro, and went into exile. While in Colombia, Alcalá set up a training camp to prepare a force to oust Maduro. According to a source, Goudreau and Alcalá discussed a plan to topple the Venezuelan president, "a tactical operation to capture the big players in Venezuela who would be handed over to the United States. Juan Guaidó [an opposition leader][26] would assume the mandate as interim president, leading free elections in Venezuela."[27]

Goudreau took responsibility for the finances, and later meetings were held in Miami, where Guaidó's "presidential commission" would explore secret ways to depose Maduro. The plan Goudreau, Alcalá, and crew eventually landed on, Operation Gideon, called for an infiltration of Venezuela at the coastal town of Macuto, roughly an hour from Caracas. One hundred Venezuelan exiles, with American ex-military-turned-private-contractor help, would incite a popular rebellion against the government.[28]

Goudreau and the Venezuelan rebels signed a contract for his services on October 16, 2019. According to the contract, Goudreau would receive $1.5 million up front as a retainer, and then $200 million after the job was done.[29]

This sounds a bit like the Bay of Pigs plan, doesn't it? It worked out great the first time.

Once they landed, the force would spend a few days in safe houses before moving to Caracas. Once there, they would stay hidden for a few more days before they began to hit their targets—the presidential Palace of Miraflores, the headquarters of Venezuela's intelligence service (SEBIN), and military jails (to free prisoners to add to their numbers). Eventually they would capture Maduro and his top lieutenants.

That's a lot of moving parts. A plan this complicated is destined to fail. And, of course, it did.

More than a month before the launch of the operation, it became clear the security for the mission was blown—Diosdado Cabello, Maduro's second-in-command, announced on Venezuelan television that the regime knew of the training camps in Colombia and named the specific people involved in the plan, including the Americans. Well, so much for that. Time to cancel the mission now, right?

Right?

Again, of course not. Even though the operation was compromised, on Friday, May 1, 2020, two boats left Colombia for Venezuela. Fifty-eight fighters were aboard . . . but only ten rifles. Within an hour of departure, one of the engines had failed.

Surely the mission would be scrapped now? But no, they still kept going.

It took almost two days to get to Macuto, and by the time they arrived, many of the fighters were seasick. Worst of all, the Venezuelan military was there, waiting for them. Eight men died, and most of the rest were captured, including two Americans, Airan Berry and Luke Denman. Goudreau wasn't there for the mission. He was stuck in Miami due to COVID travel restrictions.

He insists the plan would have worked if the timing was better. The original intent was to land at Macuto before dawn on May 3 so that they could move in under the cover of darkness. But the boats were late, likely due to the busted engine.

Instead of thanking his lucky stars he wasn't there that day, Goudreau actually *sued* for breach of contract. On October 30, 2020, a lawsuit was filed on his behalf against Juan José "JJ" Rendón, a political consultant who worked for Juan Guaidó. The suit called for $1.4 million in damages, or what Goudreau thought he was still owed for his stunningly inept operation.

This Is Why We Can't Have Nice Things

On October 2, 2022, Brazilian president Jair Bolsonaro lost his bid for reelection to his political rival and former Brazilian president, Luiz Inácio Lula de Silva. The right-wing Bolsonaro was a bit of a sore loser. Instead of participating in what should have been a peaceful transfer of power to Lula, the defeated president skipped town on December 30, just two days before he would have handed over the presidential sash (which is a big deal in Brazil). According to Bryan Pitts, the assistant director of UCLA's Latin American

Institute, Bolsonaro "really just doesn't like Lula and didn't want to hand the presidential sash over to him at the inauguration."[30]

World leaders were stunned. Brazil was supposed to be a democracy. They hadn't seen a democratically elected president skip his successor's inauguration in . . . well, actually it was only two years.

To make matters worse, Bolsonaro stoked conspiracy theories of widespread corruption and voter fraud, and refused to admit he had been defeated fairly. Whether it was the "deep state," the mainstream media, or the devious Left rigging voting machines, the election was stolen, and not legitimately won.

Despite a thorough investigation into the claim by the Brazilian military, which found no evidence of fraud, on January 8, 2023, thousands of Bolsonaro supporters rioted in Brazil's capital, Brasília, ransacking Brazil's Congress, Supreme Court, presidential offices, and other government buildings—two years almost to the day that a similar event happened here in the United States. More than one thousand people were arrested for their participation in the riot, and in mid-January 2023, the Brazilian Supreme Court approved an investigation into Bolsonaro to discern his involvement in the uprising.

Of course, as we discussed, Bolsonaro wasn't there that day. He wasn't even in the country. He'd taken his presidential plane (for the last time) northward to the land of palm trees, humidity, Zika, sunbaked tourists, and cheap souvenirs.

Ok, yes, this sounds like Brazil. But you know where he went, right?

He went to Florida. And his critics immediately pounced.[31]

Carmen Hertz, member of the Chilean Congress from the Communist Party:

Bolsonaro sheltered in Miami leading the fascist mob of his followers with the complicity of the head of the Federal District in a remake of the assault on the Capitol by Trump and his henchmen. How dangerous the ultra-right is for democracy and the lives of the citizens!

Andreína Chávez Alava, journalist from Ecuador:

Fascism uses the same tactics everywhere. Meanwhile, Bolsonaro is happy spending time in Miami, where all fascists and *gusanos* meet.*

---

* If you recall, *guasanos*, which means "worms," was Castro's favorite way to insult his Cuban-born critics.

Colombian ambassador to Mexico, Moisés Ninco Daza, via Twitter:

> Bolsonaro flees by helicopter to Miami and from there orders a failed coup attempt. A clear example of the cowardice of anti–Latin American fascism. They are and will be defeated by popular power.

The Cuban government couldn't resist this opportunity to stick it to the Right. Johana Tablada, of the Cuban Foreign Ministry, also on Twitter:

> #Bolsonaro in #Miami and his followers in #Brasilia try to force with violence in the streets what he could not achieve at the polls.

Even Lula joined the fray. Speaking at a press conference, the Brazilian president had this to say:

> This genocidal man . . . is encouraging this via social media from Miami. Everybody knows there are various speeches of the ex-president encouraging this.

Jair Bolsonaro denied the accusations, and kinda, sorta condemned the attacks—several hours after they happened. For many commentators on social media and in traditional media, this wasn't nearly enough, and his comments made "from Miami" were widely criticized.

And it's hard to blame the Bolsonaro haters for their reaction. What else did he expect when he shunned his responsibilities to his successor and instead fomented an insurgency from abroad? This is what happens when you refuse to face reality and scurry off to exile in a city so renowned for corruption, graft, violence, and a constant coddling of right-wing dictators.* This is what happens when you run away to Miami.

Except there is a plot twist here. Bolsonaro wasn't in Miami after all.

He went to Orlando. Why stay in the Magic City when you could be in a whole Magic Kingdom?

---

* Batista, Trujillo, Somoza, Perón . . .

Bolsonaro was staying in the Orlando home of former Brazilian Ultimate Fighting Championship fighter José Aldo, right down the street from Disney World. He was seen eating at an Orlando KFC and walking through an Orlando Publix.*

But in a way, it shouldn't be a surprise to Miamians. When you spend so many years developing a reputation for conspiracy and intrigue, these things can happen.

Even when it's not Miami's fault, we get the blame.

---

* The world's greatest supermarket. IYKYK, as the kids say.

EPILOGUE

Eric Driggs

This book is partially a retelling of the Cold War through the lens of our hometown, Miami, Florida. It is a reminder of how the city that is now primarily known as a tropical playground for bachelorettes and spring breakers was at one point—not too long ago—a playground for spies, adventure-seekers, and people willing to take up arms in order to go back home. Those interested in the Cold War should absolutely study and consider Miami.

It's the only place it's still going on.

Miami is also a border town, and one like no other. It doesn't sit across from another country on any land border that can clearly be seen on a map. But the lines are no less clear. It sits at a cultural border, serving as the "capital" of Latin America and a major American city. And sometimes it's hard to tell which side of that border the city's on. In many parts of Miami, if you have a question, order food, need directions, or just want to say hello, chances are the default language won't be English. There's an old joke that one of the best things about Miami is that it's so close to the United States. Or that you could tell which part of the "border" created by the county line you were on by whether salsa was something you did on a dance floor or something you dipped a chip into. As with most border towns, the licit and illicit are both well represented and coexist. From the days of Capone to the age of cocaine, the city has attracted both hardworking people and others unburdened by such mundane concepts as legality or morals.

But there are deeper, unseen borders that have shaped Miami just as much. More than almost anywhere else, Miami straddles the border between past and present. While it is a city that is without a doubt harnessing the opportunities of now, it continues to be shaped by its past. Across the sea, on the other side of that border, Havana is the opposite: a city of the past, physically and ideologically, existing in the present.

Both places have shaped each other, and me. My life, who I am, and what I believe have all been carved from the strange juxtaposition.

Both my parents' families lost their livelihoods, their reality, their country, the lives they had known. And yet, they found a new life here in a country that welcomed them with open arms. I was raised in a household that made it very clear that this country, flawed as it may be, provides rights and possibilities hard to fathom for so many across the globe. I believe this because I am a product of it. I will be forever indebted to the United States and its people for welcoming my family, for providing me with opportunities far beyond my ability to repay. But I cannot forget that my life was also shaped by Cuba, indirectly but powerfully and undeniably, as the moon shapes the tides. Nor can I forget that so many ache for what I was granted, to be free of a system guilty of the most unforgivable sin of governance: silencing the citizenry's own voice, eliminating its own will in how it shall be governed.

In Chapter 10, we referenced a song by a Cuban artist named Willy Chirino, which to me is one of the best encapsulations of the Cuban exile experience that I know of. It is a powerful retelling of his immigration to Miami, the heartache of losing one's homeland, and the hope of return. It was released in 1991, during the fall of the Soviet Union, and the song ends with Chirino listing countries that had freed themselves from autocratic governments, one by one, with the last country, passionately shouted with unbridled hope, being Cuba.

One of my most vivid memories was walking past my father, who was sitting on the floor in the living room listening to this song. I had never seen that look on his face before, or since. He was staring off, expressionless, seemingly nowhere. But I knew exactly where he was. The incredible, almost unthinkable changes that were taking place on the world stage were rekindling a hope, one that had likely been suppressed for years, locked away after so many disappointments. I know he was overtaken by memories of all that was left behind, and daring to imagine what return would look like. That feeling, the ever-present mourning of a paradise lost, and the stubborn defiance of hope in the face of it, to me, is what being a Cuban exile is.

And that experience, heartbreakingly replicated so many times, makes Miami home to some misunderstood communities. Some look to South Florida with confusion, or worse, they see a city with so many people stuck in the past, torn between where they stand and where they came from. Cubans still talking about Castro, Venezuelans, Nicaraguans growing in number, but always with an eye back home. But how could they not? How could they completely forget those they left behind, who have no idea what life is like in a system that actually protects its citizens, gives them a voice? My parents have always said that one of the biggest testaments to the United States is that it is unfathomable to most people who are born here that everyone around the world doesn't live like they do, or have the rights that they have always enjoyed. In college, I remember getting in arguments with fellow students who had been to Cuba and claimed to know more about it because they had "been there." The fact that they believed that those they spoke to were going to risk the very little they had been able to gain to speak freely with a tourist spending four days on island revealed a fundamental lack of understanding of what they had walked into, and yet strangely made me proud to be an American. You want to really know the realities in Cuba, or Venezuela, or Nicaragua, or Haiti? Go to Miami, where those who were there recently and still have family there know they can speak freely.

Miami is a place where you are constantly reminded that you should never take those blessings for granted. While writing this, I was in Miami visiting family, and I was chatting (as I always do) with my Uber driver, who was originally from Cuba. When I told him that both sides of my family fled Cuba in the early stages of the Revolution, he said: "You could build a gold statue in honor of your parents and it wouldn't come close to repaying what they did for you."

He was absolutely right.

Miami is a crazy place. You've just read about some of the history that has contributed to that craziness over the years. But it is also one of the places that can restore an appreciation of this country. And it is a city that sits on the most compelling border of all. The boundary between free and unfree, between opportunity and want.

For so many, Miami is the city on the other side.

Additional Sources

Sources referenced in the text of the book, or anything directly used for the content of the chapters, can be found in the notes section. The following is a resource for anyone who was inspired by this book to take a deeper dive into the main themes offered within. It is by no means an exhaustive list—that would require hundreds of pages of references. This is just some of what is available.

Agee, Philip. *Inside the Company*. New York: Penguin, 1975.

Allman, T. D. *Miami: City of the Future*. New York: Atlantic Monthly Press, 1987.

Anderson, Jon Lee. *Che Guevara: A Revolutionary Life*. New York: Grove Press, 1997.

Bardach, Ann Louise, ed. *Cuba: A Traveler's Literary Companion*. Berkeley, CA: Whereabouts Press, 2002.

Beschloss, Michael. *The Crisis Years: Kennedy and Khrushchev, 1960–1963*. New York: Edward Burlingame Books, 1991.

Bissell, Richard M. *Reflections of a Cold Warrior: From Yalta to the Bay of Pigs*. New Haven: Yale University Press, 1996.

Blight, James, Bruce J. Allyn, and David A. Welch. *Cuba on the Brink: Castro, the Missile Crisis and the Soviet Collapse*. New York: Pantheon Books, 1993.

Bohning, Don. *The Castro Obsession*. Dulles, VA: Potomac Books, 2005.

Bonachea, Rolando, and Nelson Valdés. *Cuba in Revolution*. Garden City, NY: Anchor Books, 1972.

————, eds. *The Selected Works of Fidel Castro, Vol. I: Revolutionary Struggle, 1947–1958*. Cambridge, MA: MIT Press, 1972.

Boot, Max. *The Road Not Taken: Edward Lansdale and the American Tragedy in Vietnam*. New York: Liveright, 2018.

Bretos, Miguel A. *Cuba & Florida: Exploration of an Historic Connection, 1539–1991*. Miami: Historical Association of Southern Florida, 1991.

Castañeda, Jorge. *Companero: The Life and Death of Che Guevara*. New York: Knopf, 1997.

Castro, Fidel. *In Defense of Socialism*. New York: Pathfinder Press, 1989.

Castro, Fidel, and Ignacio Ramonet. *Fidel Castro: My Life*. New York: Simon & Schuster, 2006.

Chomsky, Aviva. *A History of the Cuban Revolution*. Malden, MA: Wiley-Blackwell, 2011.

Corn, David. *Blond Ghost: Ted Shackley and the CIA's Crusades*. New York: Simon & Schuster, 1994.

Crispell, Brian Lewis. *Testing the Limits: George Armistead Smathers and Cold War America*. Athens, GA: University of Georgia Press, 1999.

Dobbs, Michael. *One Minute to Midnight: Kennedy, Khrushchev, and Castro on the Brink of Nuclear War*. New York: Vintage Books, 2008.

Dobrynin, Anatoly. *In Confidence: Moscow's Ambassador to America's Six Cold War Presidents*. New York: Times Books, 1995.

Eire, Carlos. *Waiting for Snow in Havana: Confessions of a Cuban Boy*. New York: Simon & Schuster, 2003.

————. *Learning to Die in Miami*. New York: Free Press, 2010.

Elliston, Jon. *Psywar on Cuba: The Declassified History of US Anti-Castro Propaganda*. New York: Ocean Press, 1999.

English, T. J. *Havana Nocturne: How the Mob Owned Cuba and Then Lost It to the Revolution*. New York: Harper, 2009.

Engstrom, David W. *Presidential Decision Making Adrift: The Carter Administration and the Mariel Boatlift*. New York: Rowman and Littlefield, 1998.

Erikson, Daniel P. *The Cuba Wars: Fidel Castro, the United States, and the Next Revolution*. New York: Bloomsbury, 2010.

Escalante, Fabian. *The Secret War: CIA Covert Operations against Cuba, 1959–1962.* New York: Ocean Press, 1995.

Garcia, Maria Cristina. *Havana USA: Cuban Exiles and Cuban Americans in South Florida, 1959–1994.* Berkeley, CA: University of California Press, 1996.

Geyer, Georgie Anne. *Guerrilla Prince.* Boston: Little, Brown, 1991.

Gjelten, Tom. *Bacardi and the Long Fight for Cuba: The Biography of a Cause.* New York: Viking, 2008.

Gonzalez-Pando, Miguel. *The Cuban Americans.* Westport, CT: Greenwood Press, 1998.

Goodwin, Richard N. *Remembering America: A Voice from the Sixties.* Boston: Little, Brown, 1988.

Greene, Graham. *Our Man in Havana.* New York: Penguin, 1958.

Grose, Peter. *Gentleman Spy: The Life of Allen Dulles.* Boston: Houghton Mifflin, 1994.

Hidalgo, Orlando Castro. *Spy for Fidel.* Miami: E. E. Seaman, 1971.

Hinckle, Warren, and William W. Turner. *The Fish Is Red: The Story of the Secret War Against Castro.* New York: Harper and Row, 1981.

Huddleston, Vicki, and Carlos Pascual. *Learning to Salsa: New Steps in US-Cuba Relations.* Washington, DC: Brookings Institution Press, 2010.

Immerman, Richard H. *The CIA in Guatemala: The Foreign Policy of Intervention.* Austin, TX: University of Texas Press, 1982.

Latell, Brian. *After Fidel: The Inside Story of Castro's Regime and Cuba's Next Leader.* New York: Palgrave Macmillan, 2005.

LeoGrande, William M., and Peter Kornbluh. *Back Channel to Cuba: The Hidden Story of Negotiations between Washington and Havana.* Chapel Hill, NC: University of North Carolina Press, 2015.

Kalugin, Oleg. *The First Chief Directorate.* New York: St. Martin's Press, 1994.

Kennedy, Robert F. *Thirteen Days: A Memoir of the Cuban Missile Crisis.* New York: W. W. Norton, 1969.

Khrushchev, Nikita. *Khrushchev Remembers.* Translated and edited by Strobe Talbott. Boston: Little, Brown, 1970.

Kirkland, Robert O. *Observing Our Hermanos de Armas: US Military Attachés in Guatemala, Cuba, and Bolivia, 1950–1964*. New York: Routledge, 2003.

Kornbluh, Peter, ed. *Bay of Pigs Declassified*. New York: New Press, 1998.

Landau, Saul. *The Guerrilla Wars of Central America*. New York: St. Martin's Press, 1993.

Levine, Robert M. *Secret Missions to Cuba*. New York: Palgrave, 2001.

Lockwood, Lee. *Castro's Cuba, Cuba's Fidel: An American Journalist's Inside Look at Today's Cuba in Text and Picture*. New York: Macmillan, 1967.

Martí, José. *Selected Writings*. Translated and edited by Ester Allen. New York: Penguin, 2002.

Martin, Edwin McCammon. *Kennedy and Latin America*. Lanham, MD: University Press of America, 1994.

Matthews, Herbert L. *Revolution in Cuba: An Essay in Understanding*. New York: Scribner's, 1975.

May, Ernest R., and Philip Zelikow, eds. *The Kennedy Tapes: Inside the White House During the Cuban Missile Crisis*. Cambridge, MA: Belknap Press of Harvard University Press, 1997.

Michener, James A., and John Kings. *Six Days in Havana*. Austin, TX: University of Texas Press, 1989.

Othen, Christopher. *The Men from Miami: American Rebels and Patriots on Both Sides of Fidel Castro's Cuban Revolution*. London: Biteback Publishing, 2022.

Pérez-Sable, Marifeli. *The United States and Cuba: Intimate Enemies*. New York: Routledge, 2010.

Portes, Alejandro, and Alex Stepick. *City on the Edge: The Transformation of Miami*. Berkeley, CA: University of California Press, 1993.

Posner, Gerald. *Miami Babylon: Crime, Wealth, and Power—a Dispatch from the Beach*. New York: Simon & Schuster, 2009.

Prellezo, Lily, and José Basulto. *Seagull One: The Amazing True Story of Brothers to the Rescue*. Gainesville, FL: University Press of Florida, 2010.

Quirk, Robert E. *Fidel Castro*. New York: W. W. Norton, 1993.

Rieff, David. *The Exile: Cuba in the Heart of Miami*. New York: Simon & Schuster, 1993.

Rivera, Mario Antonio. *Decision and Structure: US Refugee Policy in the Mariel Crisis.* New York: University Press of America, 1991.

Ruíz, Ramón Eduardo. *Cuba: The Making of a Revolution.* New York: W. W. Norton, 1970.

Russo, Gus, and Stephen Molton. *Brothers in Arms: The Kennedys, the Castros, and the Politics of Murder.* New York: Bloomsbury USA, 2008.

Schlesinger, Arthur M., Jr. *A Thousand Days: John F. Kennedy in the White House.* Boston: Houghton Mifflin, 1965.

Szulc, Tad. *Fidel: A Critical Portrait.* New York: Avon Books, 1986.

Thomas, Evan. *The Very Best Men.* New York: Simon & Schuster, 1995.

Thomas, Hugh. *Cuba: A History.* New York: Penguin, 2010.

———. *Cuba: The Pursuit of Freedom.* New York: Harper & Row, 1971.

Notes

Prologue

1. I grew up in Pinecrest, which, along with Miami Beach, Miami Gardens, Palmetto Bay, and many other places, is technically not the "City of Miami." For the purposes of this book, it's all Miami. The Miami CIA station, for the record, was in Richmond Heights.

2. Should we call this Castroism? Fidelism? We, the authors, have been debating which term to use for more than two years now. We still don't have a consensus. Neither, it seems, does anyone else. Government documents, journal articles, and the scholarly community alternate between the two.

Chapter 1: In the Apostle's Footsteps

1. "Clubs Revolucionarios," *Patria*, November 24, 1894. See Antonio Rafael de la Cova, "Fernandina Filibuster Fiasco: Birth of the 1895 Cuban War of Independence," *Florida Historical Quarterly* 82, no. 1 (summer 2003).

2. José Martí, "Montecristi Manifesto," March 25, 1895, Modern Latin America, Brown University Center for Digital Scholarship, https://library.brown.edu/create /modernlatinamerica/chapters/chapter-4-cuba/primary-documents-w-accom panying-discussion-questions/document-8-montecristi-manifesto-jose-marti-and -maximo-gomez-1895/.

3. Edwin M. Martin, Assistant Secretary for Inter-American Affairs, testifying before United States Senate, Subcommittee on Refugees and Escapees of the Committee on the Judiciary, May 23, 1963, page 5, https://hdl.handle.net/2027/umn .31951p00757998u.

4. *Cuban Counterrevolutionary Handbook*, Central Intelligence Agency, July 1964, in authors' possession.

5. "Despatch from the Embassy in Cuba to the Department of State," December 6, 1960, in John P. Glennon, ed., *Foreign Relations of the United States, 1958–1960, Cuba, Volume VI* (Washington, DC: US Government Printing Office, 1991), https://history.state.gov/historicaldocuments/frus1958-60v06/d617.

6. *Cuban Counterrevolutionary Handbook*, CIA, 347.

7. House Select Committee on Assassinations Report, vol. 10, sect. 6, 65, https://archive.org/details/HouseSelectCommitteeOnAssassinations/Volume %2010/page/n67/mode/2up.

8. Quotation from Martí's "Montecristi Manifesto," just as relevant almost sixty years later.

9. *Cuban Counterrevolutionary Handbook*, CIA, 348.

10. *Cuban Counterrevolutionary Handbook*, CIA, 465.

11. FRD internal planning documents, n.d., in Driggs Family Archive, in authors' possession.

12. History of the Cuban Navy in Exile, typed internal document, n.d. but likely 1961, in Driggs Family Archive, in authors' possession.

13. Primary document, signed by recruit, in authors' possession.

14. Grayston Lynch, *Decision for Disaster: Betrayal at the Bay of Pigs* (Washington, DC: Brassey's, 1998), 24.

15. Enrique Encinosa, *Cuba en Guerra: Historia de la Oposición Anti-Castrista, 1959–1993*, 2nd ed. (Madison, WI: Endowment for Cuban-American Studies, 1995), 72.

16. Mario J. Pentón, "Bay of Pigs Brigade Leader Gen. Erneido Oliva Dies in Exile," *Miami Herald*, January 31, 2020.

17. Lynch, *Decision for Disaster*, 24.

18. "Cuban Covert Program Report," JFK Library Typescript Copy of Badly Blurred Thermofax Copy, October 13, 1961, prepared May 30, 1975, National Security Archive, https://nsarchive.gwu.edu/document/19616-national-security -archive-doc-05-cuban-covert.

19. They were cordial enough that Miró Cardona sent Kennedy birthday wishes a few months later in May via telegram, wishing him "a very happy birthday and many more to come with triumphs and increased prestige for your country." Very thoughtful, but it's a safe bet this telegram wasn't as memorable or well received as the birthday wishes Kennedy received the following year in 1962. Those were breathlessly sung by a platinum-blonde bombshell in a glittering dress. But that is very difficult competition, and besides, it's the thought that counts.

20. Miró Cardona Resignation Letter to the Revolutionary Council of Cuba, April 9, 1963, Wilson Center Digital Archive, https://digitalarchive.wilsoncenter .org/document/resignation-letter-jose-miro-cardona-revolutionary-council-cuba.

21. House Select Committee on Assassinations Report, vol. 10, sect. 4, 48.

Chapter 2: "You Can't Mañana This Thing"

1. See Justin F. Gleichauf, "A Listening Post in Miami," Center for the Study of Intelligence, Central Intelligence Agency, www.cia.gov/static/listening -post-in-miami.pdf.

2. See Gleichauf's obituary, "Justin F. Gleichauf, 91, Agent for the CIA Who Monitored Cuba Before Missile Crisis," *Baltimore Sun*, June 21, 2003, www.balti moresun.com/news/bs-xpm-2003-06-21-0306210086-story.html.

3. Aleksandr Fursenko and Timothy Naftali, *One Hell of a Gamble: Khrushchev, Castro, and Kennedy, 1958–1964* (New York: W. W. Norton, 1997), 64.

4. David Martin, *Wilderness of Mirrors* (New York: Ballantine Books, 1980), 121.

5. Warren Hinkle and William Turner, *The Fish Is Red: The Story of the Secret War Against Castro* (New York: Harper and Row, 1981), 313.

6. "Memorandum for Deputy Director of Central Intelligence, Subject: Maheu, Robert J.," Central Intelligence Agency, June 24, 1966, National Archives, www.archives.gov/files/research/jfk/releases/104-10133-10091.pdf. The original version of thedocument has the words "the liquidation of" crossed out before the name Fidel Castro.

7. "Report on Plots to Assassinate Fidel Castro," CIA Inspector General Report, May 23, 1967, National Archives, www.archives.gov/files/research/jfk/releases/104-10213-10101.pdf.

8. CIA documents say that Maheu's initial impression of Giancana was that he was a "hard, uncouth individual who looked and acted like a common run-of-the-mill hoodlum."

9. Thomas Maier, "Inside the CIA's Plot to Kill Fidel Castro—with Mafia Help," *Politico*, February 24, 2018, www.politico.com/magazine/story/2018/02/24/fidel-castro-cia-mafia-plot-216977/.

10. "Report on Plots to Assassinate Fidel Castro," CIA.

11. "Memorandum, Subject: Maheu," CIA.

12. "Report on Plots to Assassinate Fidel Castro," CIA.

13. "Report on Plots to Assassinate Fidel Castro," CIA.

14. "Memorandum, Subject: Maheu," CIA.

15. "Report on Plots to Assassinate Fidel Castro," CIA.

16. Steve Hach, "Cold War in South Florida: Historical Resource Study," October 2004, United States National Park Service, 53, www.nps.gov/parkhistory/online_books/coldwar/florida.pdf.

17. Hach, "Cold War," 48.

18. Hach, "Cold War," 57.

19. Jim Kelly, "The Fidel Fixation," *Miami New Times*, April 17, 1997, www.miaminewtimes.com/news/the-fidel-fixation-6360874.

20. Arthur Schlesinger Jr., Memorandum for the President, February 11, 1961, National Security Archive, nsarchive2.gwu.edu/bayofpigs/19610211.pdf.

21. McGeorge Bundy, Memorandum for the President, February 8, 1961, Office of the Historian, US Department of State, history.state.gov/historicaldocuments/frus1961-63v10/d39.

22. Monte Reel, *A Brotherhood of Spies: The U-2 and the CIA's Secret War* (New York: Doubleday, 1998), 229.

23. For a wonderfully snarky version of these events, and Miami history in general, see Joan Didion, *Miami* (New York: Vintage Books, 1998). See page 83 for this story.

24. Félix Rodríguez and John Weisman, *Shadow Warrior: The CIA Hero of a Hundred Unknown Battles* (New York: Simon and Schuster, 1989), 134.

25. Richard "Dick" Goodwin, Memorandum for the President, "Subject: Conversation with Commandante Ernesto Guevara of Cuba," August 22, 1961, JFK Library, www.jfklibrary.org/asset-viewer/archivesJFKPOF/115JFKPOF-115-003.

26. Rodríguez and Weisman, *Shadow Warrior*, 92.

27. Walt Rostow, Memorandum to Secretary of Defense McNamara, "Subject: Notes on Cuba Policy," April 24, 1961, Office of the Historian, US Department of State, history.state.gov/historicaldocuments/frus1961-63v10/d172JFK Library.

28. Arthur Schlesinger Jr., Memorandum for Mr. Richard Goodwin, "Subject: Cuban Covert Plan," July 8, 1961, nsarchive.gwu.edu/document/19614-national -security-archive-doc-03-white-house. Authors' emphasis.

29. Richard "Dick" Goodwin, Memorandum for the President, November 1, 1961, nsarchive.gwu.edu/document/19618-national-security-archive-doc-07-white -house.

Chapter 3: Does the *C* in CIA Stand for *Coño*?

1. "Major General Edward G. Lansdale," Official United States Air Force Biography, United States Air Force, www.af.mil/About-Us/Biographies/Display /Article/106443/major-general-edward-g-lansdale/.

2. Those were the days before the Church and Pike Committee hearings, the House and Senate oversight committees, and before when this kind of question would have to go through a gauntlet of dozens of lawyers. For quotation, see Brian Latell, *Castro's Secrets: The CIA and Cuba's Intelligence Machine* (New York: Palgrave Macmillan, 2012), 87–88.

3. "JMWAVE Cover Facility," Central Intelligence Agency, Mary Ferrell Foundation, www.maryferrell.org/showDoc.html?docId=111597#relPageId=1.

4. "CPI Inflation Calculator, US Bureau of Labor Statistics, www.bls.gov/data /inflation_calculator.htm.

5. See Don Bohning, "The Castro Obsession," *Miami Herald*, March 20, 2005; Don Bohning, *The Castro Obsession* (Washington, DC: Potomac Books, 2005). Also, see Steve Hach, "Cold War in South Florida: Historical Resource Study," October 2004, United States National Park Service, 53, www.nps.gov/parkhistory/online_books /coldwar/florida.pdf; and Félix Rodríguez and John Weisman, *Shadow Warrior: The CIA Hero of a Hundred Unknown Battles* (New York: Simon & Schuster, 1989).

6. David Macfie, "Richmond Naval Air Station, 1942–1961," *Tequesta* XXXVII (1977).

7. See Ted Shackley, *Spymaster: My Life in the CIA*, with Richard A. Finney (Dulles, VA: Potomac Books, 2005).

8. Brian Latell, *Castro's Secrets: The CIA and Cuba's Intelligence Machine* (New York: Palgrave Macmillan, 2012), 88.

9. Edward Lansdale, "The Cuba Project," February 20, 1962, National Security Archive, nsarchive.gwu.edu/document/19622-national-security-archive-doc-11 -general-edward.

10. David Martin, *Wilderness of Mirrors* (New York: Ballantine Books, 1980), 130.

11. Edward Lansdale, "Possible Actions to Provoke, Harrass [*sic*], or Disrupt Cuba," February 1962, JFK Assassination Documents, National Archives, www .archives.gov/files/research/jfk/releases/2018/104-10333-10014.pdf.

12. Aleksandr Fursenko and Timothy Naftali, *One Hell of a Gamble: Khrush-chev, Castro, and Kennedy, 1958–1964* (New York: W. W. Norton, 1997), 148.

13. Memorandum from Chairman of the JCS Gen. Lyman Lemnitzer to Secretary of Defense Robert McNamara, "Justification for US Military Intervention in Cuba," March 13, 1962, National Security Archive, nsarchive2.gwu.edu /news/20010430/northwoods.pdf.

14. For two examples of this, see Edward Lansdale, Memorandum for the Special Group (Augmented), "Review of Operation Mongoose," July 25, 1962, National Security Archive, https://nsarchive.gwu.edu/document/19623-national -security-archive-doc-12-general-edward; and William Harvey to Edward Lans-dale, "Operation MONGOOSE—Sabotage Actions," October 11, 1962, National Security Archive, https://nsarchive.gwu.edu/document/19627-national-security-arch ive-doc-16-cia-william.

15. Justin F. Gleichauf, "A Listening Post in Miami," Center for the Study of Intelligence, Central Intelligence Agency, www.cia.gov/static/listening-post-in -miami.pdf.

16. "Chronology of Specific Events Relating to the Military Buildup in Cuba," n.d., Central Intelligence Agency, National Security Archive, https://nsarchive2 .gwu.edu/nsa/cuba_mis_cri/chron.htm.

17. Gleichauf, "A Listening Post."

18. Gleichauf, "A Listening Post."

19. Steve Hach, "Cold War in South Florida: Historical Resource Study," October 2004, United States National Park Service, www.nps.gov/parkhistory/online _books/coldwar/florida.pdf, 55.

20. Headquarters, US Army Air Defense Command, General Order 65, April 1, 1963, in authors' possession.

21. [Redacted] to Edward Lansdale, "Operation MONGOOSE Infiltration Teams," October 29, 1962, National Security Archive, https://nsarchive.gwu.edu /document/19630-national-security-archive-doc-19-cia-memo. Authors' emphasis.

22. John McCone to General Marshall S. Carter, October 30, 1962, National Security Archive, https://nsarchive.gwu.edu/document/19631-national -security-archive-doc-20-cia-director. Underline emphasis in original.

Chapter 4: The Ocho

1. Displaced Persons Act, H.R. 4567, 81st Cong. (1950). See "Statement by the President upon Signing Bill Amending the Displaced Persons Act," June 16, 1950, Harry S. Truman Library, www.trumanlibrary.gov/library/public-papers/167 /statement-president-upon-signing-bill-amending-displaced-persons-act.

2. Refugee Relief Act of 1953, Pub. L. No. 83-203, 67 Stat. 400 (1953), Summary: An Act to authorize the issuance of 240,000 special note immigrant visas, and for other purposes.

3. "White House Statement on the Termination of the Emergency Program for Hungarian Refugees," December 28, 1957, American Presidency Project,

www.presidency.ucsb.edu/documents/white-house-statement-the-termination -the-emergency-program-for-hungarian-refugees.

4. *Cuban Refugee Problem: Hearings Before the US Senate Committee on the Judiciary, Subcommittee to Investigate Problems Connected with Refugees and Escapees*, 88th Cong., first session, May 22, 1963, Hathi Trust, https://babel .hathitrust.org/cgi/pt?id=umn.31951p00757998u&view=1up&seq=10.

5. Monsignor Bryan O. Walsh, "Cuban Refugee Children," *Journal of Interamerican Studies and World Affairs* 13, no. 3/4 (July–October 1971): 382.

6. *Alfabeticemos*, National Literacy Commission (Revolutionary Government Ministry of Education, 1961), 24.

7. *Alfabeticemos*, 43.

8. *Alfabeticemos*, 50.

9. *Alfabeticemos*, 91.

10. *Alfabeticemos*, 98.

11. "Cuba: And Now the Children?" *Time*, October 6, 1961.

12. Bryan Walsh, "Cuban Refugee Children: The Origins of Operation 'Pedro Pan,'" May 7, 1970, 59, https://ufdcimages.uflib.ufl.edu/AA/00/05/48/70/00001 /BOW0047006001_1.pdf.

13. Gene Miller, "Cuban Tots, a Raggedy Ann Doll," *Evansville Press*, March 10, 1962.

14. *Cuban Refugee Problem: Hearings Before the US Senate*.

15. From "Resettlement Recap: a Periodic Report from the Cuban Refugee Center," December 1965, in authors' possession, https://digitalcollections.library .miami.edu/digital/collection/chc0218/id/450/rec/52.

16. "Resettlement Recap."

17. Fidel Castro, Speech on Fifth Anniversary of CDR, September 28, 1965, Castro Speech Database, Latin American Network Information Center (LANIC), http://lanic.utexas.edu/project/castro/db/1965/19650929.html.

18. Lyndon B. Johnson, "Remarks at the Signing of the Immigration Bill, Liberty Island, New York," October 3, 1965, American Presidency Project, www .presidency.ucsb.edu/documents/remarks-the-signing-the-immigration-bill -liberty-island-new-york.

19. Johnson, "Remarks Signing Immigration Bill."

20. Dennis Noble, "Lessons Unlearned: The Camarioca Boatlift," *Naval History* 23, no. 4 (August 2009): 44–49.

21. *Cuba's Children in Exile: The Story of the Unaccompanied Cuban Refugee Children's Program*, 1967, US Department of Health, Education, and Welfare, https://books.google.com/books?id=L6zsZEftSugC&printsec=frontcover&source =gbs_ge_summary_r&cad=0#v=onepage&q&f=false, 7.

22. Research Memorandum No. 1230, May 20, 1980, Office of the Historian, US Department of State, https://history.state.gov/historicaldocuments/frus 1964-68v32/d308.

23. US House of Representatives, *Proceedings of the Special Hearing on the Cuban Refugee Problem Held in Miami, March 14, 1963*, Hathi Trust, https://hdl .handle.net/2027/umn.31951p00757998u.

24. See "Cuban Refugee Program, December 1963," reprinted from *Welfare in Review* 1, no. 3 (September 1963), official monthly publication of the Welfare Administration, US Department of Health, Education, and Welfare, Cuban Refugee Center Records, Digital Collections, University of Miami Libraries, https://digital collections.library.miami.edu/digital/collection/chc0218/id/476/rec/1.

25. *Adjustment of Status for Cuba Refugees: Hearings Before Subcommittee No. 1 of the Committee on the Judiciary*, 89th Cong., https://books.google.com/books /about/Adjustment_of_Status_for_Cuban_Refugees.html?id=RwHMHhmeFIUC.

26. "An Act to Adjust the Status of Cuban Refugees to That of Lawful Permanent Residents of the United States, and for Other Purposes," Pub. L. No. 89-732, 80 Stat. 1161 (1966).

27. Andres Viglucci, "The Best and the Brightest: Luis Botifoll," *Miami Herald*, September 22, 1985.

28. Susan Jacoby, "The 350,000 Cubans in South Florida Make a Remarkable Success Story. Even If Castro Fell Tomorrow, Great Numbers Would Not Return," *New York Times*, September 29, 1974.

29. James Russell, "Cubans Propped Up a Sagging Economy," *Miami Herald*, June 18, 1971.

30. See Sergio Diaz-Briquets, "The Evolution and Characteristics of Cuban-Owned Firms in the United States," *Cuban Studies* 35 (2004).

31. Susan Jacoby, "Miami Sí, Cuba No," *New York Times Magazine*, September 29, 1974.

32. Russell, "Cubans Propped Up a Sagging Economy."

33. "Big Name Corporations Find S. Florida Natural 'Home,'" *Miami Herald*, June 18, 1971.

Chapter 5: Raiders of the Lost Archipelago

1. *Cuban Counterrevolutionary Handbook*, Central Intelligence Agency, July 1964, in authors' possession.

2. "Victory at Sea for Anti-Castro Rebs," *Miami News*, May 23, 1962.

3. *Cuban Counterrevolutionary Handbook*, CIA, 162.

4. "Cuba: General, 1963: April–November," President's Office Files, JFK Library, www.jfklibrary.org/asset-viewer/archives/JFKPOF/115/JFKPOF-115-002?image _identifier=JFKPOF-115-002-p0010.

5. United States Senate, Subcommittee on Refugees and Escapees of the Committee on the Judiciary, May 23, 1963, Hathi Trust, https://hdl.handle.net/2027 /umn.31951p00757998u, 86.

6. John Hugh Crimmins, interview by Ashley C. Hewett Jr., Association for Diplomatic Studies and Training Foreign Affairs Oral History Project, May 10, 1989,

www.academia.edu/7436373/The_Association_for_Diplomatic_Studies_and
_Training_Foreign_Affairs_Oral_History_Project.

7. "Sea Raiders Hit Cuba," *Life*, April 12, 1963.

8. "Telegram from the Embassy in the Soviet Union to the Department of State," March 27, 1963, Office of the Historian, US Department of State, history .state.gov/historicaldocuments/frus1961-63v11/d300.

9. "Telegram from the Embassy."

10. "Telegram from the Embassy."

11. *Department of State Bulletin* 48, no. 1240 (April 1, 1963): 600.

12. *Department of State Bulletin* 48, no. 1240 (April 1, 1963).

13. "US Strengthens Checks on Raiders," *New York Times*, April 5, 1963.

14. Miró Cardona Resignation Letter to the Revolutionary Council of Cuba, April 9, 1963, Wilson Center Digital Archive, https://digitalarchive.wilsoncenter .org/document/resignation-letter-jose-miro-cardona-revolutionary-council-cuba.

15. Miró Cardona Resignation Letter.

16. "Cuban Covert Program Report," JFK Library Typescript Copy of Badly Blurred Thermofax Copy, October 13, 1961, prepared May 30, 1975, National Security Archive, https://nsarchive.gwu.edu/document/19616-national -security-archive-doc-05-cuban-covert.

17. "Reported Landing of Commandos in Cuba," FBI Memo, June 21, 1963, National Archives, www.archives.gov/files/research/jfk/releases/2021/docid32383 740.pdf.

18. "Exile Raiders Claim Landings in Cuba; US Is 'Doubtful,'" *United Press International*, June 21, 1963.

19. "Political Situation and Prospects of Cuban Exiles in Miami," Office of Coordinator of Cuban Affairs, October 14, 1963, in authors' possession, www.maryferrell .org/showDoc.html?docId=81969yferrell.org.

20. *Cuban Counterrevolutionary Handbook*, CIA.

21. "In View of the Enforced Surrender from Comandos 'L' to US Authorities of War Materiel in Hialeah, Florida on September 21, 1963, We Issue the Following Statement," September 22, 1963, NARA Record Number 124-90106-10027, Mary Ferrell Foundation, maryferrell.org.

22. JMWAVE Cable 9087, NARA Document ID Number 1993.08.04.16:50: 14:750028, Mary Ferrell Foundation, maryferrell.org.

23. *Cuban Counterrevolutionary Handbook*, CIA, 245.

24. "Exile Slate Supported by 40,905," *Miami Herald*, May 23, 1964.

25. *Cuban Counterrevolutionary Handbook*, CIA, 440.

26. Don Bohning, "Pigs Bay Veteran Says 'Exiles Must Unite for War on Fidel," *Miami Herald*, June 16, 1964.

27. Bohning, "Pigs Bay Veteran Says."

28. Letter from Ernesto Freyre, September 25, 1963. See *Cuban Counterrevolutionary Handbook*, CIA.

29. "Anti-Fidel Castro Activities," FBI Field Office File 105-1742, July 7, 1966, Mary Ferrell Foundation, www.maryferrell.org/showDoc.html?docId=93296.

30. *Cuban Counterrevolutionary Handbook*, CIA, 444.

31. JMWAVE Cable 8530, NARA Document ID Number 1993.08.04.16:35:00 :870028, Mary Ferrell Foundation, maryferrell.org.

32. JMWAVE Cable 9016, NARA Document ID Number 1993.08.04.16:50 :14:750028, Mary Ferrell Foundation, maryferrell.org.

33. JMWAVE Cable 9557, Mary Ferrell Foundation, maryferrell.org.

34. JMWAVE Cable 8744, NARA Document ID Number 1993.08.04 .16.41:41:08:870028, Mary Ferrell Foundation, maryferrell.org.

35. JMWAVE Dispatch, Operation ZORRO, NARA Document ID Number 104-10234-10312, Mary Ferrell Foundation, maryferrell.org.

36. JMWAVE Cable 9310, "After Action Report Op SALLY XIV," Number 1998.09.23.14.09.17.890128, Mary Ferrell Foundation, maryferrell.org.

37. JMWAVE Cable 9557, NARA Document ID Number 104-10234-10017, Mary Ferrell Foundation, maryferrell.org.

Chapter 6: A Rogues' Gallery

1. "Che Makes Cuba Pitch for Improved US Ties," Associated Press, December 14, 1964.

2. "Guevara, in UN, Asserts US Is Planning Attacks," *New York Times*, December 12, 1964.

3. "Bazooka Fired at UN as Cuban Speaks; Launched in Queens, Missile Explodes in East River," *New York Times*, December 12, 1964.

4. "Bazooka Fired at UN."

5. Carlos Martinez and Don Bohning, "Bazooka Suspects Identified as Officials of Miami Unit," *Miami Herald*, December 24, 1964.

6. Charles Krueger, "Mexican Consul's Car Is Dynamited," *Miami Herald*, February 2, 1968.

7. William Montalbano, "2 Consuls Here Fear Bombings, Ask Move," *Miami Herald*, September 26, 1968.

8. Arnold Markowitz and Paul Schreiber, "Blast Rips Home of British Consul," *Miami Herald*, February 10, 1968.

9. William Montalbano, "2 Consuls."

10. Álvaro Vargas Llosa, *El Exilio Indomable* (Planeta Pub Corp: 1998), 76.

11. FBI Record Number 124-10279-10057, February 5, 1976, Mary Ferrell Foundation, maryferrell.org.

12. Don Bohning, "Bosch: Often at Loggerheads with Law, Exile Had Always Remained Free," *Miami Herald*, October 12, 1968.

13. "Air Raid a Failure, Cuban Exiles Say," *New York Times*, November 22, 1964.

14. FBI Document 124-10206-10280, October 17, 1968, Mary Ferrell Foundation, maryferrell.org.

15. FBI Document 124-10206-10280, October 17, 1968, Mary Ferrell Foundation, maryferrell.org.

16. Frank Soler, "Cuban Power Meets Press," *Miami Herald*, September 21, 1968.

17. "Cuban Power Advises the Public," from FBI Document 124-10206-10280, October 17, 1968, Mary Ferrell Foundation, maryferrell.org.

18. "Cuban Power Advises the Public."

19. "Cuban Power Advises the Public."

20. Or the downing of Cubana de Aviación Flight 455 in October 1976, which has been closely linked to Bosch and Posada.

21. Alfonso Chardy, "Militants Reuniting, but Shifting Mission," *Miami Herald*, February 23, 2008.

Chapter 7: Exporting Counterrevolution

1. Steve Hach, "Cold War in South Florida: Historical Resource Study," October 2004, United States National Park Service, www.nps.gov/parkhistory/online _books/coldwar/florida.pdf, 10.

2. Gerald K. Haines, "CIA and Guatemala Assassination Proposals, 1952–1954," CIA History Staff Analysis, June 1995, www.cia.gov/readingroom/docs /DOC_0000135796.pdf. Also, see Nicholas Cullather, "Operation PBSUCCESS: The United States and Guatemala, 1952–1954," 1994, History Staff, Center for the Study of Intelligence.

3. Alfonso Chardy, "Florida Opa-locka Field Was Once the Site of Secret CIA Base," *Miami Herald*, updated April 22, 2013.

4. "PBSUCCESS," *The SHERWOOD Tapes*, Central Intelligence Agency, www .cia.gov/readingroom/docs/DOC_0000135031.pdf, 5–7.

5. "PBSUCCESS," CIA, 2.

6. Alfonso Chardy, "Florida Opa-locka Field."

7. James Hawes and Mary Ann Koenig, *Cold War Navy Seal: My Story of Che Guevara, War in the Congo, and the Communist Threat in Africa* (New York: Skyhorse Publishing, 2018), xv–xvi.

8. Author interview with James Hawes, April 24, 2018, in *SpyCast* podcast, International Spy Museum, thecyberwire.com/podcasts/spycast/316/notes.

9. Don Hollway, "The CIA's Cuban Air Force Battles Communists in the Congo," *Aviation History* (January 2021), 60.

10. Author interview with Félix Rodríguez, August 18, 2005, in *SpyCast* podcast, International Spy Museum, thecyberwire.com/podcasts/spycast/167/notes.

11. Hawes and Koenig, *Cold War Navy Seal*, 77.

12. Hawes and Koenig, *Cold War Navy Seal*, 115.

13. Félix Rodríguez, and John Weisman, *Shadow Warrior: The CIA Hero of a Hundred Unknown Battles* (New York: Simon and Schuster, 1989), 166. Also see author interview with Rodríguez, in *SpyCast* podcast.

14. Rodríguez and Weisman, *Shadow Warrior*, 135.

15. Rodríguez and Weisman, *Shadow Warrior*, 141.

16. Rodríguez and Weisman, *Shadow Warrior*, 146.

17. Rodríguez and Weisman, *Shadow Warrior*, 15. Also, see Rodríguez podcast.

18. Rodríguez and Weisman, *Shadow Warrior*, 11.

19. Rodríguez and Weisman, *Shadow Warrior*, 173–178.

Chapter 8: Open the Gates

1. Guy Gugliotta, "Havana's Upheaval Began with a Whimper," *Miami Herald,* May 4, 1980.
2. "La Posición de Cuba," *Granma,* April 7, 1980.
3. "Declaración del Gobierno Revolucionario de Cuba," *Granma,* April 4, 1980.
4. "Nations Debate; Embassy Crowd Waits," *Miami Herald,* April 10, 1980.
5. Gugliotta, "Havana's Upheaval."
6. Lou Cannon, "Reagan Proposes 'Airlift' of Cuban Refugees," *Washington Post,* April 10, 1980.
7. *Granma,* April 22, 1980.
8. "Sea Lift from Cuba to Key West," *Newsweek,* May 5, 1980, 59.
9. "Voyage from Cuba," *Time,* May 5, 1980, 42.
10. "Noticias de Mariel," *Granma,* April 22, 1980.
11. Jimmy Carter, "League of Women Voters Remarks and a Question-and-Answer Session at the League's Biennial National Convention," May 5, 1980, the American Presidency Project, www.presidency.ucsb.edu/documents/league-women -voters-remarks-and-question-and-answer-session-the-leagues-biennial-national.
12. "Restrictions on Freedom of Expression in Cuba," Amnesty International, 2010, www.amnesty.org/en/wp-content/uploads/2021/06/amr250052010en.pdf.
13. Richard Morin, "Dade Fears Refugee Wave, Poll Shows," *Miami Herald,* May 11, 1980.
14. George Stein and Guillermo Martínez, "Little Havana Struck by Boatlift Criminals," *Miami Herald,* September 18, 1980.
15. Stein and Martínez, "Little Havana Struck."
16. See Sam Verdeja and Guillermo Martínez, *Cubans, An Epic Journey: The Struggle of Exiles for Truth and Freedom* (St. Louis, MO: Reedy Press, 2011).
17. "Members of Minority Religious Cults Considered Least Desirable as Neighbors," *Miami Herald,* January 21, 1982.

Chapter 9: Up Up Down Down Left Right Left Right B A Start

1. For more Iran-Contra information than you can probably handle, see Lawrence E. Walsh, "Final Report of the Independent Counsel for Iran/Contra Matters," United States Court of Appeals for the District of Columbia Circuit, August 4, 1993.
2. There were four total "Boland amendments": two before this, and one later. But this is the one that matters the most.
3. Walsh, "Final Report," Part I.
4. Walsh, "Final Report," Part III.
5. William J. Casey, during Oliver North Trial Testimony, April 6, 1989, in Walsh, "Final Report," chap. 15.
6. Walsh, "Final Report," Part I.
7. Walsh, "Final Report," Part I.
8. Saudi Arabia contributed $32 million between July 1984 and March 1985. Taiwan donated $2 million (total) in September 1985 and February 1986.
9. "The Enterprise and Its Finances," in Walsh, "Final Report," chap. 8.

10. "The Enterprise and Its Finances."

11. "Other Money Matters: Traveler's Checks and Cash Transactions," in Walsh, "Final Report," chap. 14.

12. "Bay of Pigs Survivors Find Common Cause with Contras," *Washington Post*, October 26, 1986.

13. "Bay of Pigs Survivors."

14. Joseph B. Treaster, "A Cuban-American 'Adviser' Tells of Combat with Nicaraguan Rebels," *New York Times*, December 22, 1986.

15. Ann Louise Bardach, *Cuba Confidential: Love and Vengeance in Miami and Havana* (New York: Vintage Books, 2002), 141.

16. "Bay of Pigs Survivors."

17. Bustillo is a particularly horrible human. If you have a strong stomach, look him up.

18. So much like the situation in Nicaragua, but the sides are flip-flopped.

19. Donald P. Gregg, in Walsh, "Final Report," chap. 29.

20. (Very) long story.

21. He was wanted for terrorism against the Cuban government in many places, including the US. Quotation from "Bay of Pigs Survivors."

22. Félix Rodríguez and John Weisman, *Shadow Warrior: The CIA Hero of a Hundred Unknown Battles* (New York: Simon and Schuster, 1989), 238.

23. He was right. The other side of the affair, the Iran side, also shows the unscrupulous nature of the Enterprise. The Iranian military paid $30 million for the arms sold to them by North and his team. Of that amount, only $12 million was given over to the United States government. The rest went to the Enterprise, whose operating expenses amounted to just about $2 million. The remainder? $16 million went into their bank accounts.

24. Rodríguez and Weisman, *Shadow Warrior*, 246–247.

25. Walsh, "Final Report," Part I.

Chapter 10: Critical Mas

1. Álvaro Vargas Llosa, *El Exilio Indomable* (Spain: Planeta Pub Corp, 1998), 53.

2. Vargas Llosa, *El Exilio Indomable*, 63.

3. June Kronholz, "'Dade Cubans' Dilemma Cited: Citizenship or Cuban Culture," *Miami Herald*, June 9, 1974.

4. *Statistical Yearbook of the Immigration and Naturalization Service Annual Report*, Immigration and Naturalization Service, 1980, table 22, https://books .google.com/books?id=Qa9a-Cho0IcC&printsec=frontcover&source=gbs_ge _summary_r&cad=0#v=onepage&q&f=false.

5. Guillermo Martínez, "Cuban-Americans Love Reagan's Latin Stand," *Miami Herald*, May 2, 1983.

6. "US Radio Broadcasting in Cuba—Policy Implications," Cuban American National Foundation, www.canf.org/the-archive/special-collections/10-125-fun dacion/690-us-radio-broadcasting-to-cuba-policy-implications-vol-1, 11.

7. The Board of International Broadcasting, Seventh Annual Report, 1981.

8. "US Radio Broadcasting in Cuba," CANF.

9. "US Radio Broadcasting in Cuba," CANF.

10. Vargas Llosa, *El Exilio Indomable*, 129.

11. CQ Almanac Online Edition, library.cqpress.com/cqalmanac.

12. CQ Almanac Online Edition, library.cqpress.com/cqalmanac.

13. Radio Broadcasting to Cuba Act, Amendments, H.R. 5427, 97th Cong. (1981–1982).

14. Helga Silva and Liz Balmaseda, "Superstar Wows Little Havana," *Miami Herald*, May 21, 1983.

15. Silva and Balmaseda, "Superstar Wows Little Havana."

16. Remarks of Jorge Mas Canosa, Cuban American National Foundation, May 20, 1983, www.canf.org/the-archive/special-collections/9-127-jorge-mas-canosa /215-speech-by-jorge-mas-canosa-regarding-the-visit-to-miami-from-president -ronald-w-reagananf.org.

17. Ronald Reagan, "Remarks at a Cuban Independence Day Celebration in Miami, Florida," May 20, 1983, American Presidency Project, www.presidency.ucsb .edu/documents/remarks-cuban-independence-day-celebration-miami-florida.

18. Ronald Reagan, "Remarks at a Cuban Independence Day Celebration in Miami, Florida."

19. Ronald Reagan, "Statement on the Radio Broadcasting to Cuba Act," October 11, 1983, American Presidency Project, www.presidency.ucsb.edu/documents /statement-the-radio-broadcasting-cuba-act.

20. Sandra Dibble, "Cuban-Americans Reap the Rewards of Diligent Effort," *Miami Herald*, May 26, 1985.

21. "The 'First Voice' of Radio Martí, the Cuban Moisés López, Died in Miami," *Miami Diario*, January 4, 2022, https://miamidiario.com/the-first-voice-of-radio -marti-the-cuban-moises-lopez-died-in-miami/; and Andres Viglucci "First Broadcast Mixes News, Sports, Entertainment," *Miami Herald*, May 21, 1985.

22. "Acting Presidential: A Miami Businessman Is Angling, Some Say, to Succeed Castro," *Wall Street Journal*, May 11, 1990.

23. Luis Feldstein Soto, "It's Ros-Lehtinen 53-47%," *Miami Herald*, August 30, 1989.

24. "Bush, Yeltsin Issued 'Declaration of New Relations,'" February 1, 1992, UPI Archives.

25. US Memorandums of Conversation, George H. W. Bush and Mikhail Gorbachev at Malta Summit, December 2–3, 1989, Wilson Center Digital Archive, https://digitalarchive.wilsoncenter.org/document/us-memorandums-conversa tion-george-h-w-bush-and-mikhail-gorbachev-malta-summit-2-3, 5.

26. Sandra Dibble, Fred Tasker, and Mimi Whitefield, "Exiles Press Soviets for Change in Cuba," *Miami Herald*, May 27, 1990.

27. Alfonso Chardy, "Exiles Plan Talks on Cuba in Moscow," *Miami Herald*, October 16, 1990. Also, see Alexander Makhov, "The Other Cuba, Which One Hears About on Meeting Emigrants in Miami," *Moscow News*, no. 38 (1990): 12.

28. Statement on Actions to Support Democracy in Cuba, April 18, 1992, from Public Papers of the President of the United States: George H. W. Bush, Office of the Secretary, White House, book I, 615–616.

29. Richard Newcomb, Office of Foreign Assets Control, Testimony Before the Subcommittee on Western Hemisphere and Peace Corps Affairs, May 22, 1995, Senate Foreign Relations Committee, 35.

30. Omnibus Export Amendments Act of 1990, H.R. 4653, 101st Cong. (1989–1990), www.congress.gov/bill/101st-congress/house-bill/4653?r=7.

31. Robert G. Torricelli, "Mas Canosa Made His New Country Pay Attention," *Miami Herald*, September 20, 2017.

32. Vargas Llosa, *El Exilio Indomable*, 219.

Chapter 11: Double Trouble

1. "Brian S. Latell," Cuban Research Institute, Steven J. Green School of International & Public Affairs, Florida International University, cri.fiu.edu/faculty/brian-latell.

2. Brian Latell, *Castro's Secrets: The CIA and Cuba's Intelligence Machine* (New York: Palgrave MacMillan, 2012), 1.

3. Latell, *Castro's Secrets*, 239. Authors' emphasis.

4. Aleksandr Fursenko and Timothy Naftali, *One Hell of a Gamble: Khrushchev, Castro, and Kennedy, 1958–1964* (New York: W. W. Norton, 1997), 97.

5. Fursenko and Naftali, *One Hell of a Gamble*, 97–98.

6. Latell, *Castro's Secrets*, 2–3.

7. Latell, *Castro's Secrets*, 10–11.

8. Latell, *Castro's Secrets*, 66.

9. Besides Aspillaga, DGI counterintelligence officer Roberto Hernández del Llano provided the US with important insight into the Cuban double agent program when he also defected in 1987.

10. Latell, *Castro's Secrets*, 37.

11. This would have been mainly in the form of defoliants, or attacks on agriculture. Not mustard gas or something like VX.

12. Dan Williams, "Duped CIA, 'Double Agents' Claim: US-Cuban Tensions Rise as Spying Charges Spiral," *Los Angeles Times*, July 26, 1987.

13. Gail Epstein Nieves, "Spy Trial Unmasks Cuba Secrets," *Miami Herald*, December 20, 2000.

14. Chris Simmons, "A Cynical End for Castro's Faux-Beloved "Cuban Five," *Cuba Confidential*, cubaconfidential.wordpress.com.

15. David Kidwell, "Contrite Cuban Spy Couple Sentenced," *Miami Herald*, February 3, 2000; Carol Rosenberg, "Defense: Cuban Spies Learned No Secrets," *Miami Herald*, June 1, 2001.

16. See Chapter 14 for the complete story.

17. Nieves, "Spy Trial."

18. Latell, *Castro's Secrets*, 71.

19. Martha Burk, "Obama and Castro: Sparring over Human Rights," *Huffington Post*, June 7, 2010, www.huffpost.com/entry/obama-and-castro-sparring _b_529606.

20. René González got released on parole in 2011. Fernando González got out in 2014. The remaining three were sent back to Cuba as part of a spy trade for Cuban Rolando Sarraff Trujillo, a DI cryptologic expert who provided the US with information about Cuban spies, including the Wasp Network. USAID contractor Alan Gross, jailed in Cuba since 2009, was also released—apparently unrelated to the spy swap, but coincidentally at the exact same time . . .

21. Nick Miroff, "Heroic Homecoming for Cuban Agents Brings Speculation About Future in Politics," *Washington Post*, January 18, 2015.

22. Sharon Krum, "The Spy Who Never Loved Me," *Guardian*, August 18, 1999.

23. Jay Weaver, "Jilted Wife of Spy Wins $7.1 Million," *Miami Herald*, March 10, 2001.

24. Latell, *Castro's Secrets*, 8.

25. Latell, *Castro's Secrets*, 6.

26. For an in-depth interview about Montes and FBI counterintelligence in general, check out author Vince Houghton's interview with the FBI agent who arrested Montes, Pete Lapp, in *SpyCast* podcast, International Spy Museum, the cyberwire.com/podcasts/spycast/365/notes.

27. For a comprehensive account of the Montes story, see feature article by Jim Popkin, "Ana Montes Did Much Harm Spying for Cuba. Chances Are, You Haven't Heard of Her," *Washington Post*, April 18, 2013.

28. There are still several numbers stations in operation. Some still might be used by Cuban intelligence. You can find multiple websites that link to them.

Chapter 12: All Politics Is International

1. "The Rafter Crisis of 1994 and the US Response," Digital Exhibits, University of Miami Libraries, https://scholar.library.miami.edu/digital/exhibits/show /guantanamo/crisis.

2. For a great article on the rafter's life in Guantánamo, see Fabiola Santiago, "A Revisit to the Cuban Balsero Crisis and the People Who Found Freedom in America," *Miami Herald*, September 8, 2014.

3. Andorra Bruno, "US Policy on Cuban Migrants: In Brief," Congressional Research Service, December 16, 2016, https://crsreports.congress.gov/product /pdf/R/R44714.

4. "The Day When 'Wet Foot, Dry Foot' Became Policy and Changed Immigration," *Miami Herald*, January 12, 2017.

5. "The Day When 'Wet Foot.'"

6. Caroline McCulloch, "The Helms-Burton Act: Then and Now," Association for the Study of the Cuban Economy (ASCE), Cuba in Transition, 2021, www .ascecuba.org.

7. Vicki Huddleston, *Our Woman in Havana: A Diplomat's Chronicle of America's Long Struggle with Castro's Cuba* (New York: Overlook Press, 2018), 194.

8. Patrick J. Kiger, "Squeeze Play: The United States, Cuba, and the Helms-Burton Act," Center for Public Integrity, https://cloudfront-files-1.publicintegrity.org/legacy_projects/pdf_reports/SQUEEZEPLAY.pdf, 1–2.

9. McCulloch, "Helms-Burton Act," 92.

10. Kiger, "Squeeze Play," 5.

11. Kiger, "Squeeze Play," 6.

12. Kiger, "Squeeze Play," 12.

13. McCulloch, "Helms-Burton Act," 94–95.

14. Ann Louise Bardach, *Cuba Confidential: Love and Vengeance in Miami and Havana* (New York: Vintage Books, 2002), 74.

15. Bardach, *Cuba Confidential*, 90.

16. Bardach, *Cuba Confidential*, 96–97.

17. Bardach, *Cuba Confidential*, 17.

18. Bardach, *Cuba Confidential*, 80–81.

19. Bardach, *Cuba Confidential*, 291.

20. Bardach, *Cuba Confidential*, 301–302.

21. From "Fidel: oldado de las Ideas," Cubadebate, May 12, 2013, www.fidelcastro.cu/es/valoraciones/un-padre.

22. David Adams, "Elian Swings Cuban Voters Back to GOP," *Tampa Bay Times*, November 5, 2000.

Chapter 13: Schrödinger's Castro

1. Andres Viglucci, "False Rumors of Castro's Death Snowball Through Cuban Miami," *Miami Herald*, January 8, 1986.

2. Anthony Boadle, "Castro's Prognosis 'Very Serious,'" Reuters, January 21, 2007.

3. "Rumors of Castro's Death Persist, Except in Cuba," *Miami Herald*, September 1, 2007.

4. See "FIDEL: Soldier of Ideas," www.comandanteenjefe.org.

5. Rory Carroll, "Castro's Disappearance Fuels New Health Fears," *Guardian*, January 15, 2009.

6. Haroon Siddique, "Argentine President Dismisses Fidel Castro Health Rumours," *Guardian*, January 22, 2009.

7. Tere Figueras Negrete and Kathleen McGrory, "Rumors of Castro's Death Set Social Media Sites on Fire," *Miami Herald*, October 13, 2012.

8. "Chávez visita a Castro, en plena tormenta de rumores sobre su salud deteriorada," *ABC*, October 18, 2012, www.abc.es/internacional/abci-fidel-castro-estado-moribundo-201210180000_noticia.html.

9. Fidel Castro Ruz, "Fidel Castro está agonizando," Fidel: Soldado de las Ideas, October 21, 2012, www.fidelcastro.cu/es/articulos/fidel-castro-esta-agonizando.

10. "Celebration, Sorrow and Slights Greet News of Castro's Death," Associated Press, November 26, 2016.

11. Daniel Chang, Patricia Mazzei, David Ovalle, and David Smiley, "Castro's Death Brings Hope, Healing in Miami," *Miami Herald*, November 27, 2016.

12. "Rumors of Castro's Death Persist, Except in Cuba," *Miami Herald*, September 1, 2007.

13. "Celebration, Sorrow Mingle After Death of Fidel Castro," Associated Press, November 26, 2016.

14. Luiz Inácio Lula da Silva, "Lula aponta Fidel Castro como o 'maior de todos os latino-americanos,' Mundo, G1, November 26, 2016, https://g1.globo.com/mundo/noticia/2016/11/lula-aponta-fidel-castro-como-o-maior-de-todos-os-latino-americanos.html.

15. "In Cuba, Days of Mourning for Fidel Castro," CNN, November 22, 2016, https://edition.cnn.com/videos/world/2016/11/27/fidel-castro-cuba-reaction-robertson-newday-lok.cnn.

Chapter 14: A Wretched Hive of Scum and Villainy

1. This poetic refrain is from "International Intrigue Makes Miami the New 'Casablanca,'" *New York Times*, December 29, 1984.

2. Abby Goodnough, "US Pushes Anti-Castro TV, but Is Anyone Watching?" *New York Times*, September 27, 2006.

3. David Fahrenthold, "Grounded TV Martí Plane a Monument to the Limits of American Austerity," *Washington Post*, September 2, 2013.

4. Tim Elfrink, "TV Martí's New Plan for Toppling Castro: Spamming Cuban Cell Phones," *Miami New Times*, October 24, 2011.

5. Nora Gámez Torres, "Radio and TV Martí Sneaked in Same Forbidden Technology That Landed Alan Gross in Cuban Jail," *Miami Herald*, updated March 30, 2018.

6. Jerry Iannelli, "US Government Has Plans to Spread Hidden Facebook Propaganda in Cuba," *Miami New Times*, August 21, 2018.

7. Broadcasting Board of Governors, 2019 Congressional Budget Justification, US Agency for Global Media, www.usagm.gov/wp-content/uploads/2018/02/BBGBudget_FY19_CBJ_2-7-18_Final.pdf.

8. Joshua Goodman and Terry Spencer, "Ex-Miami US Rep. David Rivera Arrested in Venezuela Probe," Associated Press, December 6, 2022.

9. See Jay Weaver, "Ex-chief of Venezuela's Highest Court Charged with Diverting Millions in Bribes to Miami," *Miami Herald*, January 26, 2023.

10. Hillary Hoffower, "Inside Florida's 'Little Moscow,' Where Russian Money Flows Thanks to 'Rich Daddies' Snapping up Real Estate," *Insider*, March 6, 2022, www.businessinsider.com/florida-little-moscow-sunny-isles-miami-russian-money-real-estate-2022-3.

11. Nicholas Nehamas, "Before Donald Trump Attacked Foreigners, He Helped to Sell Them Condos," *Miami Herald*, updated October 15, 2016.

12. Nicholas Nehamas, "How Secret Offshore Money Helps Fuel Miami's Luxury Real-Estate Boom," *Miami Herald*, updated September 6, 2018.

13. Nehamas, "Before Donald Trump."

14. Nathan Layne et al., "Moscow on the Beach: Russian Elite Invested Nearly $100 Million in Trump Buildings," Reuters, March 17, 2017.

15. Nehamas, "Before Donald Trump."

16. Layne et al., "Moscow on the Beach."

17. Michael Wilner, "As Biden Targets Russian Assets over Ukraine, Elite Money Remains Parked on Florida Shores," *Miami Herald*, updated February 24, 2022.

18. Layne et al., "Moscow on the Beach."

19. See Wilner, "As Biden Targets."

20. Nehamas, "How Secret Offshore Money."

21. Hoffower, "Inside Florida's 'Little Moscow.'"

22. See Jay Weaver and Daniela Castro, "Scientist Turned Bumbling Miami Spy for Russia Gets 4 Years in Cloak-and-Dagger Caper," *Miami Herald*, updated June 21, 2022; or "Individual Pleads Guilty to Acting Within the United States on Behalf of Russian Government," Office of Public Affairs, US Department of Justice, February 16, 2022, www.justice.gov/opa/pr/individual-pleads-guilty -acting-within-united-states-behalf-russian-government; see Michael Wilner and Ben Weider, "Putin Says Russians Living Large in Miami, French Riviera Are Traitors to the Motherland," *Miami Herald*, March 17, 2022.

23. For more, see Jacqueline Charles, Antonio Maria Delgado, and Jay Weaver, "How Money, Drugs and a Foreign Embassy Played Parts in the Murder of Haiti's President," *Miami Herald*, updated December 7, 2022; Tom Driesbach, "Mystery Surrounds Florida Company Suspected in Assassination of Haiti's President," NPR, July 16, 2021; and Frances Robles and Anatoly Kurmanaev, "US Charges a Suspect in Assassination of Haiti's President," *New York Times*, updated January 5, 2022.

24. Linda Pressley, "'Bay of Piglets': A 'Bizarre' Plot to Capture a President," BBC, July 30, 2020.

25. Antonio Maria Delgado et al., "Venezuela Coup Plotters Met at Trump Doral. Central Figure Says US Officials Knew of Plan," *Miami Herald*, October 30, 2020.

26. Starting in January 2019, the Trump administration began calling Guaidó the legitimate president of Venezuela.

27. Pressley, "'Bay of Piglets.'"

28. Delgado et al., "Venezuela Coup Plotters."

29. Pressley, "'Bay of Piglets.'"

30. Sergio Olmos, "Bolsonaro Backers in Florida Decry What They See as a Stolen Election in Brazil," NPR, January 25, 2023.

31. Quotations taken from Nora Gámez Torres, "How Miami Got an Undeserved Central Role in Brazil Riots, Accusations Against Former Leader," *Miami Herald*, January 9, 2023.

Index

Index